Designing Alternative Assessments for Interdisciplinary Curriculum in Middle and Secondary Schools

RICHARD E. MAURER

Tuckahoe Union Free School District
Eastchester, New York

Allyn and Bacon
Boston London Toronto Sydney Tokyo Singapore

For my parents, and for Jeannette and Regina,
and especially for Elizabeth

Copyright © 1996 by Allyn & Bacon
A Simon & Schuster Company
Needham Heights, Massachusetts 02194

Library of Congress Cataloging-in-Publication Data

Maurer, Richard E.
    Designing alternative assessments for interdisciplinary curriculum
in middle and secondary schools / Richard E. Maurer
      p. cm.
    Includes bibliographical references and index.
    ISBN 0-205-17393-4
    1. Educational tests and measurements—United States.
2. Interdisciplinary approach in education—United States.
3. Curriculum evaluation—United States I. Title.
LB3051.M459 1996
371.2′6′0973—dc20   95-15017
                                 CIP

Printed in the United States of America
10 9 8 7 6 5 4 3 2 1   99 98 97 96 95

Contents

Preface   v

Part One   Designing Interdisciplinary Assessments   1

1   Establishing the Nature of Authentic Assessment Strategies   3
What Is Authentic Assessment?   3
How Did It Begin?   4
Work Force 2000   9
Research Findings in Cognitive and Developmental Psychology   11
Summary   19
References   20

2   Determining Interdisciplinary Curriculum Standards   23
Setting Standards   24
Choosing an Interdisciplinary Theme   33
Examples of Interdisciplinary Standards   38
Controversy Surrounding Standards   41
Instructing for High Standards   43
Summary   53
References   53

3   Creating Alternative Assessment Tasks   57
Purposes of Alternative Assessments   60
Types of Alternative Assessments   62
Qualities of Alternative Assessments   71
Problems in Designing Assessment Tasks   76
Planning for the Assessment Task   79
Summary   85
References   86

4   Developing Measurement Criteria   89
Measurement   89
Types of Measurement   101
Reflections   111
Summary   117
References   118

Part Two   Interdisciplinary Assessments   119

Wallops Island Field Study   122
School–Business Partnership   128
Algebra II   130
Learning Journals in the History Classroom   141
Senior Honors British Literature Portfolio   153

Senior Research Portfolio   153
Writing as a Process   156
Diet and Food Facts   158
Oak Park 2013   165
Schoolwide Portfolios   170
Career Certificate Program (CCP)   174
Expressive Arts   181
Mini-Business Community   183
Science Projects   195
Science Portfolios   202
Water Water Everywhere   205
American Society   210
Science Thinking Journal   217
Weather   218
Cultural Comparisons   220
USA: Melting Pot of the World   221
Where Do Floridians Come From?   222

Appendixes

Appendix A   Increasing Parent and Community Participation in Schools   225

Appendix B   Blue Ribbon Schools   230

Appendix C   Blue Ribbon Schools Program   234

Appendix D   Model Sixth-Grade Language Arts Assessments   236

Index   246

Preface

My experience with interdisciplinary curriculum, first as a teacher, then as a principal, and now as a superintendent of schools, has given me a perspective on the role and function, the strengths and weaknesses of this integrated approach to teaching curriculum content. In my book, *Designing Interdisciplinary Curriculum in the Middle, Junior High, and High Schools* (Allyn and Bacon, 1994), I discussed at length the role, function, and strengths of interdisciplinary curriculum and provided detailed examples of 42 actual curricula used by nationally recognized schools. In my research for that book and from my own experience, I found that one of the primary weaknesses of current interdisciplinary projects is the lack of an appropriate assessment system to determine what a student has learned. Many teachers design and implement sophisticated interdisciplinary projects but fail to develop an evaluation system that can authentically reveal what a student has gained from the project. In many cases, the evaluation system does not assess the integrated nature of the curriculum but reverts back to testing in the content area. Standardized tests and many state minimum competency tests share this deficiency. For example, a class of seventh-graders, after completing a two-week interdisciplinary project working in small teams to create a colonial newspaper, are graded separately by their English, history, science, and math teachers, using an A-through-F system. This assessment system does not adequately report to the student or to the parents and community how the student has truly performed in creating the newspaper project.

Clearly, with the growing use of interdisciplinary curriculum in our nation's schools, there is a need to provide a more authentic assessment system. Current innovations in performance-based assessments provide direction for designing a more compatible assessment system. In my three years as an evaluator for the Department of Education's National Blue Ribbon Schools Program, I have had the opportunity to review hundreds of curriculum innovations from outstanding elementary, middle, junior high, and high schools from rural, suburban, urban, private, parochial, and public schools across our nation. In this rich collection of innovations, I discovered schools that have attempted to address the need to design assessment systems that can authentically evaluate student progress in an interdisciplinary curriculum mode. These examples are worth sharing with other educators across the country as they themselves struggle to implement more authentic curriculum and assessment systems.

The book is divided into two parts. In Part One, "Designing Interdisciplinary Assessments," you will learn how to construct alternative assessment systems that can measure interdisciplinary curricula. This part describes the design process as one of developing a four-step taxonomy or design: Standards, Assessment Task, Measurement, and Reflection. In each of the chapters, special attention is devoted to including parents and community members in the process of designing curriculum and assessment systems. Appendix A provides three methods for involving the community more in your school or school district innovations.

Chapter 1 helps you understand the nature of the current trend toward using alternative assessments. You will be exposed to three major influences on the current reform movement in testing and evaluation: (1) the demand for "higher" standards from Congress, from the state legislatures, from your own local school board; (2) the international competition to develop a more competent work force for the twenty-first century; and (3) trends in developmental and psychological research.

In Chapter 2 you will learn how to design interdisciplinary curriculum standards. The emphasis is on how to design curriculum when you know beforehand what you want your students to be able to accomplish at the end. Too many interdisciplinary projects are sophisticated and fun but are not linked to school district, school, or grade-level standards. As part of this chapter, you will see the importance of effective instruction in teaching interdisciplinary curriculum.

In Chapter 3 you learn how to create the actual assessment instrument—that is, the task the student must complete as part of the curriculum project. These tasks typically fall into one of three areas: products, performances, or exhibitions. You will see how to build quality into each task, how to avoid problems, and how to implement the task itself.

Chapter 4 provides methods for measuring the task the student has completed: what should be measured; who should measure; what the scoring system should look like; and how to establish reliability, validity, and generalizability in the measurement process.

This book is a hands-on guide to designing and implementing an alternative assessment system for your interdisciplinary curriculum. Throughout this section you will find tables, charts, and procedure guides to help you implement each of the steps in designing an alternative assessment system. Numerous examples of curriculum and assessments from state and national curriculum standards committees and from local schools are illustrated as examples for each of the design steps. References have been provided at the end of each chapter to assist you in locating further research and readings.

In Part Two you will find 22 examples of interdisciplinary curriculum and assessments from schools that were recognized by the Department of Education as Blue Ribbon Schools during 1993. These examples include different developmental aspects of what was discussed in Part One. Keep in mind that with each of these examples you have tried and true procedures. These are not systems designed in a laboratory or workshop but, rather, procedures being used by teachers today. You may find fault with parts of them or may find them incomplete. Remember that designing systems for change and actually implementing them in a classroom is a very difficult process. These examples work for the teachers who use them. They will work for you as well.

When you attempt to design and implement your own interdisciplinary curriculum and assessment system, read Part One and review the examples in Part Two for ideas. If the need arises, contact the teachers who designed the examples; addresses and phone numbers are provided. In some cases, you will find that the curriculum and assessment system may have been updated or a newer system developed.

Appendix C describes the Blue Ribbon Schools Program from which these examples have been chosen. For the reader interested in how a number of interdisciplinary units and assessments can be sequenced to cover a particular grade-level curriculum, Appendix D provides four additional examples.

I would like to thank the staff of the Blue Ribbon Schools Program and, in particular, the recently retired director of the School Recognition Division at the U.S. Department of Education, Jean Narayanan, for her assistance and cooperation. I also thank the principals and teachers of the nationally recognized schools represented here for sharing their materials. May you continue to be a source of inspiration to our nation's schools. I want to thank Frances K. Kochan for reviewing the manuscript. Finally, thank you to Mother Nature for producing in 1994 one of the worst winters in a decade in the Northeast. You forced me to stay at home and write.

Part One
Designing Interdisciplinary Assessments

1 Establishing the Nature of Authentic Assessment Strategies

What Is Authentic Assessment?

Authentic assessment means testing students by requiring them to show what they have learned in a context that is congruent with real-life experience. Usually these demonstrations are performances closely tied to specific course standards. The standards themselves warrant major investment of time and instruction. They usually are referred to as exit standards—the essential things required of students before they move to the next level, grade, or school. The performances may take the form of projects, exhibitions, or portfolios. They are multifaceted and also measured over time, usually over a school year. They are closely tied to the instructional process, not part of the "end of the year" recall of knowledge. With authentic assessments there may be many forms of "right" answer, with scores resembling a range of achievement rather than simply passing or failing. Teachers often have examples, models, or benchmarks which the student can view before hand. There are no surprise questions because the student and teacher work together closely to improve the quality of the student's work.

One example of an authentic assessment comes from an eighth-grade mathematics class

> Students will use a computer spreadsheet for the purposes of compiling, comparing, graphing, and analyzing data.

Here the standard is clearly stated, is essential to learning, can be measured over time, has multiple forms for a response, and is closely tied to instruction. The assessment is authentic because it requires a student to do something—create a spreadsheet—using the mathematical skills acquired in the course. The measurement scale to grade these spreadsheets could be complex, measuring different skills at the same time. Further, the assessment assumes that the students have the basic skills and advances the testing to require a performance base or application of higher level thinking.

Compare this authentic assessment to a traditional basic competency mathematical test question:

> Compute the following problem: $3x + 4 = 44$
>   a) 8
>   b) 10
>   c) 12
>   d) None of the above

The differences between the two types of assessments are dramatic. In the former example, understanding is demonstrated by performance, in the latter example, memorization is required for a formula computation. The remainder of this chapter will illustrate further how this vast difference came about.

How Did It Begin?

No one person or institution can be singled out as the founder of authentic assessment. Unlike many recent trends in education, authentic assessment has no one root. Many different trends in education have led to the development of authentic assessment, which emerged as a natural outgrowth of the nurturing efforts of many different people working at different levels of educational reform.

At least three major movements have had a significant effect on the recent rise of the authentic assessment movement: (1) demands for higher standards, (2) work force 2000, and (3) cognitive and developmental psychological research. Each of these movements have influenced the development of authentic assessment in different ways. Each begins from a different conceptual base and draws on this base to make recommendations to educators. Common recommendation coming from each of these movements have promoted the emerging trend toward authentic assessment. It would benefit the reader to understand the conceptual basis of these three movements.

Demands for Higher Standards

Demands for higher standards have been heard periodically throughout the history of education in the United States. The current call dates back to the Commission on Excellence and its publication in 1983 of *A Nation at Risk: The Imperative for Educational Reform.* This single document has produced a ripple effect or, more aptly, a tidal wave of educational reform legislation throughout the country. Virtually every state adopted mandatory changes in how our children were to be educated. Without exception, the driving force behind this legislation was the introduction of more testing and examinations. The theory was that if school districts and ultimately teachers were held accountable through testing, then the standards of the educational process would rise.

This was the top-down or "stick" approach to educational reform. Throughout most of the 1980s, the demand for higher standards was heard throughout the educational establishment. The Education Commission of the States (1983) reported that a common denominator of this first wave of reform was legislating, regulating, and mandating higher standards. Kirst (1990) talks about some of the key assumptions of this wave of reform. One assumption was the link between high educational standards and an economic edge in the global market. Another assumption was that the organization of schools did not need to change, just the way we managed the instructional and assessment process.

Looking at other countries known for their outstanding student achievement, we find (Resnick & Nolan, 1995) that few of them use multiple-choice items as their instrument for testing high standards. In France, students qualify for the Brevet certificate; in the Netherlands, students take national exams. Neither country uses multiple-choice or short-answer questions as the main feature of their achievement exams. In Germany, teachers prepare and grade their own exams. In the United States, on the other hand, we who are looking to develop world-class curriculum standards rely almost exclusively on less than world-class standards for our assessments.

Initially, the publication of various different commission and task force reports had little day-to-day effect on classroom teachers. Reform from the top took its time to reach the classroom. Many educators viewed reform as a process in which they were not consulted. Parents and most community members were ignored as well. Often, educators viewed the reforms as a form of teacher bashing. Rather than having the front-line troops, the classroom teachers and building-level administrators, as an integral part of the reform effort, a deep mistrust developed between the educators and the bureaucrats in state legislatures and state education departments. When reform efforts did arrive at the school doorstep, they usually took the form of more regulations and more testing. Pressure to improve test scores became an accountability issue. This pressure became intense in some areas as test scores of school districts and individual schools were compared with one another in the press. Raising standards was one thing; to be held publicly accountable for poor or declining standards was quite another. Classroom teachers and building principals did not want to be held accountable for what they could not totally control.

With intense pressure to raise standards and improve test scores, school administrators and teachers began to look carefully at testing procedures. Most tests were either mandated state exams or standardized tests from large national companies. Teachers viewed state exams as having standards set at the minimum competency level. These ridiculously low "passing" levels were nonetheless held as standards, which affected curriculum development and instructional delivery. Instruction followed the exam format, prompting the use of worksheets incorporating fill-in-the-blank, multiple-choice, skill and drill, or simple report writing as part of the child's daily experience. Rather than raising the educational achievement of our students, such top-down legislation only reinforced minimal standards. Linda Darling-Hammond (1993) cites officials of the National Assessment of Educational Progress, the National Research Council, and the National Councils of Teachers of English and Mathematics, among others, as blaming for a decline in higher order thinking and performance.

The view of the national standardized exams was very similar. Minimum competency was emphasized at the expense of higher order thinking skills. Teachers viewed, and still view these exams as unrelated to what they teach. Most of the exams do not have sections on writing, reading for comparison and contrast, projects, displays, or performances. They do have multiple-choice answers, which allow students to guess and still be correct about 25 percent of the time. Many teachers dismissed the standardized test as a chore one had to deal with. The test results seldom were returned early enough in the school year to affect instruction. When they were returned and analyzed, the teachers felt the test items were so far removed from what they did in the classroom that the results were meaningless. Many teachers left standardized test results alone, to be dealt with by administrators and/or district directors of research and evaluation.

Educators responses to the demand for higher standards were to attack the test on which they were being measured. Mitchell (1992) summarizes many of the reasons for educators' disdain of standardized tests.

1. These tests only ask students to select a response. Students do not contribute their own thinking.
2. Each question implies that there is only one right answer. In real life, however, many problems fall into a gray area.
3. The tests are based on what was memorized or, to use Bloom's (1956) taxonomy of the cognitive domain, on the first level of knowledge, the recitation of facts. There is no opportunity to show understanding.
4. The national test companies determine what should be tested, not the classroom teacher.
5. The test does not record what a student can *do* with the knowledge.
6. Students study for the test ("Is it going to be on the test?") rather than to gain wisdom.

The evidence (Fuhrman, 1994) is in that although student achievement increased slightly during the 1980s, the gains have not been dramatic. The Scholastic Aptitude Test (SAT) increased 16 points between 1980 and 1985 but lost 10 points between 1987 and 1991. National Assessment of Educational Progress (NAEP) scores remained stable. Mastery of basic skills, not analytic and reasoning skills, was emphasized and measured over this period.

Educators decided (Hawley, 1990) to take hold of the reform movement and make their mark. Left out of the first wave, educators were determined to shape the crest of the second wave of educational reform which came in the late 1980s with a strong advocacy for addressing the concerns of children at risk and minority children, and for investing in the improvement of teaching and the reorganization of schools. There was a new emphasis on empowering teachers and administrators in the schools to decide how best to raise the achievement levels of all students. There was an emphasis on including parents as primary stakeholders in the educational process. The opening of the schoolhouse door to parents and community groups was to have a profound effect on how schools were run, not only at the local level but at the State level as well.

From the beginning, the issue of assessment was a dominant one. The Carnegie Forum (1986) was one of the first groups that called for improved testing methods linked more closely with what was going on in the classroom. Different state education departments, under the influence of the teachers in the respective states, again changed the form of assessment being mandated. Joining the authentic assessment bandwagon were the states of Maryland, Vermont, Kentucky, Michigan, California, and Arizona, to name but a few. These states have mandated authentic assessments and have discarded older forms of state assessments of basic competencies. Recently, all these states have had to slow down their reform efforts to some degree as it has become apparent that parents and community groups were once again being left at the sidelines.

The federal government entered the debate in 1990, when President Bush and the governors established six national education goals to be reached by the year 2000:

1. Ensuring that children came to school ready to learn
2. Setting the high school graduation rate at 90 percent
3. Encouraging maintenance of competency standards in the core academic subjects in grades 4, 8, and 12
4. Establishing U.S. students as first in the world in science and mathematics
5. Reaching full adult literacy and readiness to complete in a global economy
6. Keeping schools free of violence, drugs, and firearms.

The federal government did not stop here. Citing the fact (U.S. Department of Education, 1993) that two-thirds of the nation's citizens see a crisis in education and a need for higher school standards, on March 31, 1994, President Clinton signed into law Goals 2000: Educate America Act. This law won bipartisan support and was the first major school reform legislation in more than a decade. It aims to reinvent U.S. schools by creating a framework for establishing high academic and skill standards. At the core of Goals 2000 are these principles:

1. Establish higher expectations for all students. All students can learn more than what we ask them.
2. Promote new approaches to teaching. Teacher preparation and professional development programs will be overhauled and improved.
3. Make schools accountable. Provide schools with flexibility but hold them accountable for results.
4. Build partnerships among parents, community members, business, labor, and private and nonprofit groups.

In addition to adding two new goals, teacher preparation and partnerships, to the original six, Goals 2000 asks for a partnership of federal, state, and local groups. This partnership would help state and community schools to develop and implement a comprehensive improvement plan to raise standards, encourage the development of a new generation of student performance assessment, and support the creation of voluntary national occupational standards. Clearly, the federal government has established its presence in the current reform movement.

The organized teacher voice is also being heard. Strong influence from educators is reflected in the rating the teachers gave for setting high standards and a stronger examination system. The Metropolitan Life Insurance Company's survey of *The American Teacher* (1993) reports that a large majority of teachers favor establishing standards for students. The highest rating (80 percent support, including 42 percent who *strongly* support) is seen in their desire to have eighth-graders pass an exam in order to go on to high school. The second highest rating was for establishing national standards for what students know (81 percent support). Less surprising was the evidence that only 61 percent support and only 17 percent strongly support a national system to measure students' and schools' progress in meeting national standards.

National networks of educators were also established. Groups like the Coalition of Essential Schools, the New Standards Project, Foxfire Outreach, Effective Schools, and many others became strong national movements. Though different in specifics, they all shared the common belief that schools needed to be reorganized to meet the needs of students. There was and still is in these networks a solid belief that those educators closest to the students, the teachers and the administrators of school buildings, should be empowered to make decisions. In addition, these networks viewed assessment as an integral part of the instructional process. Though advocating high standards for all students, they also pushed through a reform of testing procedures.

The State Education Leader (1992) reported on sixteen major national reform movements according to a number of criteria. Of the sixteen movements, only three did not have authentic assessment as a major system component. The New Standards Project (1994) is one example of how authentic assessment has been incorporated as a major system of educational reform. Its focus is to develop national standards and performance-based assessments in math, science, English, and history. The curriculum units will be interdisciplinary and will be made available to states and school districts to be used as formal assessment programs. The key to student assessment will be a variety of open-ended questions, projects, journals, dramatizations, and portfolios. Approximately 50 percent of the students in the United States are involved in various pilot activities. The first of these assessments for everyone's use should be published shortly.

National curriculum groups also took the initiative and began to produce major overalls of curriculum. The first published was the new mathematics standards from the National Council of the Teachers of Mathematics (NCTM). The American Association for the Advancement of Science (AAAS) has published its new standards in *Benchmarks for Science Literacy:*

Project 2061. Other groups will be publishing new curriculum standards soon. All the standards published so far and all those being readied advocate for new performance-based assessments.

To counterbalance the weaknesses of standardized testing, many educators adopted a dual or parallel system of accountability. Worthen (1993) explains the rationale for this move by saying that most educators doubted whether a single assessment can or should be used to measure instruction and also be used to hold standards accountable. In addition, classroom teachers felt that the assessments they use every day in the classroom were more valid indicators of student academic growth. So much confidence is placed in this type of assessment that decisions about instruction in the classroom every day are based on their results. In this spirit, teachers developed assessments that were more congruent with the instructional process. These assessments were based on the belief that assessment is part of being a lifelong leader; that it is open ended and cumulative; that it has applications beyond the classroom; and, most important, that it is part of learning, not an end product. Ironically, as we shall see later, authentic assessments not only measure higher standards but also drive the instructional process toward producing students who can function at a higher, more complex level of thinking. Thus, assessments began pushing teaching and learning in the direction of concepts, application, and student responsibility for learning.

Having two parallel systems of assessment based on two different conceptual viewpoints creates tension and discord in teachers. Nowhere is this more carefully explained than in Linda Darling-Hammond's (1993) description of competing models of reform. On the one hand, students are viewed as standardized and educational treatments and assessments as prescribed. On the other hand, students are seen as having a diversity of learning styles; different intelligences; and different social, cultural, and emotional dispositions on which they connect knowledge. Assessment then moves from being standard and limited to being flexible and authentic. This tension will most likely increase both within schools and at the state level as the different stakeholders—teachers, parents, politicians, administrators, and business—become more involved and advocate their particular vision of what schools should teach and how they should measure achievement and be held accountable. Yet, on a positive note, evidence (Smith, Fuhrman, & O'Day, 1994) suggests that if challenging and high-quality standards are implemented properly, student achievement, the quality of teachers and schools, and educational equity in our nation will vastly improve.

Work Force 2000

In both the first and second reform waves of educational reform, there has been a strong assumption that the nation's economic health is closely linked with higher standards for our country's educational system. The impetus for the *Nation at Risk* report came more from economic factors than from educational concerns. The popular press (Kohlberg & Smith, 1992) has consistently compared worker preparation and education in the United States to that of its economic rivals throughout the world. In most cases, the United States has been portrayed as lagging behind in preparing a work force with world-class standards. Private institutions voiced similar themes, especially reports issued by the Carnegie Council on Adolescent Development (1989) and the National Center on Education and the Economy (1990). The message is clear to the political and business leaders of our nation. Develop an educational system that produces students who can enter the work force with standards that are not only equal to but exceed those of our economic rivals—or face the consequences of a declining standard of living in the United States.

The federal government took a lead in meeting this challenge. In March 1992 the U.S. Secretary of Labor published a comprehensive document called the Secretary's Commission on Achieving Necessary Skills (SCANS). This report laid the foundations for the necessary skills and competencies that have been identified as critical to producing a work force ready for the next century. It is noteworthy that this report came from the Labor Department, not the Education Department.

The report describes five competencies necessary for effective job performance:

1. *Resources:*   Student can identify, organize, plan, and allocate resources.
2. *Interpersonal:* Student can work with others, lead, negotiate, and communicate.
3. *Information:*   Student can acquire, organize, interpret, and use information.
4. *Systems:*   Student can understand, monitor, and improve complex systems.
5. *Technology:*   Student can select, apply, and maintain a variety of technologies.

The Department of Labor and the Education Department teamed up in October 1993 to support a bill in Congress called the School-to-Work Opportunity Act. This bill would provide funding to combine academic and occupational learning—a key proposal of the SCANS commission advocated a year and half earlier. Essentially, this bill would provide seed money to help partnerships of the business community, teachers, and others to coordinate classroom lessons with job activities. As with the assumptions of the SCANS report, the proponents of this bill believe that work-based learning, integrated with schoolwork, can give students the world-class standards to be major competitors in the U.S. work force. The secretaries of both labor and education view this bill as a small step in motivating and supporting state and local initiatives to link school and work.

Various states have developed similar proposals to meet the demand to produce a world-class work force. In New York State, for example, former Governor Mario Cuomo was instrumental in promoting a join venture between business and schools. In September 1992 the state published *Education That Works: Creating Career Pathways for New York State Youths*. Although it focuses on high school level work force preparation, it is clear in its language that, to achieve the necessary changes, the entire educational organization, K–12, will have to be reformed to meet the challenge of the new initiative.

The report is similar to ideas being advocated at the national and other state levels. It demands higher standards, makes recommendations for school reorganization, and outlines funding procedures for the changes. At the core of its proposal is the development of a New Career Pathways Certificate, defined as follows:

> The New Career Pathways Certificate should be instituted to certify mastery at world-class level of the fundamental academics and work-readiness skills needed for entry to the workplace and continuing education. (Cuomo, 1992)

In its implementation, the new program would require students to earn a Career Pathways Certificate (CPC) as a prerequisite for either a high school diploma or a Professional and Technical Certificate. The Career Pathways Certificate would certify a mastery of fundamental skills and knowledge and would be required to enter the workplace. The key point here is that the state education department would be in the direct business of certifying whether or not an adolescent can work. Beyond the CPC would be either a high school diploma and work-related schooling or a Professional or Technical Certificate in a particular occupational field.

The fundamental concept supporting all the national and state initiatives in preparing a work force for the next century is the need to be able first to measure against some standard and then to testify that a student has, indeed, achieved a given level of academic and/or technical expertise. The assumption is that the federal or state governments must be able to produce valid and credible assessments to accomplish these steps. Many of these reports explicitly support the development and implementation of authentic assessments such as student performances, portfolios, projects, and/or demonstrations of knowledge and skills. There is, however, little discussion in any of these reports of how to go about developing these authentic assessments.

Research Findings in Cognitive and Developmental Psychology

Remember what you were told about right brain and left brain? A major breakthrough in the study of how the brain works (Sperry, 1968) demonstrated how the brain has specific regions for different neurological functions. We were told that those who are dominated by the left hemisphere of the brain are logical and rational in their approach to situations. Conversely, those who are dominated by the right hemisphere are more intuitive and emotional in orientation. Other research (Restak, 1979) reported findings that strongly indicate that the brain constructs reality, that it builds models of the world. These models act as internal representations on the basis of which we judge new knowledge. Tversky and Kahneman (1974) have shown that individuals reason by mentally constructing analogies, associations, and metaphors. This and other cognitive research provided us with a neurological basis for understanding human perception and learning. These findings, though major discoveries, had little immediate effect on educational research and even less effect on what went on inside the classroom. This situation, as we shall see, will not last long.

In another area, developmental psychology was undergoing major changes as well. American psychology had been dominated by the theoretical view known as *behaviorism*. B. F. Skinner (1953) was the foremost voice for the use of reinforcement and shaping to teach children and others correct responses. Skinner saw behavior as a function of the environment and believed that one can predict and control behavior by making systematic changes in the environment.

Schools often adopted behaviorism as a theory of learning. Students were taught to behave by a system of rewards and punishments. They were taught to learn by exposing them to specific subskills first, then the completed product; by modeling the correct and only response; by memorization of facts, repetition, lecture, and presentations; and, finally, by measurement or testing as separate from instruction. Nowadays one can see behaviorism in the use of computers solely to teach skills by rewarding, shaping, and sequencing the delivery of students' self-taught tasks.

Primarily in response to the brilliant observations of Piaget (1967, 1974), there was a transformational shift in theory about how children develop and learn. Rather than viewing a child's learning process as one of external manipulation by a variety of highly sophisticated stimuli and responses, Piaget felt that each child was an individual and must construct his or her own form of knowledge over time. For example, among his many ideas over fifty years of research was his belief in three definite stages of cognitive growth—sensorimotor, preoperational, and operational thinking. These stages are widely known but, surprisingly, could not be transformed for classroom use. Another Piagetian idea was the belief that individuals seek cognitive equilibrium when presented with something that is in contrast with what they already know. Again, this is a concept often studied but not of immediate use to classroom teachers. Although these and many others of Piaget's ideas are being questioned today, there is no doubt that he opened the door to the human mind as never seen before. Beyond the door, the view was that of an individual actively engaged in perceiving, representing, constructing, and reorganizing the world.

Most major theorists of human development today embrace a view of cognitive development that is far more complex than anyone, including Piaget, initially envisioned. Gardner (1991) describes the view as follows.

> The deep problem for the developmentalist attempting a synthesis is to understand the relationships among the constraints imposed by nature, the constraints imposed by culture, and the degree of human inventiveness that nonetheless manages to emerge.

Despite this complexity, the results of research in cognitive psychology and developmental psychology, mentioned earlier, had a profound effect on the educator and greatly influenced, perhaps forever, the nature of teaching and learning as we now know it. A number of changes were introduced into the classroom based on the findings of the current research. Each of these changes requires a vastly different view of how we test and measure student acquisition of knowledge. Some of the more significant changes that have evolved in education are described here with a primary orientation toward explaining their impact on the development of the authentic assessment movement.

Multiple Intelligences

The theory of multiple intelligences was first introduced by Gardner (1983) in his book *Frames of Mind: The Theory of Multiple Intelligences*. This presented a lengthy justification and explanation of the need for educators to expand their perception of what the term *intelligence* really means. In the paperback version of this book (1985), Gardner defines what he means by intelligence.

> An intelligence is the ability to solve problems, or to create products, that are valued within one or more cultural settings.

Building on solid evidence from neuropsychology and developmental psychology, Gardner developed a biological basis of intelligence that is significantly different from what we now know. Gardner believes that there is persuasive evidence that specific areas of the nervous system serve complex human functions, such as musical or mathematical ability. Further, the evidence supports the belief that different individuals can develop a strength in one specific area over that of others. Depending on the intensity of this neurological development, one can have a unique "intelligence." In addition, culture and environmental factors play a significant role in the individualization of these unique intelligences.

Gardner advocates for a view that encompasses seven, not just one, form of unique intelligence. Drawing from past cognitive and developmental research, he believes that people learn, represent, and use knowledge in many different ways. This diversity does not undermine the strength of what intelligence really is but, rather, amplifies it to include a host of different characteristics. These seven intelligences are briefly outlined here to show the reader the true diversity of representations an individual can learn, remember, and ultimately perform or exhibit to show what they know:

1. *Linguistic intelligence:* This is primarily an auditory or oral ability to communicate. The poet would be exemplified as the individual who has mastered the art and craft of expressing and communicating ideas through words. The ability to communicate the word is an area of intelligence that requires one who can use language as a tool to express to others experiences, emotions, and ideas in a clear, concise, and meaningful way.

2. *Musical intelligence:* This is one of the earliest intelligences to develop. It encompasses the components of pitch or melody, rhythm, and timbre, or the characteristic qualities of a tone. The ability to compose is also part of this intelligence. Working with tones, rhythm, and form, the individual constructs a musical piece that symbolizes for him or her a perfect synthesis.

3. *Logical-mathematical intelligence:* The central gift of the mathematician is the ability to handle long chains of reasoning. The mathematician discovers an idea and then draws out its implications. Closely tied to this skill is the study of science. The scientist also can relate to this intelligence in that the order of abstract reasoning is needed to discover the order in the vast amount of data or observations being created.

4. *Spatial intelligence:* This is the ability to perceive the visual world, to perform transformations and modifications on one's perception, and to re-create the experience. In contrast to linguistic intelligence, which is primarily verbal, spatial intelligence is imagistic. Artists exhibit this form of intelligence.

5. *Bodily-kinesthetic intelligence:* The ability to use one's body in a skillful way and the ability to use objects with fine and gross motor coordination characterize this type of intelligence. These functions may exist separately but they usually are part of the same manifestation of this intelligence. Expressions such as demonstrated by the dancer, actor, mime, athlete, and the inventor are illustrations of this form of intelligence.

6. *Personal intelligence:* This is one manifestation of the ability to notice and make distinctions among individuals, particularly in movement, temperament, motivation, and intentions. Intrapersonal intelligence is the ability to look at and understand oneself.

7. *Interpersonal intelligence:* This is the ability to understand others.

The very nature of multiple intelligences requires us to view individuals as developmentally and cognitively different. It is logical to assume that individuals can best understand new knowledge through their primary intelligence. The curriculum entry points for new knowledge need to be offered in a diverse fashion so as to be congruent with the respective intelligences of the students. Students' grasp of knowledge can further be strengthened by providing guides or apprenticeships to students through this primary intelligence map and later through other entry points. The curriculum emphasis should be less on basic skills and mimetic learning and more on assurances that a student can transfer the knowledge learned to new and similar situations.

Multiple intelligence theory also implies that students will show quite different forms or representations of knowledge and competency. The standardized written test forms used to assess so many students today cannot possibly meet the demands of a rich curriculum that is teaching students for understanding. The emphasis on assessment in such curricula should be on students' performances for understanding. In such schools, projects, exhibitions, and demonstrations would abound to reflect a deep level of understanding as well as the broad range of student intelligences.

This is the challenge that multiple intelligence theory presents to the authentic assessment movement. Gardner (1991), in a follow-up to his initial book, presents some ideas on how schools should teach children. Getting into the mind of the child and trying to understand the child's view of knowledge from within will profoundly alter an educator's instructional method. The seven intelligences are maps from which the educator can chart a course of understanding of the student's world. It would follow that educators will need to change the curriculum to provide students with an understanding of knowledge, build community support, and search out authentic forms of assessment through which students can represent their understanding.

Gardner has provided models of alternative assessment in the ARTS PROPEL project in the Pittsburgh schools. Here the focus is on process not product. Students take on the responsibility of understanding the knowledge. Evidence of understanding is seen in journals, process-folios, and other self monitoring methods.

Interdisciplinary Curriculum

Defined as the organization and transfer of knowledge under a unified or interdisciplinary theme, interdisciplinary curriculum has a long history in American education. Vars (1991) traces the evolving nature of this concept back to the nineteenth century, when the concept of *core curriculum* was first introduced. The popularity of this concept rises and falls as educators try to deal with changing societal demands, "back-to-basics" movements, and student needs. Currently, interdisciplinary curriculum is popular in the educational community and finds a theoretical case in recent cognitive psychology.

Most state and national reform initiatives have advocated the incorporation of interdisciplinary studies in the design of curriculum and instruction. These efforts include America 2000 Schools; the prototype designs funded by the New American Schools Development Corporation; the efforts of national curriculum associations such as the American Association for the Advancement of Science (AAAS) in its Project 2061 and the National Council of Teachers of Mathematics (NCTM); and the various state reform initiatives.

Interdisciplinary curriculum can take many different forms. A continuum of integration, from simplest to most complex, is convenient to utilize.

Correlated

At Upper Darby High School in Upper Darby, Pennsylvania, a unit called "Pursuing the Dream: Puritans and Immigration" will find the history teacher teaching from *A Nation of Immigrants* and the English teacher from *Giants in the Earth.*

Multidisciplinary

A course that weaves the content area of different subjects into a unified course of study is an example of this design. This course either can be taught by one teacher or can involve several teachers coming into the class. In historical terms, this design would be a "core." At Anacortes High School in Anacortes, Washington, a unit called "Like the Stars That Never Set: A Study of Native American Cultures of the Pacific Northwest" helps students understand the history of Washington State as well as the entire nation by understanding the Native American people who lived here before the white settlers.

Interdisciplinary

This approach organizes curriculum around broad themes which, by their nature, contain elements of most areas of knowledge. At Bloomfield Hills Middle School in Bloomfield Hills, Michigan, one of the "Kaleidoscope" unit is called "Touch the Earth." Students form groups to investigate such themes as "Made from the Earth," "Save the Earth," and "Sounds from the Earth." At Brewster Middle School in Camp Lejeune, North Carolina, the theme of patriotism is developed in a "Spirit of America" interdisciplinary unit.

Integrated Day

This design, involving an extensive reorganization of the entire school includes the entire staff and every student. At Cross Keys Middle School in Florissant, Missouri, a complex interdisciplinary unit called "Historic Dig" takes place over a six-day period. Students gain an understanding of culture by participating in group activities related to the period or culture they are studying.

The importance of the interdisciplinary curriculum movement to the development of alternative assessment lies in the challenge the movement presents to formal standardized testing. With interdisciplinary courses, it is difficult for teachers to isolate knowledge into specific content areas. Some teachers will implement an interdisciplinary study unit with a team of other teachers, only to revert back to the content domain area for testing. But more and more teachers are willing to continue the interdisciplinary curriculum and instruction theme into testing. Having broken the mold in content organization and delivery, they have the mind set to continue to do so in testing by developing creative and truly alternative forms of assessments. Freed from the content arena of isolated facts and recall, these assessments can easily move into cognitive integrated areas of analysis, synthesis, and evaluation. Teachers who use interdisciplinary approaches often require students to show understanding by performing or exhibiting.

For more detailed information on interdisciplinary curriculum movement, see Jacobs (1989) for a concise explanation, Maurer (1994) for examples of interdisciplinary curriculum in 42 award-winning middle/junior high schools and high schools, and Beane (1990) for a philosophical analysis of interdisciplinary curriculum design.

The Constructivist Paradigm

Research in cognitive psychology portrays learning as needing complex, diverse, and concrete experiences in which students make connections between inner mental representations and external perceptions and experiences. There are many different names for this type of learning. Phrases like "making connections," "educating for insight," "understanding performances," "authentic instruction," and "thinking-centered learning," define learning as an active generative process that places the student, not the teacher, at the center of the teaching and learning experience.

At the core of this paradigm is the belief that students construct understanding of the world about them. This process is a deep one in that it allows the student to process information in relation to what is already known, whether this past knowledge is correct or incorrect. Caine and Caine (1991) describe the process as one where the search for meaning is innate, involving not only cognitive processes but also emotional ones; where the process is one of building patterns consciously and unconsciously; and where memory is best engaged when facts and skills are part of natural discovery and creativity in the specific authentic context of learning. Perkins (1993–1994) focuses on describing constructivist learning as a process where students engage in higher or thinking skills: analyzing, critiquing, defending, asking what-if questions, and exploring other points of view. Such active thinking allows students to construct elaborate webs of connections that produce deep understanding and more efficient long-term memory.

Brooks and Brooks (1993) contrast a traditional classroom with a classroom involving constructivist teaching. In traditional classrooms, the curriculum is presented from part to whole, with emphasis on basic skills, curricular activities relying heavily on textbooks and workbooks, and assessment of student learning as separate from teaching. Assessment occurs almost entirely through testing. Constructivist classrooms, on the other hand, present curriculum from whole to part with an emphasis on big concepts, curricular activities relying heavily on primary sources of data and manipulative materials, and assessment of student learning as interwoven with teaching and occurring through observation and student exhibitions and portfolios.

For those readers interested in measuring the standards of a true constructivist classroom, Newmann and Wehlage (1993) describe five standards, each one measured on a scale from low (1) to high (5). The five standards are the presence of higher order thinking skills, depth of knowledge, connectedness to the world beyond the classroom, substantive conversation, and social support for student achievement.

The constructivist teacher presents a direct challenge to traditional forms of assessment. Recall of isolated bits of information not related to the direct learning context does not assess deep understanding. Such assessments are driven by the course content coverage. The question is: "What can you remember of all the information covered or studied in this course?" Authentic assessment measures what the student has internalized about the learning process. The question becomes "What can you show, tell, do, or write for me that demonstrates what you know?" Assessment is a natural process that carries over from activities in the classroom. Assessment in the context of the learning process happens over time, provides the student and teacher with feedback on progress made, and always involves action or performances.

One curriculum initiative that has grown from the development of the constructivist paradigm is the whole language movement. This approach views literacy development as an active process where the student learns phonetics, pramatics, semantics, and syntax at the same time, not as isolated skills. Language development is total immersion; it is holistic. A whole language elementary school teacher attempts to connect a student with reading and writing from the first day of school. Students read and write about their reading in journals, all the while making connections between what they know and new information. Creating books and stories is part of authentic instruction. In a science classroom at the secondary level, the teacher has the students working in microscopes the first week of school. Learning about the parts of the microscope and its history can come later. The goal is to have the students involved in hands-on science and connecting what they know about nature with what they discover using the microscope.

Assessment in the whole language classroom is authentic because it measures instruction that is authentic. Goodman, Goodman, and Hood (1989) define the process as ongoing, something that happens in the course of teaching and learning. Both self-evaluation and peer evaluation are part of the assessment process. Whole language teachers use interaction between themselves and the students, observation of a student's work, and analysis of changes in student behavior as an indication of developing knowledge and competence.

Summary

A teacher interested in whether a student can transfer what is known to solve a problem in a different but real context is one who is interested in using an assessment tool that is authentic. Such a teacher tries to understand the meanings students assign to ideas by investigating how students use understanding for performance.

The initiative for authentic assessment has come from many different movements, three of which were defined to some degree in this chapter. The first is the emphasis on higher standards, which has prompted a significant change in how schools do business. Disagreement on what these standards are has fueled debates from Congress to state legislatures to local school board meetings, and major national reform movements have been born from the ensuing controversy.

One can understand the great interest in standards if one considers the radical change that the establishment of national standards will cause. Since the founding of this nation, education has been left to the local level of government to define and fund. National standards will dismantle over two hundred years of educational politics and culture. Whether or not national standards come, the debate has focused educators not only on the outcomes but also on the measurement process. The use of standardized tests and minimum competency tests is under attack. These are seen as cheap approaches that are ineffective in raising the educational quality of our nation's schools. The use of the type of assessments that teachers use in the classroom every day to measure student comprehension and growth is being advocated as more authentic in the context of the instructional process.

The United States is striving to be first in the world in establishing a competitive and competent work force. This movement, known as Work Force 2000, is the second major influence on assessment. The original initiative for educational reform came primarily from a concern for the nation's economic health. As Japan, then Germany, and now the Pacific Rim countries achieve strong economic growth, the United States feels its leadership position is being threatened. This concern became focused on our nation's schools as perhaps the one institution that has caused the decline and also the one institution that can restore the nation's economic health. The U.S. Departments of Labor and Education have teamed up to promote the establishment of world-class benchmark standards for our country's youth. This movement is significant in that it links worker preparation very closely to the instructional and assessment process within our schools. Because the interest is in the quality of an individual's work, the emphasis is on authentic assessment. That is, a student should be able to demonstrate how knowledge can be applied to complete certain tasks that are directly related to skills required for the workplace. The apprenticeship model is often cited as a process whereby a student is assessed continually and in context of a real-life task.

The third major influence comes from recent research in developmental and cognitive psychology. At first, this research was confined to professional journals, but in the past decade the findings have reached into most classrooms and have changed forever what we know about how children learn. We now know that children learn by connecting new knowledge to what they already know. Mental representations of the world influence perception and assimilation of new knowledge. The learning process itself involves the student in searching for patterns and relationships. Students construct knowledge by applying thinking skills and generating new knowledge that can be applied to authentic contexts. Some of the instructional changes that have been developed from this view of learning have been the theory of multiple intelligences, a reemphasis on interdisciplinary curriculum, and the constructivist paradigm influences on curriculum development.

All three of these influences—standards, Work Force 2000, and the constructivist paradigm—advocate the use of assessments that are based on having students demonstrate what they know and can do in the context of real world experience. Assessment of individuals should reflect what we now know how students learn. The assessment process should help, not check, a student seeking understanding for performance. The authentic assessment movement is a major paradigm shift. It challenges what we think we know about how students learn and what students should learn. It is not an easy change to swallow.

The remaining chapters will help the reader design authentic assessments that meet the needs of the student, teacher, parent, and community.

References

Beane, J. A. (1990). *A middle school curriculum: From rhetoric to reality*. Columbus, OH: National Middle School Association.

Bloom, B. (1956). *Taxonomy of education objectives: Handbook I: Cognitive domain*. New York: David McKay.

Brooks, J. G., & Brooks, M. (1993). *The case for constructivist classrooms*. Alexandria, VA: Association for Supervision and Curriculum Development.

Caine, R. N., & Caine, G. (1991). *Teaching and the human brain*. Alexandria, VA: Association for Supervision and Curriculum Development.

Carnegie Forum. (1986). *A nation prepared: Teachers for the 21st century*. New York: Carnegie Forum.

Carnegie Council on Adolescent Development. (1989). *Turning points: Preparing American youth for the 21st century. The report of the Task Force on Education of Young Adolescents*. Washington, DC: The Council.

Chomsky, N. (1980). *Rules and representation*. New York: Columbia University Press.

Cuomo, M. (1992, September). *Education That Works: Creating Career Pathways for New York State Youths*. Albany: New York State Governor's Office.

Darling-Hammond, L. (1993, June). Reframing the school reform agenda. *Phi Delta Kappan*, 753–761.

Darling-Hammond, L. (1993, November). Setting standards for students: The case for authentic assessment. *NASSP Bulletin, 77*, 18–26.

Education Commission of the States Task Force on Education for Economic Growth. (1983). *Action for excellence*. Denver, CO: Education Commission of the States.

Fuhrman, S. H. (1994). Legislatures and education policy. In R. F. Elmore & S. H. Fuhrman (Eds.), *The governance of curriculum*. Alexandria, VA: Association for Supervision and Curriculum Development.

Gardner, H. (1983, 1985 paperback). *Frames of mind: The theory of multiple intelligences*. New York: Basic Books.

Gardner, H. (1991). *The unschooled mind: How children think and how schools should teach*. New York: Basic Books.

Goodman, K., Goodman, Y., & Hood, W. (1989). *The whole language evaluation book*. Portsmouth, NH: Heinemann.

Hawley, W. (1990). Preparing students from today's families for tomorrow's cognitive challenges. In S. B. Bacharach (Ed.), *Education reform: Making sense of it all*. Boston: Allyn and Bacon.

Jacobs, H. H. (Ed.). (1989). *Interdisciplinary curriculum: Design and implementation*. Alexandria, VA: Association for Supervision and Curriculum Development.

Kirst, M. W. (1990). The crash of the first wave. In S. B. Bacharach (Ed.), *Education reform: Making sense of it all*. Boston: Allyn and Bacon.

Kohlberg, W. H., & Smith, F. C. (1992). Forum: A new track for blue-collar workers. *New York Times*. February 9.

Maurer, R. E. (1994). *Designing interdisciplinary curriculum in middle, junior high, and high schools*. Boston: Allyn and Bacon.

Metropolitan Life Insurance Company. (1993). *The American teacher 1993: Teachers respond to President Clinton's educational proposals*. New York: Metropolitan Life Insurance Company.

Mitchell, R. (1992). *Testing for learning*. New York: Free Press.

National Center on Education and the Economy. Commission on the Skills of the American Workforce. (1990, June). *America's choice: High skills or low wages!* Rochester, NY: The Commission.

National Commission on Excellence in Education. (1983). *A nation at risk: The imperative for educational reform*. Washington, DC: U.S. Department of Education.

Newmann, F. M., & Wehlage, G. (1993, April). Five standards of authentic instruction. *Educational Leadership, 7*, 8–12.

New Standards Project. (1994). Washington, DC: National Center on Education and the Economy.

Perkins, D. (1991, October). Educating for insight. *Educational Leadership, 49*, 4–8.

Perkins, D. (1993–1994). Thinking centered learning. *Educational Leadership, 51*, 84–85.

Piaget, J. (1967). *The child's conception of the world.* Totowa, NJ: Littlefield, Adams.

Piaget, J. (1974). *To understand is to ivnent: The future of education.* New York: Grossman.

Resnick, L., & Nolan, K. (1995). Where in the world are world class standards: *Educational Leadership, 52*, 6–10.

Restak, R. M. (1979). *The brain: The last frontier.* New York: Doubleday.

Secretary's Commission on Achieving Necessary Skills (SCANS), U.S. Department of Labor. (1992, March). *Learning a living: Schools, competence, and jobs.* Washington, DC: The Commission.

Skinner, B. F. (1953). Some contributions of an experimental analysis of behavior to psychology as a whole. *American Psychologist, 8*, 69–78.

Smith, M. S., Fuhrman, S. H., & O'Day, J. (1994). National curriculum standards: Are they desirable and feasible? In R. F. Elmore & S. H. Fuhrman (Eds.), *The governance of curriculum.* Alexandria, VA: Association for Supervision and Curriculum Development.

Sperry, R. (1968). Hemisphere disconnection and unity in conscious awareness. *American Psychologist, 23*, 723–733.

The State Education Leader. (1992, Fall). A guide to systems change initiatives. Denver, CO: Education Commission of the States.

Tversky, A., & Kahneman, D. (1974). Judgment under certainty: Heuristics and biases. *Science*, p. 1124.

U.S. Department of Education. (1993). *The Goals 2000 Educate America Act of 1994.* Washington, DC: U.S. Government Printing Office.

Vars, G. (1991). Integrated curriculum: Historical perspective. *Educational Leadership, 49*, 14–15.

Worthen, B. (1993, February). Critical issues that will determine the future of alternative assessment. *Phi Delta Kappan*, pp. 444–456.

2 Determining Interdisciplinary Curriculum Standards

After having examined the issues that have led to the development of alternative assessments, with this chapter we begin to design actual alternative assessments for interdisciplinary curricula. The first step is to establish a taxonomy or planning guide for this process. Each assessment should have at least five major components. The following four-step taxonomy of alternative assessment will guide us through the design process.

1. *Standards:* First, establish the knowledge and/or skills you would like the students to attain as a result of your instruction. These become the standard you will use to determine not only the instruction but also the assessment process. Once the standards are established, you can build interdisciplinary themes from them.

2. *Assessment task:* This is the work the student must accomplish to demonstrate mastery of the curriculum standard previously established. This work is usually the culminating activity of the instructional process but also can be a collection of activities accomplished over a specific period of time. These assessments should be authentic in that they require students to connect the learning activities to tasks that demonstrate proficiency in a real context. They may be projects, exhibitions, a performance, or a portfolio.

3. *Measurements:* This includes the specific criteria on which the task will be judged. These criteria provide the mark to aim for and should be available to the student beforehand. They answer the question: "What is this student's performance in relation to the defined outcome, to the individual students, and to others in the class?"

4. *Reflection:* After the instructional unit has been completed, including the assessment piece, take some time to review the entire process, especially with respect to its reliability, validity, and generalizability.

It is helpful to follow the taxonomy presented here in designing the initial authentic assessments. Once you have some experience with the process, you may want to personalize this taxonomy to meet your own needs.

This chapter focuses on the first stage of the taxonomy: determining the interdisciplinary curriculum standards you want to establish. Subsequent chapters will deal with the other three stages.

Setting Standards

In Chapter 1 I discussed the effect the standards movement had on the development of the authentic assessment initiative. Here I will define, explain, and show how to construct standards. The term *standards*, for the purposes of this discussion, is synonymous with *outcomes, frameworks,* or *benchmarks.* Defined as an observable or measurable result in the area of what we expect students to know, to do, and to be like, an outcome or standard is set before instruction begins. A standard is aimed at the student, not the curriculum. The question is, "What can we expect of the student?," not "What curriculum material do we have to cover?" (paradoxically, a standard or outcome must be both broad and specific at the same time—broad enough to be flexible in defining how a student reaches it, yet specific enough to define what skills will be engaged. The standard we develop will drive all our decisions about curriculum, instruction, and ultimately assessment. Next I will describe the decision that must be made about curriculum and instruction. In Chapter 3 I will show how assessment decisions are made.

Currently there is controversy over what standards should be included in the curriculum. As parents and community members have become more involved in the educational reform movement, decisions about what students should know are no longer left in the hands of educators or politicians.

The two chief entry points for parent and community involvement have been the nature of high-stakes assessments and the inclusion of nonacademic standards. As standards have become more closely tied to evaluation, the controversy has only increased. High-stakes assessments become an issue if students are going to be held accountable for achievement in order to go on to the next grade or even to graduate. Most of us went through an educational system where passing a course was sufficient for moving up or accumulating a certain number of credits met the criterion for graduation. The emphasis on student accountability prompts concerns as to whether schools and teachers are capable of delivering quality instruction to help students meet these new and usually more stringent standards. There is a fear that kids will be hurt in the process.

The second issue concerns the inclusion of nonacademic areas in standards/assessment reform. Many parents question whether schools should be holding students accountable for standards in values, ethics, human relations, and other nonacademic areas. The issue of safeguarding the family and individual domain from public institutional intrusion has been raised. Businesses question whether schools should not spend more time dealing with core academic subjects rather than what they see as peripheral subjects.

In this book I will focus on academic standards. You will see in the next chapter that the focus on assessment, at least at this stage of development, does not advocate high-stakes testing. A second feature of this book is the deep-seated belief that curriculum standards cannot be mandated from the process of standard setting—teachers, parents, community members, administrators, and students—be committed, trained, and motivated to make the standards achievable.

A standard should be developed in a hierarchical format. The first step is to develop exit standards. From these we develop program standards, then course standards, and finally unit standards. Exit standards—the broad goals we wish students to achieve before they leave our school—should be set for the entire school district. They are the "wants" of the educational staff. The achievement of exit standards should virtually ensure that students will achieve future success. For this reason, exit standards should be developed by a broad constituency representing all the stakeholders in the district. This broad involvement enables everyone to feel part of the process and empowers those involved with the students with a mission that clearly defines what is expected of all students in the school district. An exit standard ("The Criteria of Outcome-Based Education," 1992) directly reflects the knowledge, competencies, and orientations individuals need to function successfully in this world.

A few examples of exit standards follows:

Self-directed learners
Collaborative workers
Community contributors
Quality producers
Well read individuals
Complex thinkers who discover, access, integrate, and use available resources and information to reason, make decisions, and create solutions for complex problems in a variety of contexts
Effective communicators who convey thoughts, competencies, and feelings to others through a variety of methods

Exit standards force students to create new knowledge, not just consume others' knowledge. If exit outcomes are truly to drive instruction and assessment, then they must move students away from curriculum that is based on memorizing many facts, that emphasizes review for recall, that covers easy items followed by harder ones, that covers material chronologically, and that is tied to a textbook.

How to Develop Standards

The following process may be followed in designing exit standards. As you proceed through the process, place a check mark on what you have accomplished.

_____ 1. With as broad a constituency as possible, involving representatives of as many stakeholder groups in your school district as you can, develop a district planning team. Members should come from the teaching, secretarial, administrative, custodial, PTA, community, business, recreational, and social groups. A group of 15 to 20 members is appropriate.

_____ 2. At the first meeting, have the group decide how it will make decisions. A consensus building model is ideal, but a contingency plan should exist for dealing with controversy. A voting procedure should also be defined.

_____ 3. Ask members of the representative group to brainstorm what they would like each student in the district to be able to do when he or she graduates from the last grade in the district. In most cases, this would be what the group expects twelfth-grade graduates to be able to do.

_____ 4. From the brainstorm list, consolidate the various answers under different broad headings. Hold discussions about the meaning of these terms, words, or concepts.

_____ 5. Ask the group to decide on a list of standards they would like all graduates to meet when they exit from the district. The list should not be voluminous but should reflect broad areas of the group's interest. These outcomes then become the proposed exit standards of the district.

_____ 6. Hold public meetings on the exit standards. Have members of the various stakeholder groups explain the outcomes to their respective constituents.

_____ 7. Assemble the district planning group for a final meeting to make any necessary adjustments in the exit standards.

Once the exit standards are clearly defined, you need to develop program standards, which specify further how to reach the exit standards. Commonly, program standards are linked closely to curriculum guidelines in areas such as math, science, or social studies. Many schools develop program standards at the departmental level and represent them as department standards. In addition, program standards may contain statements about what the student will do, include connections to other subject areas, and incorporate higher order thinking skills. Most program standards begin with action verbs emphasizing their performance orientation. An example of program standards for mathematics follows:

1. Develop critical thinking through a variety of methods to solve problems found in all aspects of life, including consumer, political, social, and environmental issues.
2. Connect mathematics with its different components and to other subjects, establishing its relevance to life situations.
3. Create and communicate solutions to new problems by applying previous knowledge and experience in mathematics.

These program standards require a student to accomplish certain tasks in mathematics that are directly related to the exit standard established. A program standard should indicate that if a student accomplishes the defined task, then the exit standard will be achieved. For example, if a student can accomplish program standard #2, connecting mathematics with other subjects to show relevance to life situations, then the exit standard requiring a student to be successful in complex thinking (listed earlier) will be achieved. The specifics of how this program standard will be completed is left to the definition of the course standard.

Course standards are specific and further define what is required of the student. They are built from the program and exit standards already stated. A course standard will tell the student what he or she will accomplish by the end of the course time, whether the duration is a year, semester, quarter, or week. After reading a course standard, you should be able to describe to someone exactly what you will be able to do at the end of the course. Course standards do not tell you what you will cover, read, or study. They tell you what you will *do*. The emphasis is on performance.

Building course standards using action verbs is an excellent way to ensure that the development of functions such as higher order thinking skills. Bloom (1956) outlines six levels of mental functioning, ranging from basic facts to higher order thinking. Each level is listed here, with verbs that describe the inherent mental processes:

1. *Knowledge:* list, cite, arrange, label, group, pick, quote, say, show, spell, write, recite, identify, match
2. *Comprehension:* change, convert, moderate, restate, infer, define, outline, propose, calculate, project
3. *Application:* relate, utilize, solve, operate, manipulate, put to use, make use of, explain how, classify
4. *Analysis:* uncover, examine, deduce, inspect, search, test for, compare, contrast
5. *Synthesis:* create, combine, reorganize, generate, make up, brainstorm, generalize, predict, organize solutions, organize concepts, diagram, add to

6. *Evaluation:* judge, decide, rank, reject, determine, critique, state opinion about, select from equally appealing alternatives, conduct an evaluation

To incorporate higher order thinking skills in your course standard, choose action verbs representingt the last three levels of mental functioning: analysis, synthesis, and evaluation. This does not preclude teaching in the other domains such as knowledge and comprehension, as these are necessary to accomplish if students are to reach the higher levels. The point is that you do not want to stay stuck at the basic levels.

A mathematical course standard developed from the mathematics program standard #2 ("Connect mathematics with its different components and to other subjects, establishing its relevance to life situations.") described earlier is:

Students will use a computer spreadsheet for the purposes of compiling, comparing, graphing, and analyzing data.

This course standard is written clearly, and the verbs used require students to make use of higher order thinking skills. At the end of the course, each student will have a product to show.

Course standards are the core knowledge of the curriculum. The curriculum is usually much broader than the course outcomes. An analogy to the old computer floppy disk seen in Figure 2-1 serves us well here. The core course standards are represented by the hole in the center. These are the common critical course standards shared by all teachers teaching the course. The remainder of the disk represents other aspects of the curriculum. This model leaves room for teachers to teach material that is particularly important to them while still maintaining a common core. It is this core that constitutes the measured course standards. In Chapter 3 I will discuss various means to measure this core.

How to Establish Course Standards

Following the steps listed here, join with other teachers in your school or in your district who teach the same course. Using the program and exit standards already established, the next step is to design the core standards you want to establish for your course. Check each step as you plan.

____ 1. Gather the course syllabus, any state standards available, textbooks, and other printed or software material you have related to your particular course.

____ 2. With other teachers, review the collected material and decide what you would like your students to know by the end of the

FIGURE 2-1   The Relationship of Core Curriculum Standards to Curriculum

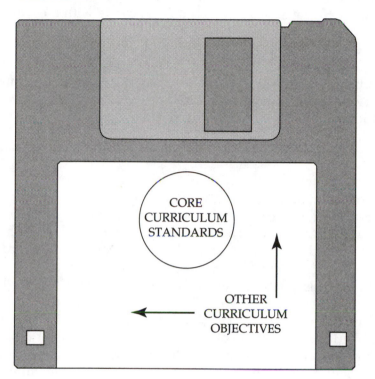

course. List everything you discuss. You are still at the brainstorming stage.

_____ 3.   Decide as a team to choose three or four things (for full-year courses, fewer things for shorter courses) you feel should be at the curriculum core. This process will take some time. Consider that these are the essential or most crucial things a student should know as a result of your course. They are the most crucial for moving on to the next grade or school level.

_____ 4.   Decide as a team how a student could demonstrate understanding of the knowledge you have decided is most crucial. Choose action verbs to describe what the student will do, say, perform, or demonstrate. The emphasis in your discussions should be on developing performances of understanding for these core outcomes.

_____ 5.   Review the descriptions that your team has written. If some of them seem to be too complicated for students to perform or involve tasks that are too simple, discard the core outcome chosen and choose one of those that was high on the list but not initially picked. Repeat step #4 for this outcome.

_____ **6.** Share your core course outcomes with teachers from other disciplines in your school, district, or grade. If you are part of an interdisciplinary team of teachers, share these course outcomes with the team.

7. If necessary, determine whether some of the course standards from the different disciplines can be integrated to form interdisciplinary course standards. (For examaple, a colonial history outcome in history can be combined with a writing outcome in English to require students to write a colonial newspaper article.)

The final step in the process of developing course standards is to provide a draft document for review by representatives of parents and the community. Most parents and community members do not have the time or background to be involved in developing course standards. You need knowledge of the curriculum scope and sequence to be a contributing member in this phase. However, these core course standards should be reviewed with representatives of parents and of other teachers in the building. One school district used a PTA meeting for this purpose. Another school had the teachers explain the course standards at a back-to-school evening. A faculty meeting or grade-level meeting can be used to assist a staff review. Making the review process at the draft-forming stage is important because it tells parents and community members that you have not finalized the course standards, nor have you excluded others from the process. In giving other staff members time to review your standards, you offer the possibilities of building interdisciplinary connections in the curriculum. The following chart can serve as a guide.

Course Review Guide

This guide can be given to the review team members before the meeting. At the meeting, team members can share their thoughts and develop a common review guide response. Question #4 can be used to answers concerns at the local school district level.

_____ **1.** Do the course standards relate to the exit   YES   NO
standards? How? _____

_____

2. Do the course standards have connections to   YES   NO
other curriculum standards or disciplines in
the building or grade level? Which ones? _____

_____

_____ **3.** Are the standards written in clear simple   YES   NO
       language? If NO, rewrite them here.

_____

_____

_____ **4.** Do the standards _____ ?   YES   NO

       Comment _____

       _____

       Summary: Do you recommend adoption   YES   NO
       of this standard?

       _____

       _____

Once you have developed course standards, you need to be aware that they are not set in stone. They should be reviewed, revised, and updated every year. Curriculum does not stay static, nor do teachers teach the same material every year. Do not assume that because you reviewed and incorporated parent feedback the first time, you therefore do not have to review the process each year. Parents and parent groups change in a school or school district. The review should be done yearly. In the following chart you will see how some course standards changed from year to year. They have become, in most cases, clearer and less value-oriented.

Initial	*Revised*
Students demonstrate understanding of number concepts.	Students demonstrate number concepts and use numbers appropriately and accurately.
Students identify and describe systems, subsystems, and components and their interactions by completing tasks and/or creating products.	Students identify and analyze systems and the ways their components work together to affect each other.
All children should be able to acquire basic skills in music reading.	Students will be able to demonstrate a level of understanding in their individual music area, culminating in performance or a product.

Unit standards come next. They are written by the teacher to describe a specific subskill a student will be able to accomplish in a short period of time—a week or a month—in a course. This subskill will be added to other skills developed and, when the subskills are applied together, will enable the student to accomplish the task defined in the total course standard. Individual teachers can take responsibility for writing unit standards. Unit standards can be different for teachers who share the same course standards.

To accomplish the mathematical course standard involving spreadsheets a teacher would have to take time in the planning to develop specific unit standards. For example, there would have to be a unit on computers.

Students will be able to access the spreadsheet program on the computer and create a simple spreadsheet using one mathematical formula.

Another unit will have to be created to teach students how to compile or collect data to be incorporated into the spreadsheet.

Students will be able to access information and data from a database on the computer and be able to arrange the data in a certain order.

One can see from the logical order of building outcomes or standards that one starts from the top and works down:

Exit standards
Program standards
Course standards
Unit standards

This arrangement provides a very closely aligned curriculum, which directs a student toward achieving the broad goals of the district—the exit standards. There is no room in this type of planning for not knowing where the students will be at the end of the course, whether all the material will be covered, whether a student can accomplish it, and whether the material in the course is important or crucial. Questions like "Will this be on the test?" or "Did I miss anything important in yesterday's class?" or "What do I have to know this for?" will not be asked.

In summary, setting a standard is a process that requires many steps. In planning, you have to begin where you want to end up. Once this is determined, you know the standard or standards you want your students to have when they leave you. The rest of your planning is not guesswork. It carefully builds down by defining, specifying, and finally stating what a student will do at each stage. The curriculum alignment is tight and can be carefully planned and documented along the way. Parents and community members are involved in establishing the exit standards and reviewing the course standards.

Choosing an Interdisciplinary Theme

Determining the theme of the interdisciplinary curriculum unit is a process that builds from establishing the exit and program standards. You cannot choose an interdisciplinary theme until you know where you want to go with the instruction. Often we read about exciting interdisciplinary projects in schools, but they are just that—projects. They appear as abnormalities in the curriculum sequence and remain outside the "real" curriculum content. Gardner and Mansilla-Boix (1994) present a strong case for the need to maintain the integrity of the disciplines, not subject areas that determine how we schedule students day-to-day. Discipline areas are those that constitute the way we think about life. Sizer (1992) believes that, at the high school level, knowledge should be distinguished into just three or four disciplinary areas—language, history, arts, math, and science. Boyer (1993) talks about twenty-first-century school curriculum being organized around only seven areas: birth, growth, and death; language; aesthetics; time and space; social webs; producing and consuming; and morality and ethics. The disciplines represent the different models of how we view life. They are connected just as knowledge about the world is connected. From the disciplines we build our interdisciplinary themes.

Depending on the grade level you teach, the process will vary but should lead to the same conclusion. An elementary-grade teacher who teaches most of the core subject areas alone will have an easier job choosing a theme than a secondary-level teacher who needs to consult with other subject area teachers on the same grade level. On the other hand, an elementary teacher may want to consult with other grade-level teachers in the building or district to present a unified thematic instruction for all students at the same grade level. And a secondary-level teacher may decide to go it alone with an interdisciplinary theme by establishing a course within a course he or she is teaching.

The first factor to consider in choosing a theme is related to the student's world view. Beane (1990) talks about organizing interdisciplinary themes by blending the concerns of the students with concerns about issues in the larger world. For example, a theme on wellness would blend students' personal concerns with the larger issues of nutrition, disease, stress, and public health. Arnold (1993) presents a similar view in which the student is empowered to make decisions about which themes should be allowed in an interdisciplinary unit. He believes that themes should allow students to assume some control over their own learning by exercising initiative and responsibility, should help them make sense of themselves and their world, and should allow all students to contribute to the well-being of others while at the same time helping them feel needed and useful.

A second factor in choosing a theme is to look for a primary principle, not just a topic. A theme should be a universal concept. In language arts, for example, a theme would be the study of identity, rather than a more limited topic such as heroes or heroines. In social studies it would be a study of human needs rather than something specific like the long houses of the Iroquois. Brophy and Alleman (1991) list some principles for the design, selection, and evaluation of curriculum activities. Some of these are as follows:

- *Goal relevance:* Activities should be built around powerful ideas, key concepts, and generalizations. Teachers should avoid isolated activities or themes taken out of context. For example, studying "leadership" is preferable to cutting out paper axes and cherries on George Washington's birthday.
- *Multiple goals:* Themes should connect major ideas from various subjects. These themes should engage students in critical thinking and decision making; they should be current and should be seen as authentic. Thus, a colonial newspaper project connecting social studies and language arts can be part of larger theme on communication. Writing should be emphasized in such a project, not just creating art for the paper's masthead.

A third factor is what Perkins (1986) calls "understanding performances." He believes we need to design themes out of generative topics or topics that connect knowledge. These are the themes that engage students deeply by emphasizing connection-making performances within and across subject matter knowledge. They demand that students explain, find evidence, and give examples. These performances build and show student understanding.

Stevenson and Carr (1993) believe that organizing a theme around a culminating event can help teachers focus on the theme. This event, be it a performance, presentation, product, or outing, can aprovide the structure from which students can engage the subject matter enthusiastically and deeply.

A fourth factor can be referred to calendar mapping or sequencing. Jacobs (1991) believes a good place to begin choosing a theme is to look at the curriculum calendar that is now followed. Teachers can discover when students are studying the different units in the different subjects, sequence those units that are most similar so that they are taught at the same time, eliminate repetitious coverage of the same material, identify those units that have broad themes evident, and target those units that lend themselves to performance-based assessment.

Other factors—feasibility, cost, level of difficulty—also need to be considered. Try to find a theme that captures the four major criteria described here: relevance to students, primary principles, multiple goals, and appropriate sequencing.

The easiest way to begin is to use a mapping grid, which presents in a pictorial fashion the scope and sequence of the theme. Maurer (1994); Van Patten, Chao, and Reigeluth (1986); and Fogarty (1991) present a number of different methods to map an interdisciplinary theme. Vars (1993) presents a coamprehensive monograph on how to use mapping as a technique as well as how to reformat the daily structure of the school to meet the needs of interdisciplinary curriculum. The most common mapping procedure is the *webbing sequence*. For example, suppose that three elementary school teachers have teamed up to plan an interdisciplinary theme. The teachers represent the separate subject content areas of math, science, language arts, and social studies. They agree on "energy" as a theme. Then they begin by mapping how this broad theme can be taught. Their use of the webbing sequence is illustrated in Figure 2-2.

In the center is the theme, ENERGY. From this radiates the four major subject areas. From each of these are listed a host of activities the teachers can do to teach around the major theme. This webbing represents the brainstorming process. The next step is to decide how much time to spend on this unit—a few days, a week, two weeks, a month. This time factor will limit the scope of the theme. Once the final list of activities is agreed to, the staff needs to ask each other these questions:

1. Is the theme relevant to the personal interests of the students, both in concept and in terms of activities chosen?
2. Is the theme involved with a primary principle and not just a topic?
3. Do the theme and the subsequent activities involve multiple goals?
4. Is the theme current and relevant to today's society?
5. Are higher order thinking skills engaged in some of the activities?
6. Is there an attempt to teach for understanding where the students have to demonstrate mastery of the specific skills and concepts?
7. Do the activities associated with the theme actually support the theme and are they sequenced in terms of time so that there is order and no repetition?

FIGURE 2-2   A Web Sequence to Illustrate an Interdisciplinary Theme

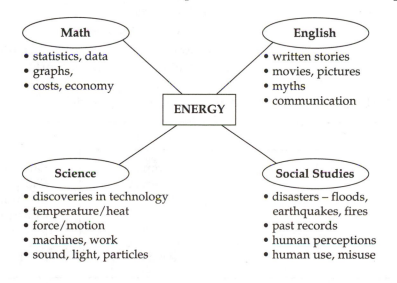

For curriculum that involves an interdisciplinary theme, developing standards follows the same process. The exit outcomes and the program outcomes should already be established for the district or school. Exit outcomes are universal "wants" for the students, regardless of the interdisciplinary curriculum. Program outcomes, as mentioned, are linked to the specific disciplines and support the exit outcomes. For interdisciplinary curriculum to be meaningful, it must be based on the knowledge base of the chief disciplines. It is at the course outcome level that we can clearly define the interdisciplinary theme.

To build a set of course standards for the ENERGY interdisciplinary theme, we can organize our information using Table 2-1. This table is organized into three parts: concepts, strategy, and content. Under "concepts," we place our interdisciplinary theme, ENERGY. Concepts embody the larger picture we are attempting to teach. The "strategy" section tells us what the student will do. The action verb *do* is included here to describe the process students will undertake to understand the content. In this case we have chosen tasks such as "compare and contrast" for the elementary grade levels and "analysis" for the upper grade levels. The last section includes the course content. This material can be taken from a textbook or a curriculum syllabus. The content here is earthquakes, equipment, environmental building, and human perception.

Aligning this curriculum from top to bottom, the sequence would be organized as follows:

Exit standard: Independent thinker

Program standard: *Middle school and high school:*
Understand and demonstrate the interactions of science, technology, and society, and the possibilities and limits of science and technology in explaining the natural world.

Elementary school:
Develop an awareness of how science and technology discoveries in today's life can explain events in the natural world.

TABLE 2-1   Course Outcome Development Model

Concept	*Strategy*	*Content*
ENERGY	Compare Contrast	Earthquake Equipment Environment Construction Perception
	Analyze	Earth templates

Course standard: *Middle school and high school:*
Students will compare and contrast the effects of the performance of seismograph instruments on predicting earthquakes, building construction, and people's view of living in earthquake-prone regions.

Elementary school:
Students will be able to analyze the effects of force and motion of the earth's templates and brainstorm solutions to problems this may cause.

Unit standard: *Middle and high school:*
Students will be able to orally describe how a seismograph instrument works.

Elementary school:
Students will be able to describe orally the function of earth templates.

The exit standard here is something wanted for all students in the district, regardless of age. The program standards are differentiated to allow for different tasks based on age. In the upper grades, students should understand and demonstrate interrelations and pros and cons of science, technology, and society. In the lower grades, students are expected to be aware of and able to explain natural events in their real world using science and technology. In both cases, the program outcomes will allow students to become independent thinkers.

The course standards are clearly defined here in terms of what students will be able to do in an interdisciplinary setting. Using action verbs, they tell us that a secondary student will be able to use higher order thinking skills such as comparing, contrasting, and predicting against three additional factors: earthquakes, construction, and human perceptions. At the elementary level, the higher order thinking skills of analyzing and brainstorming will be applied to force and motion under the earth and to solving human problems. This course will not be taught in a week or two. There is a wealth of information to be understood, skills to learn, and projects to be completed. It is evident that the course uses interdisciplinary connections and requires students to do things (demonstrate and explain). Though specific in description, these outcomes are written to allow flexibility for the student to choose different means to demonstrate proficiency on this standard. For one student it may be a project, for another a videotape or even a traditional term paper. Several students may join together to plan and execute these tasks, thus introducing a collaborative element to the project.

The unit standard here demonstrates how a teacher would break the course standard down into smaller planning units. In this example, only the first unit standard is presented. These units are performance-based as well. In the secondary unit, students would need to know how the seismographic instrument works in order to complete the tasks in the course standards. At the elementary level, knowledge of the movement of the earth's templates is necessary before anything else can be done to fulfill the course standard. Teachers at both levels would need many different unit outcomes all aimed at helping students complete the course standard.

Examples of Interdisciplinary Standards

As mentioned in Chapter 1, there is a major emphasis on establishing standards for students. There seems to be no lack of standards from which to choose. So many standards are being generated, in fact, that there is bound to be a collision sooner or later.

All fifty states have developed standards. An excellent summary and comparison of the different states' curriculum standards can be found in *Education Week* (April 1995). A similar excellent summary and comparison of the ten different national commissions and professional groups designing standards can be found in the same issue of this publication.

The federal government is promoting Goals 2000, another attempt to set standards at the national level. There are attempts to create a sort of clearinghouse for all these goals by such groups as the Council of Chief State School Officers and the Council for Basic Education.

A very good guide to the standards movement can be found in Ravitch's (1995) *National Standards in American Education: A Citizen's Guide.* Here she describes the origins of the move to establish national standards and assessments, examines the rationale for such standards, defines standards and their purposes, and analyzes current federal and state activities. This is a good resource for parents and/or school board members to read.

To develop standards for your district, school, or class, it may be helpful to look at standards others have already developed. You may want to copy some ideas or at least use them as guides. Listed here are various types of standards already in place.

Toronto Board of Education

Program Standards in Language and Video—Grade 8

- Use language appropriately as a means of communication and an instrument of thought.
- Show an understanding of purpose, content, and audience in preparing a talk.
- Express ideas in a variety of forms including talk.

- Explain and express personal interpretations of new learning.
- Become aware through self-evaluation of personal strengths and weaknesses.
- Develop values related to personal and ethical beliefs and to the common welfare of society.

Course Standards in Language and Video—Grade 8

Students will prepare and deliver a two-minute talk for television on a chosen topic. The talk will be videotaped and should be designed to interest and persuade the audience and display evidence of social, moral, and political responsibility.

Alma Public Schools

Exit Standards

1. Displays self-esteem as a learner and a person.
2. Exhibits cognitive learning:
   a. Masters essential skills.
   b. Learns on an extended basis.
   c. Progresses from low to high cognitive levels.

3. Possesses process skills:
   a. Solves problems.
   b. Communicates effectively.
   c. Makes decisions in a logical, mature manner.
   d. Demonstrates accountability.
   e. Understands group processes.

4. Learns in a self-directed manner.
5. Shows concern for others.
6. Demonstrates emotional, social, and physical well-being.

New York State Curriculum and Assessment Frameworks for Language Arts

Program Standard #3

The student will write, listen, and speak for social interaction.

Course Standard #4 (Commencement—High School)

As a group, create an annotated reading list of 25 books you believe should be read by all high school students before graduation. For each entry, include a critical review written by one or more members of your group. Group members must agree on the selections and assure a balance of fiction and nonfiction, a range of genres, and authorship representing a range of cultures.

Johnson City (New York) School District

Exit Standard
Self-directed learner:

- Is creative.
- Understands and uses knowledge.
- Can use the tools of the disciplines.
- Has attitudes supportive of inquiry.
- Has a clear values system.
- Has knowledge of self as a learner.
- Has an adequate self-concept.
- Can take charge of his or her own learning.

Kentucky State Education Department

Exit Standards

Goal 1: Apply basic communication and mathematical skills in situations similar to what students will experience in life.
Goal 2: Apply core concepts and principles from mathematics, science, social studies, arts, and practical living studies to situations similar to what students will experience in life.
Goal 3: Demonstrate self-sufficiency.
Goal 4: Demonstrate responsible citizenship.
Goal 5: Think and solve problems.
Goal 6: Integrate knowledge across disciplines.

National History Standards Project

Program Standard
Students should know the causes of the American Revolution, the ideas and interests involved in forging the revolutionary movement, and the reasons for the American victory.

Course Standards
Students will reconstruct the arguments among patriots and loyalists about independence and draw conclusions about how the decision to declare independence was reached.

Wyandotte Public Schools (Wyandotte, Michigan)

Course Standard for First Grade
The average student will demonstrate knowledge of basic care and responsibilities pertaining to his or her body.

State of Hawaii Performance Standards

Life Science Program Standard (K–3)
Students will understand the structures and functions of animal and plant parts.

Life Science Course Standard (K–3)
Students will be able to group plants and animals by structures and characteristics.

- Students will be able to observe measurable and nonmeasurable characteristics including texture, shape, size, smell, sound, and temperature.

National Council for Science Standards

Program Standards
Students should know the major discoveries in science and technology, some of their social and economic effects, and the major scientists and inventors associated with them.

Course Standard (Grade 3–4)
Students will be able to create a timeline tracing the development of the wheel and simple tools in the ancient world, and subsequent developments of technological inventions, control of the elements, and work.

Controversy Surrounding Standards

One would think that defining high standards for students would be popular with most Americans. Indeed, the business community, parents, and educators, have called for higher standards in our educational system. Agreeing on which standards we will set for our students, however, has caused significant controversy. Many states and school districts have found themselves under intense attack in trying to define what they mean by the standards they have set. The different critiques can be grouped according to three different perspectives: community opposition, professional opposition, and loss of control.

Community Opposition

This perspective takes many views. Most commonly criticism comes from religious fundamentalists, political conservatives, and parents of gifted students. Religious fundamentalists may believe that some educational standards meddle with values and social concerns that properly belong to the family. Their concern is that if schools start defining, measuring, and holding students accountable for values, then the schools will have entered into a new and dangerous area of education.

Olson (1993) presents a detailed report outlining the views of religious fundamentalists and politically conservative groups. One example cited is some of the value-laden terminology (e.g., *self-worth* in the state of Pennsylvania) used to write some standards. Particularly hard hit is the outcome-based education (OBE) movement. It is seen as a behavior modification curriculum that teaches students values that the school has decided are "right." Kelly (1993) defends OBE by saying that it does not teach nor does it advocate teaching values. It is a philosophy of organizing curriculum and instruction, not an actual curriculum. Values, he claims, *are* taught in schools, and most people agree that they should be taught. He cites justice, kindness, and honesty as a few examples of universal values that all communities should teach. Other values, he says, should be left to the local community's discretion. Spady (1993) defends OBE also by saying that it advocates that students demonstrate successful performance in the use of knowledge, competence, and performance motivation, not just values.

Parents of gifted students may view the new standards as a "dumbing down" of the curriculum. They may feel that these standards were established to bring slower, less high achieving students up to par with average or bright students. The standards, in this view, do nothing for bright students. In fact, as written, they hold students back. The state of Connecticut (Judson, 1994) has met intense opposition from parents who fear that smaller suburban schools will suffer because the standards are set so low for inner-city schools whose students traditionally lag behind in achievement. The demise of mastery learning in the Chicago public schools was due largely to this same perception. Yet Boschee and Baron (1994) report on several school districts that have actually improved test scores and student achievement after implementing an OBE program. They feel those who are reporting a dumbing down of the curriculum are not looking at the research reporting strong academic gains through OBE.

Professional Opposition

Another point of view from the educational profession itself is that expressed by Cizek (1993), who believes that educators have devoted so much time and effort to trying to enhance students' self-esteem that the profession has been reluctant to demand high standards whereby some students may actually fail. Ina this view, a concern to protect students' self-image from the impact failure or of fear of failure has eroded standards. Many educators believe that standards should be set very high. If many or even most students fail to reach them, there will be an impetus for the schools to improve instruction. Another view is that of McKernan (1993), who believes that predetermining curriculum outcomes undermines the possibility that educational experiences might be valuable for their own sake.

Education has value in process and exploration, not just in product or pre-determined sequence. OBE, McKernan feels, reduces teaching and learning to human engineering. He disputes the notion that knowledge can be broken down and believes instead that knowledge is open-ended inquiry, not just mastery of facts.

Other professionals (Viadero, 1995) question whether authentic assessments can ever be implemented on the state or national level because their very nature makes standardization impossible.

The OBE movement (Center for Outcome-Based Education, 1994) has attacked vigorously the belief that its organization of curriculum is a reduction of standards. OBE advocates state that criticism is often aimed at schools and districts that say they are implementing OBE but, in fact, have misadopted the philosophy. Calling these schools "hucksters," the movement has divorced itself from what they view as an OBE fad wherein everyone is claiming to be using OBE. OBE has adopted a new name, Partners for Quality Learning, to avoid being associated with poor replications.

Loss of Control

Who controls the development of standards has also become a major concern. The education profession itself is split on this issue. Some (Sizer, 1992) believe that school districts or regions should set exit standards for students. These writers believe that states should not have the power to control what students learn. Rather, the function of the state should be to help local districts in achieving and maintaining through some measure of accountability a quality educational program that all students can learn. Advocates of multicultural education support increased local control as well. They believe that curriculum content should reflect the cultural richness and contributions of the minority groups the community represents.

On the other side of the argument, the teacher unions (New York State United Teachers, 1993) believe that states should set core curriculum which might make up 60 to 70 percent of the total curriculum. This ratio allows for local flexibility but ensures quality education for all students, provides continuity for students who move from district to district, and focuses the direction of preservice and inservice teacher training on specific curriculum outcomes.

Instructing for High Standards

Having established the standards we require for our students, it is time to discuss the instructional program that would facilitate meeting these standards. In recent reports in the press, federal courts have found that the delivery system of instruction is so unequal that students in some schools are deprived of their right to a free and equal education. Many questions arise: Do teachers have an in-depth grasp of the curriculum content? Are teachers trained to deliver the new curriculum standards? Are there sufficient supplies and materials available for students? Is the school effectively organized to deliver the instruction? These questions need to be asked before any assessment system holds students accountable. In the area of effective instruction, the research is rich with attributes. The reader no doubt has access to much of this literature. Three processes, however, should be mentioned here because they have proved to have close correlation with students demonstrating high standards.

Proficiency Learning

This is a systematic approach to curriculum, instruction, and assessment that is based on the idea that all children can achieve high standards providing that there are multiple ways for students to reach the standards and sufficient time for them to do so. The curriculum system discussed earlier in this chapter consists essentially of a top-down planning of goals and student outcomes, from exit standards to program standards, course standards, and finally unit standards. The curriculum materials are used in a logical manner to support the attainment of the goals.

Proficiency learning (Block, Efthim, & Burns, 1989) divides the curriculum into units of instruction, focuses instruction on these goals, adjusts instructional time to meet students' needs, and uses various forms of feedback and correction for students who need help to show proficiency. Although standards are designed from the top down, the instruction is delivered from the bottom up. For students who demonstrate earlier attainment of proficiency, the teacher provides curriculum enrichment units. One of the key elements of proficiency learning instruction is the manipulation of time. Carrol (1963) has demonstrated that time is a factor in student learning. In proficiency learning, each student uses as much time as necessary to master the standard before moving onto the next standard. For students who move very quickly, time is adjusted so that they do not spend unnecessary time learning the requirements. Learning is a managed process with two variables: time and multiple ways of gaining achievement.

The assessment component utilizes formative testing periodically throughout instruction to show the teacher where the student is in relation to performance standards. Using the results of the testing, the teacher can adjust the instruction by offering correctives to help the student. The process of teach–test–teach becomes individualized, thereby ensuring that all students attain mastery.

One key to implementing a proficiency learning model is to predefine *mastery* as attainment of a certain test score, a certain mark on a scoring rubric (e.g., 4 on a scale of 1 to 10, with 1 being poor and 10 being excellent), or a certain number of completions (e.g., swimming 9 laps). Most experts say that mastery is in the 80 to 90 percent range.

Table 2-2 illustrates how one would organize instruction to provide for a learning environment that emphasizes proficiency. The longitudinal line

TABLE 2-2   Proficiency Learning Instructional Alignment

	< teach >				assess		< reteach>		reassess
1	2	3	4	5	6	7	8	9	

Note: Numbers from 1 to 9 indicate the number of weeks.

indicates how many weeks it would take to teach a particular unit of instruction. In this case, the unit would be nine weeks long. The unit has a predetermined standard and measurement that determines how students will demonstrate mastery. The first five weeks of instruction are devoted to teaching the unit curriculum. Some teachers like to include a pretest or diagnostic test in the first week, but this is optional. At the eighth week, there is a formative assessment. Students need to show where they are in terms achieving the standard. On the basis of this information, the teacher makes some decisions. The instruction for weeks 6 through 9 is then geared toward reteaching the material. Students who have failed to show sufficient gains toward proficiency on the formative assessment are given correctives to help them understand the curriculum. For students who have already shown proficiency at the six-week mark, enrichment curriculum activities are offered. At the end of the ninth week's unit, all students are reassessed. At this time, it is expected that all students would have reached the predetermined mark of mastery (whether it be 80 percent, 85 percent, or 90 percent) and that some will have far exceeded this mark. The teacher then uses the information he or she has on the unit standards and plans on teaching another unit of instruction using a similar nine-week plan. As each unit is accomplished, the standards build on each other so that progress is made toward achieving the total course standard. The instruction is planned and delivered from the bottom up.

One of the major criticisms of this model of learning is that a teacher can inadvertently "dumb down" the curriculum. Carried to an extreme, this model can hurt students. For example, a teacher who is too anxious to ensure that all his or her students become proficient on a task may teach it over and over again despite boredom of the brighter students. A common practice is to reteach a concept only once. Then, if a student or students have not understood the material, it is time to move on and provide support outside the classroom.

In the real world, many critics say, time is not a variable. Problems need to be solved and decisions made by a deadline. In another example of poor implementation of this model, in order for all students to learn, the curriculum becomes so weak and the standards so minimal in terms of performance that although all children learn, the brighter students are not challenged.

Steps toward Planning Proficiency

Check each step as you progress through your planning and delivery of curriculum. At the conclusion of this process, you should have implemented an instructional plan for achieving high standards.

_____ **1.** Choose the unit standard you will teach. Be sure the standard is aligned with the total course standards and moves the student toward achieving an exit standard. If you have not completed this step, refer back to the section in this chapter on "How to Establish Course Standards."

_____ **2.** Construct an ungraded pretest or diagnostic test. This formative assessment should include items that will demonstrate components of the unit standard. The results of this test will allow you to show gains in student and class achievement based on instruction.

_____ **3.** Plan which instructional materials and techniques you will use to deliver the lesson. Included in this plan are items you have chosen after determining from the pretest which students will need special attention to achieve the unit standard.

_____ **4.** Map out a six- to eight-week instructional plan. Include specific weeks in which the formative assessment will take place. There may be more than one formative assessment.

_____ **5.** Determine the level of mastery you will accept from a student to determine if proficiency on the standard has been reached. As mentioned, this can be a score, a completion, or a demonstration based on a rubric scale.

_____ **6.** Orient the students to your total instructional plan. The students should know what the unit standard is, how you will know they have reached it, how you will help them get there, how the standard will be measured, and when they will know they have reached a proficient level.

_____ **7.** Implement the instructional plan.

_____ **8.** At the predetermined point, give a formative assessment.

_____ **9.** Score the formative assessment and judge student achievement levels to date.

_____ **10.** Assign correctives or enrichment activities to students as needed.

_____ **11.** Reteach the course material.

_____ **12.** Give a summative assessment based on the unit standard. Grade students for mastery.

Critical Thinking Skills

Critical thinking is the mental restructuring of perception from the five senses to form new ideas or beliefs based on a logical thought process that is objective and sequential. Presseisen (1992) refers to four aspects of higher order thinking that interact with one another in curriculum development.

1. *Cognition:* Mental acts by which long-term knowledge is acquired and remembered. These are perception, attention, learning, memory, reasoning, language, and emotion.
2. *Metacognition:* The learner's knowledge or awareness of his or her own cognitive processes and products and the ability to regulate them.
3. *Conation:* Motivational striving or attempting to do something directly with a learning experience.
4. *Epistemology:* The different ways knowledge is characterized and the methods associated with defining and generating content.

Because most of the standards, particularly the course standards, involve performances where students must use higher level thinking skills, there is significant discussion in the research as to how these higher level critical thinking skills should be taught. At one end of the spectrum are those (Hirsch, 1987) who believe that curriculum content is most important and that instructional emphasis should be on predetermined objective content that is important for any well-educated person. At the other end are those (Michalko, 1991; DeBono, 1985) who believe that higher level thinking skills can be taught in isolation from content. Their assumption is that one's mental faculties can be stretched and made more critical by performing a number of thinking exercises. Between these two poles are those who believe in a synthesis of views. Inherent in this belief is the need first to identify those higher order thinking skills necessary to learn, then to teach these skills at the pure skill level, and finally to infuse them with the curriculum content area. In such an instructional program, the student is taught various methods to organize, process, and use information from any curriculum area. For a review of different methods of teaching thinking, Costa (1985) provides an excellent resource.

For our purposes, there are two methods used to teach students the processes of thinking critically. Both occupy the middle ground of the spectrum just described. That is, they advocate the following process:

1. Identify those critical thinking skills you want students to be able to use.
2. Design and teach the specific thinking skill.
3. Design assessments to determine if the thinking skill has been mastered.
4. Infuse or integrate the thinking skills with the curriculum content.

The first method is that developed by Beyer (1991) and described in *Teaching Thinking Skills: A Handbook for Secondary School Teachers* and *Teaching Thinking Skills: A Handbook for Elementary School Teachers*. Beyer defines *thinking skills* as precisely delineated mental operations applied in different combinations to produce meaning, insight, and new knowledge. He lists dozens of thinking skills, such as remembering, distinguishing the relevant from the irrelevant, classifying, predicting, judging the strength of a claim, synthesizing, inferring, and making relationships. In defining each skill, he cites the skill's attributes, its procedures, rules, and declarative knowledge or criteria (conditions of attainment). For example, Beyer describes the thinking skill *predicting* as follows:

Predicting*

Definition   Stating in advance what will probably happen next: forecasting, extrapolating, foretelling, prophesizing, projecting.

Procedure

1. State and clearly define what the prediction is to be about.
2. Collect data relevant to the prediction to be made.
3. Recall information already known about the topic.
4. Identify a pattern, trend, or repetition in the recalled data.
5. Map the perceived patterns on the given data to imagine the next possible instances of the perceived patterns.
6. Determine the probability that each imagined outcome will actually occur.
7. Select the outcome most likely to occur.

Rules

1. When to use?
   - In hypothesizing or inferring about any topic or subject
   - In forming new categories or groups of any data

*Adapted from *Developing a Thinking Skills Program* by Barry Beyer (Boston: Allyn and Bacon, 1988), p. 344. Used with permission.

2. How to start?
   - Ask yourself, "What could happen (or be true) next?"
   - Arrange the data on paper or in a diagram.

3. What to do if . . .
   - little relevant information exists? Think of similar situations, of problems in the past, or of analogies.
   - it is difficult to generate possible outcomes? Brainstorm as many solutions as possible without regard to probabilities.

Knowledge

1. Comparing, contrasting
2. Various types of patterns (temporal, spatial, numerical, cause–effect, functional, etc.)
3. Probabilities
4. Potential intervening conditions, variations, and influences related to the subject
5. Historical and logical situations/problems/conditions

The second method of teaching thinking skills is that developed by the Maryland Center for Thinking Studies (1992). This method uses an interdisciplinary approach by incorporating stories, facts and phenomena from different sources, places, people, current events, social and political issues, experiments as the content for teaching thinking skills. In addition there are directions for the teacher to help students use many of the multiple intelligences discussed in Chapter 1. The goal of all the thinking skills instruction is to have students generate their own knowledge and be held accountable for their own learning. An example of how the thinking skill "predicting" is taught will illustrate this method, in which the skill is taught by the teacher prior to its inclusion into a curriculum content area.

Predicting*

Grade Level   7/8

Objectives   Students will construct a working definition of the word *prediction.* Students will list the steps that lead to making a prediction.

Procedures

1. In an envelope, place the frames of a comic strip. Remove the last frame.

---

*Adapted from the Maryland Center for Thinking Skills, *Lesson Plans, Volume 4: Predicting,* p. 91. Used with permission.

2. Distribute the envelopes to pairs of students. Have them arrange the frames in the order they wish. Ask each pair to write or draw the last frame from their prediction.

3. The teacher should share with the class the last frame of the comic strip. Students then compare their own predictions.

4. Ask the pairs and then ask each pair to join another pair to answer and share answers to the following questions:
   a. What would happen if you did not do your homework?
   b. What will you do next summer?
   c. What will happen on (a given holiday)?
   d. What do you think would happen if the gravity of the earth was doubled?
   The teacher can generate additional questions of this nature.

5. Discuss answers as a general class. Emphasize that some information is needed before predictions can be made.

6. Develop with the class a list of words that describe what happened in their discussions. Concentrate on the word *predicting*. What words did students use in their discussion that were similar to *predicting*?

7. Ask students to list the steps involved in making a prediction. Ask students to define the word *predicting*.

Because the use of critcal thinking skills is essential to the successful completion of the curriculum standards, the teacher needs to plan carefully to ensure that students have a working knowledge of the necessary thinking skills. The following steps are recommended to help in this process.

How to Include Thinking Skills in the Instruction

Check each step as you progress through your planning and delivery of curriculum. At the conclusion, you should have implemented an instructional plan for teaching critical thinking skills.

_____ 1. Determine which critical thinking skills will be required to complete the different course standards. Make a list of them using the verb phrases that are actually used to describe the standards (e.g., "Students will compare and contrast . . .".

_____ 2. Choose one of the thinking skills to teach this month or quarter.

_____ 3. Plan the sequence of teaching the skill by deciding the date the skill will first be introduced, the dates it will be reinforced, and how you will determine that students are competent in using it.

_____ 4. Decide in which curriculum content the thinking skills will be integrated. In an interdisciplinary format the social studies teacher may decide to include the skill in the first quarter, the English teacher will reinforce the skill in the second quarter, and the science teacher in the third quarter. In a truly integrated school, the skills sequence can be delegated to each grade level (in fourth grade, comparing and contrasting will be taught, in fifth grade predicting, etc.).

_____ 5. Teach the chosen skill. (You may choose Beyer's examples, examples from the Maryland Center for Thinking Skills, or examples from another skills series.)

_____ 6. Assess the students' use of the skill.

_____ 7. Integrate the skill in the chosen curriculum content.

Cooperative Learning

Cooperative learning is an instructional strategy that can be of great use in helping students achieve high standards. The concept has been part of staff development programs nationwide. Proper use of the procedure involves teams of students with different levels of ability and skills using a variety of learning activities to promote understanding of a subject. Each team member is responsible not only for learning the material but also for helping teammates learn.

Cooperative learning has been demonstrated to assist in promoting positive relations among students, improve peer coaching, establish school environments where learning and high standards are valued, promote positive school discipline, and improve critical thinking skills (Slavin, 1987, Webb, 1993). It is the last factor that interests us. Think of the expression, "Two heads are better than one." This applies to the teaching of critical thinking and mastery learning as well. Johnson and Johnson (1989) report a positive correlation between working cooperatively in groups and students' achievement and level of reasoning. Students working in cooperative learning groups used more higher level thinking skills than did students working individually.

In designing instruction for successful student completion of the standards, you will find many opportunities to use cooperative work groups. Some of the activities involved in the instructional phase of the standards should involve students working in cooperative groups. Johnson and Johnson (1992) report reasons for promoting cooperative groups. Among the strongest are increased use of oral summarizing, explaining, and elaborating on what one knows adds long-term retention; divergent thinking and critical thinking are stimulated by members' different perspectives and approaches to assignment completions; gathering information and understanding the cognitive and emotional perspectives of others in the groups forces individuals to retain and manipulate different perspectives in the mind at the same time; and, finally, the public expression of one's ideas and reasoning results in group members critically evaluating and monitoring the group's problem-solving process.

The use of cooperative groups to foster critical thinking is well explained in an excellent series of bulletins published by the International Thinking Assessment Network (Duff, 1992). Among the many excellent ideas is the inclusion process, described as a process where students are trained first in focus lessons and then in application lessons. The second step, called *applications,* is important for the use of cooperative groups. Here students work as teams to help teach, monitor, and evaluate the use of critical thinking skills to problem-solve. The use of a "critical observer" in a three-person group provides feedback to the members on use of the particular skill being mastered. This monitoring provides metacognition, which allows group members to refine and/or confirm their strategy for applying effectively the thinking skill in relation to the content to be learned. After many practice activities, the students create Performance Assessment Matrixes (PAM) to assess their own ability to apply the thinking skill. The PAM is a performance assessment in that it asks students to look for particular key phrases used in association with a skill and to rate the group's use on a scale from 1 to 3.

One caution is needed in the use of cooperative learning. Many say they use the procedure, but fewer have been trained comprehensively in its use. Parents may be skeptical about cooperative groups if they feel their child is being deprived of direct instruction from the teacher. The misuse of cooperative learning can cause serious problems with a teacher's instructional delivery system. On the other hand, students in the 1990s need to be trained to work collaboratively. Many businesses are organized in teams, and collaborative work assignments are becoming the norm. If workers cannot be part of a team, they are less highly valued. When medium to large companies downsize, they do not reduce the work force by individuals; rather, they eliminate whole teams that are unproductive or no longer fit into the corporate structure. Thus, schools have an obligation to provide students with skills in cooperative learning

Summary

This chapter presented the first step in the four-step taxonomy or planning guide for designing authentic assessment for interdisciplinary curriculum. This step involved developing the interdisciplinary curriculum standards that you will eventually measure with the assessment tasks. This chapter defined and explained curriculum standards and showed how to construct exit standards for the graduate, program or department standards, course standards, and the basic curriculum unit standard. The process of choosing an interdisciplinary theme for the curriculum standards was demonstrated, with particular emphasis on considering the four factors of relevance to students: primary principles, multiple goals, and appropriate sequencing. An example using "Energy" as a common interdisciplinary theme was provided for both secondary and elementary schools. The chapter concluded with a section on designing instruction to help students demonstrate successful completion of the curriculum standards. A learning model emphasizing proficiency, critical thinking skills, and cooperative learning was discussed as the key to delivering an instructional program that ensures that all students learn and demonstrate high curriculum standards.

Next, having determined the process of setting high standards, it is time to look at various methods we can use to measure them.

References

Arnold, J. (1993, Fall). A curriculum to empower young adolescents. *Midpoints*. Columbus, OH: National Middle School Association.

Beane, J. A. (1990). *A middle school curriculum: From rhetoric to reality*. Columbus, OH: National Middle School Association.

Beyer, B. K. (1991). *Teaching thinking skills: A handbook for secondary school teachers*. Boston: Allyn and Bacon.

Block, J. H., Efthim, H. E., & Burns, R. B. (1989). *Building effective mastery learning schools*. New York: Longman.

Bloom, B. (1956). *Taxonomy of educational objectives: Handbook I. Cognitive domain*. New York: David McKay.

Boschee, F., & Baron, M. (1994, February). Outcome-based hype. *Education Week*, p. 31.

Boyer, E. (1993). *Twenty-first-century schools*. Talk presented at a meeting of the Association for Supervision and Curriculum and Development, Washington, DC.

Brophy, J., & Alleman, J. (1991, May). Activities as instructional tools: A framework for analysis and evaluation. *Educational Researcher*, pp. 9–23.

Carrol, J. B. (1963). A model of school learning. *Teachers College Record, 64*, 723–733.

Center for Outcome-Based Education. (1994). A new alliance: Partners for quality learning. *COBE News, 2*.

Coming up to standards: What students should know and be able to do across the disciplines. (1995). *Education Week, 14*(29), 52–70.

Costa, A. (Ed.). (1985). *Developing minds: A resource book for teaching thinking*. Alexandria, VA: Association for Supervision and Curriculum Development.

The criteria of outcome-based education. (1992, Spring). *Outcomes*, p. 29.Davidson, N., & Worsham, T. (Eds.). (1992). *Enhancing thinking through cooperative learning*. New York: Teachers College Press.

DeBono, E. (1985). The CoRT thinking program. In J. W. Segal, S. F. Chipman, & R. Glaser (Eds.), *Thinking and learning skills: Volume I. Relating instruction to research*. Hillsdale, NJ: Erlbaum.

Duff, S. C. (Ed.). (1992, May). Assessing classroom thinking in action: Alternatives to the paper and pencil test. *The International Thinking Assessment Network Bulletin #2*. Baltimore, MD.

Fogarty, R. (1991). *The mindful school: How to integrate the curricula*. Palatine, IL: Skylight Publishing.

Gardner, H., & Mansilla-Boix, V. (1994, February). Teaching for understanding—Within and across disciplines. *Educational Leadership*.

Hirsch, E. D., Jr. (1987). The essential elements of literacy. *Education Week*, 6.

Jacobs, H. H. (1991, October). Planning for curriculum integration. *Educational Leadership*.

Johnson, D. W., & Johnson, R. T. (1989). *Cooperation and competition*. Edina, MN: Interaction Book Company.

Johnson, D. W., & Johnson, R. T. (1992). Encouraging thinking through constructive controversy. In N. Davidson & T. Worsham (Eds.), *Enhancing thinking through cooperative learning* (p. 120). New York: Teachers College Press.

Judson, G. (1994, January 9). Movement to revise education is attacked. *New York Times*, p. 21.

Kelly, T. (1993, Fall). Of good and evil. *Outcomes*, 12.

Maryland Center for Thinking Studies. (1992). *Predicting, Lesson Plans*, Vol. 4.

Maurer, R. (1994). *Designing interdisciplinary curriculum in middle, junior high, and high schools*. Boston: Allyn and Bacon.

McKenna, J. (1993). Perspectives and imperatives: Some limitations of outcome-based education. *Journal of Curriculum and Supervision*, p. 343.

Michalko, M. (1991). *Thinkertoys: A handbook of business creativity for the '90's*. Berkeley, CA: Ten Speed Press.

New York State United Teachers. *The NYSUT perspective: A response to the Curriculum and Assessment Council interim report*. Albany: New York State United Teachers.

Olson, L. (1993, December). Who's afraid of O.B.E.? *Education Week*, p. 25.

Perkins, D. (1986). *Knowledge as design*. Hillsdale, NJ: Erlbaum.

Presseisen, B. F. (1992). Thinking skills in the curriculum. In J. W. Keefe & H. J. Walberg (Eds.), *Teaching for thinking*. Reston, VA: National Association of Secondary School Principals.

Ravitch, D. (1995). *National standards in American education: A citizen's guide*. Washington, DC: Brookings Institution.

Sizer, T. (1992). *Horace's school*. Boston: Houghton Mifflin.

Slavin, R. E. (1987). Best-evidence synthesis: An alternative to meta-analytic and traditional reviews. In W. R. Shadish & C. S. Reichardt (Eds.), *Evaluation studies: Review annual* (Vol. 12). Newbury Park, CA: Sage.

Spady, W. (1993). Issue. *Update*. Alexandria, VA: Association for Supervision and Curriculum Development.

Standards times 50. (1995). *Education Week*, 14(29), 15–70.

Stevenson, C., & Carr, J. (1993). *Integrated studies in middle grades: Dancing through walls*. New York: Teachers College Press.

Van Patten, J., Chao, C., & Reigeluth, C. (1986). A review of strategies for sequencing and synthesizing instruction. *Review of Educational Research, 56,* 437–471.

Vars, G. F. (1993). *Interdisciplinary teaching: Why and how.* Columbus, OH: National Middle School Association.

Viadero, D. (1995). Even as popularity soars, portfolios encounter roadblocks. *Education Week, 14,* 28, 8–9.

Webb, N. M. (1993). *Collaborative group versus individual assessment in mathematics: Group process and outcomes.* Los Angeles: University of California.

Worsham, T. (1993). *Assessing classroom thinking in action: Making students believers in their ability to think better.* Paper presented to the annual convention of the Supervision and Curriculum Development, Washington, DC.

3 Creating Alternative Assessment Tasks

*E*nvision yourself in a class of students actively engaged in interviewing senior citizens about their experiences coming to America. You hear the older adults talking about their feelings and dreams as immigrants in a new land of opportunity. The students you see are busy asking questions, taking notes, conversing with each other about what to do or say next, and attempting to make their senior citizen guests as comfortable as possible.

You are viewing students involved in an interdisciplinary course on immigration. How are you going to evaluate this class activity? More precisely, among all the activities going on, what are the most important things students are doing, what new knowledge has been acquired, how has it been processed, and does this new knowledge have any meaning in the context of the real world.

Giving the students a multiple-choice or fill-in-the-blanks test will not give you the answers to these questions. A classroom activity like this one, where students are discovering and building relationships among the facts and data they have acquired in the instructional process and are using these to produce or create new knowledge, compels you to seek new forms of measurement.

This chapter will help you develop alternative assessment tasks. It will provide examples and specific information about creating alternative assessments. This is the second step of the taxonomy of design introduced in Chapter 2. After exploring the process of establishing interdisciplinary curriculum standards, the next step in our design process is to develop assessment tasks to accompany these new standards. In the next chapter we will complete the design taxonomy by discussing the measurement and reflection phase. We are at this point in our four-step design taxonomy:

- Standards
- Assessment tasks*
- Measurement
- Reflection

It is important for clarification to define what we mean by the terms assessment, evaluation and reporting. The terms are used interchangeably but really mean different things.

---

*Teacher observation of interview.

Assessment

Defined as a comprehensive and multifaceted analysis of performance (Cronbach, 1960), assessment is a collection of data; interviews; questionnaires; ratings; samples of student work; recordings of student, peer, and/or teacher observations; and even tests. Inherent in any assessment is the notion that judgment is based on the integration of many different sources of information gathered over time. The judgment is personal in that the judge makes a prediction about student performance on the basis of the assessment collection. How the judge uses the score is the most important thing. For example, a teacher observing the classroom of students interviewing senior citizens described previously uses the following assessments to gather information about a student.

- Senior citizen postinterview rating of student
- Student-written summary of the interview
- Teacher-administered essay question about immigration in the context of the interview

From these four different sources, the teacher will have gathered information about the students' performance during and after (summary) of the interview. The teacher now has the task of converting this information into a meaningful summary and analysis for the student. The teacher-administered test is just one part of the assessment collection. On the basis of this process, the student should gain important information about his or her performance during the interview and a judgment on how well he or she has been able to use this information to begin to understand the immigration experience in American history.

This book is devoted to demonstrating how to design assessments. Many different forms of assessment will be illustrated and explained. The teacher or administrator can choose which assessment or assessments will be used to gather information on a student. The end result, however, will be the gathering of information to make a judgment about a student's performance.

Evaluation

This is a process that involves activities such as summarizing, making decisions, comparing, and ensuring accountability. Hill and Ruptic (1994) cite the main difference between assessment and evaluation as follows: Evaluation means that students are judged on their own personal growth and in comparison to widely held expectations for a particular grade or age group. Examples of evaluations are teacher-made tests, tests at the end of the chapters in textbooks, state exams, and standardized tests. All these have a place in evaluation. Moreover, teachers may choose to use information collected by these assessments as part of the evaluation. In this case, the assessment information is only one piece of the instruments used for evaluation. The constraint of evaluations based solely on tests, however, is that the role of student judgment outside of the test questions does not exist, the role of the teacher is that of a scorer not a judge, and the context of learning experience is narrowed considerably to fit the test questions. The problem with tests of this nature is that they no longer are authentic to the classroom.

In the classroom described earlier, the teacher can evaluate the students' understanding of immigration on the basis of their performance or can choose to evaluate the students' recall of information and facts. In the former case, the evaluation will incorporate information from different assessments. In the latter case, the teacher may choose to evaluate students on the end-of-the-chapter test on immigration and may regard the interview process as an important experience but not vital to the evaluation process.

Reporting

This is a process of interpreting and communicating what you know about a student. Haney (1991) summarizes a number of research studies showing that teachers and administrators typically misinterpret reports of student progress. For example, adults and students themselves often mistakenly believe that the report card is the evaluation. The report card, however, is not the evaluation but only a means of interpreting or reporting on students' performance. It is a public expression to the student, the parent, and the community of what the teacher knows about the student. The form the report card takes or the graph that the standardized test results use defines the evaluation. For example, there is usually only one place on a secondary-level report card to record a students' grade in any subject. A "B" for English tells you only that the teacher evaluated your child's knowledge of English as deserving a "B." Exactly what the "B" means is unclear in most cases. At the elementary level, Language Arts is usually rated on a three-point scale: Exemplary, Satisfactory, or Unsatisfactory. If your child receives an "Unsatisfactory" in the subskill of spelling, you are not sure if this is the teacher's evaluation of your child's knowledge of spelling words compared to him or herself, compared to the class, or compared to the norms in the spelling book. In any case, the reporting of student information should not be viewed as the evaluation.

Using the senior citizen interview example, the teachers involved in the instruction will have a difficult time reporting to students or parents what students have gained from this experience. The report card format, whether secondary or elementary, usually does not allow teachers from different disciplines to report on students' understanding outside their subject area. There is probably no way to have the senior citizens report on how the students conducted the interview. If the teacher is going to report in an authentic manner what went on during the interviews, then a new form of reporting needs to be created. The teacher may decide to evaluate the students on different criteria using information gained from the different assessments collected. As part of the reporting, these assessments may be displayed at a parent evening conference so the parents themselves can make evaluations from the information. In the report form, the teacher needs to be clear that the student is being evaluated on criteria based on some external measure. In other words, if a student receives an "Exemplary" rating for the teacher observation of the interview, there should be a narrative describing what characteristics of an interview makes it "exemplary."

In summary, assessing is gathering information to make a judgment, evaluation is the actual judgment phase, and reporting is the communicating of the judgment.

Purposes of Alternative Assessments

Earlier I discussed the purposes of authentic assessment. It is important to outline these purposes again before we begin the process of creating alternative assessments. There are four agreed-on purposes (Chittenden, 1991), an assessment task can serve one or more purposes at the same time. For the sake of clarity, however, we will differentiate the four purposes.

Keeping Track

A teacher may want to gather information about a student for the purpose of keeping track of *what* the student has accomplished during the school year. This is a form of monitoring in that the assessment task is designed to provide the teacher with information. Examples would be journal writing, reading logs, and various types of portfolio collections.

Checking Up

This is a formative function of the assessment task in that it provides the teacher with information as to *where* the student is in gaining understanding about the curriculum. This purpose is similar to that of the formative tests advocated by Worthen and Sanders (1987) as a means of providing information useful to improve the program. This type of assessment task is used intermittently to gain information while an interdisciplinary unit is in progress. Examples are tests, essays, rough drafts, the first phase of a science experiment, and student proposals. Teachers use this kind of information to change the focus of the instructional program periodically so that the skills students need to gain or the understanding that needs to develop can occur.

Finding Out

This purpose is unique to assessment tasks. It is the teacher's attempt to discover *how* the student has created meaning from the instruction that has occurred. This meaning can be intensely personal for each student as the student takes the new knowledge and first discovers the relationship to old knowledge or experiences he or she may have had, then takes this new meaning and cognitively creates a new knowledge base. Peshkin (1993) refers to this purpose as the interpretation outcome. Here the assessment task helps students explain or create generalizations, develop new concepts, elaborate on existing concepts, provide insights, clarify complexity, and ultimately develop theory. Such tasks as creating a product, completing a performance, or demonstrating an exhibition of what has been learned will provide the teacher with evidence of these outcomes. This purpose helps the teacher individualize the curriculum to meet the needs of each child.

Summing Up

This purpose of assessment is to provide *judgment* information to the student, parent, or community. This is the accountability purpose (Engel, 1990), which is required for reporting. Usually it is the final word on whether a student has been able to demonstrate understanding. A clear example would be whether a student passes the performance portion of the driving test in order to obtain a state driver's license. Another example would be successfully completing the senior essay required for graduation. This type of assessment task has high stakes, as seen in the use the state of Vermont writing and mathematics assessment tasks and in the British Standard Assessment Tasks (SATs).

The following exercise is designed to help you discover the purpose of your authentic assessment tasks. It may provide some clarity in focusing the various elements of your assessment tasks.

Determining the Purpose of Your Assessment Task

Please complete the following sentence.

_____ 1. The reasons I am creating alternative assessment tasks for my students are _____

  _____

  _____

_____ 2. As you review what you wrote, look for the following clues. These clues will help assist in defining the purpose of the alternative assessment.
  • If the reason is to determine *what* information the student has completed, then the purpose of your assessment is to:

                                                        KEEP TRACK

- If the reason is to determine *where* the student is at in the curriculum, then the purpose of your assessment is to:
  CHECK UP

- If the reason for your assessment is to determine *how* the student has constructed meaning from the curriculum, then the purpose of the assessment is to:
  FIND OUT

- If the reason for your assessment is to make a *judgment* call about the student's performance, then the purpose of your assessment is to:
  SUM UP

- If you have multiple reasons for giving assessment tasks, then your purposes are a combination of some or even all of the above.

Whatever your purpose in creating the assessment task, review your responses after you have created the task to make sure that you have indeed met the purpose you intended.

Assessment tasks have multiple purposes depending on the intent of the creator. They are primarily information-gathering instruments that give the teacher insight into the learning process of each individual child. These assessment tasks are not based on rote recitation but, rather, require students to demonstrate understanding performance. A comparison of the different purposes and the terms used with various alternative assessments follows:

Terms	Function	Purpose
Assessing	Gathering	Find out, check up, keep track
Evaluating	Judging	Sum up
Reporting	Communicating	Find out

Types of Alternative Assessment

We can easily group the different types of alternative assessment into three categories: products, performances, and portfolios. Keeping the different examples within one category, however, is an impossible task. A slight variation in the assessment tasks can change the type of assessment. For example, a one-act play written for a twelfth-grade English class is a product. But the actual production of the play is an example of a performance. Finally, the insertion of the play into the student's language arts folder is an example of a portfolio. In the research, the different types of alternative assessment are described differently depending on one's orientation. McDonald (1993) talk about the products as *exhibitions* or *platforms*, words they use interchangeably. They believe that schools need to plan backwards: First, decide what type of product, exhibition, or platform best illustrates the school's goals and achievement standards. Establish these as important, and plan your instruction so that all students can reach and produce these products, exhibitions, or platforms. Feur and Fulton (1993) describe common forms of what they refer to as performance assessment: constructed-response items, writing, exhibitions, experiments, and portfolios. The classification used is not meaningful in the long run but is helpful in understanding the process by sorting out the many options from which you can choose in creating alternative assessment tasks. I will illustrate next some products, performances, and portfolios.

Products

Products are assessment tasks that require students to produce or create something to demonstrate some of the understanding they have developed in the interdisciplinary curriculum units. I say *some* because no one assessment task can possibly incorporate all of the curriculum outcomes in a study unit. Choose which product would best give you a window into a student's thinking and feelings. Later in the chapter I will discuss planning stages and demonstrate the steps involved.

Products can be written essays, stories, poems, journals, or term or research papers. They can be three-dimensional—science fair projects, art exhibitions, technology demonstrations, baked goods, sewing projects, newspapers, maps, video productions. They can even fit more conventional models of testing—filling in the blanks, solving math problems, labeling a map or chart, or completing short written responses. Listed here are a number of product-type assessment tasks used with interdisciplinary curriculum units. Their construction provides an insight into how products can be used in designing alternative assessments.

Environmental Theme: Mathematics 8, Computer, and Language Arts (Ossining, New York)
Using actual data supplied by the Office of Education and the National Air and Space Museum, students create and interpret a graph of ozone levels over the Antarctic for each day of the year 1987. Students enter all 365 pieces of information on a spreadsheet, check the accuracy of their input by using computer functions, and use the average function to determine the mean level of ozone for a fourteen-day period. Students create a graph on the computer, making decisions such as the type of graph (horizontal line, vertical line, bar, circle) and the maximum and minimum points on the graph. Students read and discuss information from *Blue Planet* (available from the Office of Education, National Air and Space Museum, Smithsonian Institution, Washington, DC 20560) so they can understand what ozone is. The final task is to transfer the graph to the graphics software where it is displayed with the appropriate title and the student's interpretation of the results.

Language Arts, Social Studies (William Floyd School District, New York)
The objective of this unit is to have the students examine the effects of historical events on society. Using the book *My Brother Sam is Dead*, students keep a journal and examine different topics over an eight-day period. Two days of journal writing are devoted to social issues effected by the American revolution, such as prejudice, freedom of speech, the death penalty, or terrorism. One day is devoted to a social issue mentioned in the book. One day examines a social issue that the student feels is important today. One entry examines the process by which the student learned about the social issue. Entries include why the student was interested in the topic, what made the student realize this was an important issue today, how students found information on this issue, and how they feel the issue is dealt with. Two entries cover topics of student choice. One of these may be the student's reaction to the book. The final entry reflects what students have learned by completing the assignment.

Building a Dog Pen, Grade 10 (Connecticut State Department of Education)
This project allows students to understand the relation between the area and perimeter of polygons. The problem begins with a man, Mr. Garcia, who buys 80 feet of chain link fence to build a dog pen for his new dog, Cosco. The question to students is: What is the largest pen he can build using exactly 80 feet of fence? Students work as individuals and then as groups using graphs, drawings, tables, and calculators for the project. A visual display and an oral presentation in front of the class are required. The second part of the problem is: What would the shape of the fenced area be (circle, square, rectangle, or triangle) that will allow him to use most of his 80 feet of fence in building a free-standing dog pen if his backyard is only 36 square feet?

Developing Product Assessments
Listed here are some ways students can present, justify, describe, or explain what they have created: create an advertising campaign, teach to others, role-play a famous historical figure, design and implement an experiment to test an hypothesis, build prototypes of a community development project, draw a map of a modern or historic place, write a story or play about some event, write a musical piece, build a model, start a collection, or design a cultural display of a county. Projects are often seen in elementary schools but are rarer at the secondary level. At the higher grade levels, long-term projects where students research, plan, develop prototypes, and reflect on what they are doing are preferred. Often high school students get into a project and then lose sight of the purpose. At the elementary level, projects should be designed in stages so that students are not overwhelmed with the complexity of the tasks. In every case the criteria for scoring the project should be made available to students before the project is begun.

Performances

Performances are different from products in that they usually require that students demonstrate their knowledge. Performances can be designed at two levels. The simplest is the application level: Can a student, after studying auto body repair at a vocational technical training site, actually repair a damaged automobile? The second level is more sophisticated in that it requires a student to generate new knowledge based on what has been studied. For example, a fifth-grader may want to direct a play with fellow classmates based on his or her interpretation of a story. As with products, it is impossible to have students demonstrate every standard in the curriculum standards. A sampling must be taken.

Examples of performances are dances, musical performances or exhibitions; science lab or fair demonstrations; tests of performances such as driving, swimming, computer keyboarding, or gymnastics; videotaping or television production, debates, mock trials, oral speeches or presentations and oral descriptions of events, posters, experiments, products, fund raising, and community service. Here are a number of performance type alternative assessment tasks designed with interdisciplinary themes.

*Move Over Rosie: English, Science, Math (Memorial Middle School, Region 15, Middlebury, Connecticut)**

Everybody has seen the commercial featuring Rosie the waitress in the diner with the sage of the paper towels. A big, clumsy guy comes into the diner and spills something, and Rosie comes to the rescue with paper towels to clean up the mess. Rosie is advertising a certain brand of paper towel. The question for students is: Is this brand of paper towel actually a better product? Or is there another brand that the students feel is better at cleaning up spills? Which is the best paper towel?

The task for the students is to create a television commercial that gives accurate, indisputable information about a product. The purpose of the task is to have people select a product on the basis of information arrived at through scientific means. Students are given directions on how to test the various paper towels. They use the scientific process of making a hypothesis, designing an experiment to test the hypothesis, collecting data in a form of data table, converting the data to a graph, analyzing the data, and drawing a conclusion.

The second step is to develop a commercial for the product the students feel is the best. This means writing a script, including dialogue and action; gathering props, equipment, and costumes; rehearsing the commercial; making any revision; filming the final version; and finally evaluating their own performance.

*Used with permission of the Region 15 Public Schools, serving Middlebury and Southbury, Connecticut.

Geography/Geology Field Trip: Third and Fourth Grades
(University for Vermont/School Districts in Vermont)
A fourth-grade class of students who had taken a geography/geology field trip as part of their science curriculum has to make a presentation to this year's third-graders about what they might see on the same trip, what they would learn, what would surprise them, and what questions to ask.

Community Service: Multidisciplinary Unit
(Glendale High School, Glendale, Arizona)
This unit involves students in three different tasks related to community service:

1. Students will design a personal action plan that describes the activity purposes, a timeline, a rationale for the selection including the specific benefits to others and/or to the environment, specific benefits to self, why this service was chosen, and a description of the challenges inherent in completion of the proposed community service.
2. Students will write a journal that includes the approved personal action plan and a series of entries, one for each occasion on which the community service activity is investigated, planned and performed. Each entry will document activities, experiences, and corresponding personal reflections.
3. Students will complete a written self-evaluation focusing on the degree to which the intended outcomes were achieved, making recommendations for future performance of the community service, and analyzing what the student learned about self and others.
4. Students will collect an external evaluation written by an authorized individual who can observe a student's performance of community service. This external evaluation will verify successful performance of the community service.

Walden III Rite of Passage (ROPE), Racine, Wisconsin
This high school requires seniors to make six oral presentations based on written reports and products the students have developed during their four years at the school. Presentations are required in these areas: (1) mathematics knowledge and skills, (2) knowledge of the U.S. government, (3) personal proficiency, (4) knowledge of geography, (5) evidence of completion of a physical challenge, and (6) demonstration of competency in English (written and spoken). As an example, knowledge of the U.S. government can be shown by a discussion of the purpose of government; the individual's relation to the state; the ideals, functions, and problems of American political institutions; and selected contemporary issues and political events.

Developing Performances

Performances are exhibitions of student understanding of the curriculum. They should flow from the student's creativity, not what adults feel the performance should look like. An example of what an exhibition is *not* the school play. Here the director has a major say in how a writer's play will be interpreted by the different actors. The student has few opportunities to show his or her own understanding or interpretation. Burke (1993) points out a series of steps one should take in helping a student get started with a performance. Among them is the need to show the student what a past exemplary performance looked like. By showing examples, you can explain the purpose of the performance and help the students brainstorm a list of criteria that make this performance an exemplary model. Students should have a choice of topics and of the mode of the exhibition. By planning backward from what the exhibition will look like, the student can determine materials, resources, and behaviors he or she will need to complete the task successfully. We have all seen exhibitions in classrooms. The difference with these tasks, however, is that the course standards, as reflected in the rating scores, are adhered to from the beginning. The exhibition is not a demonstration of how well the student can act or show off. It is a demonstration of the understanding of the course curriculum. One way to keep this focus tight is to have the judging panel ask the student after the performance a series of critical questions about the *content* of the demonstration.

Portfolios

A portfolio is a collection of student work representing a wide range of student performances. It comprises pieces of student work that demonstrate what they have learned and what they can do with what they have learned. In most portfolios you can find either the students "best pieces," works that are the final product, or "works in progress," drafts of a final product as it evolved and improved over time. The decision about what goes into a portfolio usually involves the student and the teacher but can, in some cases, involve the parent as well. Another common term used to describe this type of assessment task is *processfolio*. Gardner (1991), in particular, uses this term because it represents the idea that a portfolio constitutes a "map" of the work done. It includes any notes or papers relevant to the initial concept of the project and all subsequent drafts, sketches, and notes.

Five typical models of portfolios are described by Rhoades and McCabe (1992): group, personal, school career (reflecting a student's quality achievement during the K–12 years), class portfolio (representing quality products of a single class), and program quality portfolio (compilation of student work that reflects the quality of the school's program). There are many well-written sources on how to design and use portfolios. Among them you might want to refer to Glazer and Brown (1993); Harp (1993); Goodman, Goodman, and Hood (1989); and Tierney, Carter, and Desai (1991).

In addition, the quarterly publication of the Portfolio Assessment Clearinghouse, *Portfolio News*, provides 20 to 30 pages of information on the subject. Arts Propel has available four handbooks on a cooperative research project involving the Pittsburgh Public Schools, Harvard Project Zero, and the Educational Testing Service (ETS).*

Multidisciplinary Portfolio, Grade 4 (State of Kentucky)

A major part of the educational reform movement in Kentucky is the three-part Kentucky Instructional Results Information System (KIRIS). One part requires that each student's best work be collected throughout the school year. In 1991–1992, each fourth-grader was required to develop a writing portfolio including seven areas: (1) a table of contents; (2) a best piece; (3) a letter to a reviewer written by the student explaining why she or he selected the best piece and how the piece was developed; (4) one short story, poem, or play; (5) one personal narrative; (6) one piece supporting or defending a position or solving a problem; and (7) one prose piece from a content area other than English or Language Arts. In this new assessment program, no child "fails." Instead, the assessment results place him or her into one of four performance levels: novice, apprentice, proficient, or distinguished. The lowest level, novice, recognizes the child as a beginner, not a failure.

Writing Interdisciplinary Portfolio, Fourth through Eighth Grade (State of Vermont)

In the state of Vermont, starting in the school year 1991–1992, every student in grades 4 through 8 has been required to have a writing portfolio. The portfolio includes two types of products: a collection of six pieces of writing and a writing assessment given statewide. Every student's portfolio must contain the following information: (1) a table of contents; (2) a best piece; (3) a letter; (4) a poem, short story, play, or personal narrative; (5) a personal response to a cultural, media, or sports exhibit or event, book, current event, or math or science problem; (6) one prose piece from any curriculum area other than English for fourth-graders and three prose pieces from any curriculum area other than English for eighth-graders; and (7) the writing piece produced from the statewide assessment program.

Mathematics Portfolio—Seventh Grade (Syracuse City Schools, Syracuse, New York)

The math portfolio for every seventh-grader in the Syracuse city schools is a collection of the best work of each student. It can be used as an assessment instrument to determine promotion. It should include the following:

Portfolio News is available from Winfield Cooper, San Dieguto High Schoiol District, 710 Encinitas Boulevard, Encinitas, CA 92024. Arts Propel's handbooks are available from the Educational Testing Service, 18-R, Princeton, NJ 08541.

1. Samples for each quarter from five different elements with a minimum of 4 tests and/or quizzes, 5 writing assignments, 1 project, 5 homework assignments, and 5 classwork assignments. The samples should be selected by the teacher and the student and should reflect the best work done for each quarter.
2. Standardized test scores.
3. The pretest, midterm, and final tests.

The project in the portfolio covers the "connection" standard of the seventh-grade math curriculum. This standard calls for the use of mathematical thinking and modeling to solve problems in such areas as art, music, science, history, technology, and home and careers.

Interdisciplinary Portfolio Assessment: Grade 4
(Tribute Public School, Tribute Ohio)

This portfolio is based on 18 components and scored on a rubric of Excellent, Good, Acceptable, Unacceptable. The components are: (1) annual reading log; (2) three oral teacher–student conferences on the reading log; (3) one process composition based on the reading log title; (4) end-of-the-year written critique of the reading log; (5) summary of end-of-the unit/level test results; (6) videotape of two speaking experiences; (7) spelling progress chart; (8) process compositions; (9) one "best piece" process composition; (10) district-scored writing assessment, followed by conferences; (11) one water-color painting correlated with social studies; (12) health research project on substance abuse; (13) three homework examples (each from a different subject); (14) quarter summary of physical education log; (15) district math assessment followed by conference; (16) responses to three open-ended math questions (conference); (17) visual and written descriptions of three "best experiments" in science; and (18) district science assessment followed by a conference.

Developing Portfolio Assessments

Portfolios must be part of the classroom instruction. Decide how often and which type of materials you want to place in the portfolio and how this information will help you adopt your instructional delivery system so that all children have the opportunity to reach proficiency. Students must contribute items to the portfolio on an ongoing basis, not all at once at the semester break or at the end of the year. With portfolios, we are interested in the longitudinal development of student knowledge, not just one event. The purpose of the portfolio needs to be explained from the outset so students and parents know what will be included and how it will be scored. Ask parents and other community members what they would like to see in the portfolio as evidence of student accomplishments. Portfolios should be sent home for parent review at different times during the school year. This would be an ideal time for parent involvement in rating aspects of the portfolio, an idea discussed at length in the next chapter.

In designing portfolios, you can use three different ways to show progress in student learning.

1. September and June entries show progress over time. This design could be modified to include entries at the quarter, semester, month, or trimester. Viewing this type of system, you can make judgments using a pre- and posttests for evaluation. For parents, the comparison can be a concrete visual display of how their child improved over the time period. Most elementary school teacher–parent conferences involve the teacher showing the parent some of the student's work. The difference with this portfolio system is that there would be a comparison over time of the student's ability, and perhaps a comparative rating.

2. An anecdotal record of observations by the student, the teacher, or others over a period of time is a concrete way to show students' progress. Anecdotal material is valid because it contains the rich experience of students' day-to-day attempts to understand the knowledge. The written observations of a student, accompanied by the teacher's commentary, provide important individualized feedback. The disadvantage for the outside reader is that the written material is unprocessed and must be read in its entirety to provide the big picture of change. It takes patience to read through months of journal writings.

3. Examples of classroom work can be collected over a period of time. This type of portfolio may contain videos, drawings, copies of exams, and other such material reflecting the breadth of students' understanding of the curriculum. A storage box or large container may be needed to keep the collectibles in the portfolios. Many parents are accustomed to this type of portfolio, especially in elementary schools, where in June children bring home a pile of work, drawings, and projects that the teacher has collected over the course of the year. The difference here is that the collected works are "best examples" and are rated for assessment. The teacher and/or the students can play a role in deciding what items should go into the portfolio.

Experts recommend a balance in the use of assessment tasks. Gardner (1991a) supports a national examining system based on three parts: performance-based examinations, content-level products, and portfolios or processfolios. The New Standards Project (Tucker & Resnick, 1990) also supports the inclusion of multiple forms of assessment tasks. They advocate the use of product assessment tasks to examine school district, school, or grade-level program performance and the use of portfolios to grade individual student performance. Most of the state initiatives, such as those in Maryland, Arizona, California, Vermont, Kentucky, and New York, have developed or are well on their way to developing assessment tasks that involve all three types of alternative assessment: products, performances, and portfolios.

Qualities of Alternative Assessments

The building blocks of alternative assessment tasks can be described in terms of nine different qualities. Most of the research in this area agrees on these common core qualities. They are listed here together with reflections on how they could be incorporated in the examples described in the previous section. They are framed as questions to ask yourself as you build your own assessment tasks.

1. *Are the tasks linked to the exit standards and/or the course standards?*

The purpose of establishing standards initially is to allow direction in planning curriculum and instructional delivery. Assessment tasks that engage students in meaningful activities are worthless unless they help you meet the standards that have been set. Often the course standards are so specific that they practically hand you the guide for the assessment task. In other cases, the assessment task needs to be developed from a number of available worthwhile options. In selecting the task, keep your eye on the matching standards.

The assessment tasks for mathematics in the Syracuse middle schools illustrate how closely the task and the standard are aligned. The portfolio collects information on students based on the four (National Council of Teachers of Mathematics (NCTM standards: problem solving, communication, reasoning, and connections. The work collected is very specific in that it collects information at the course level about the program standards. For example, a program standard and one of the underlying course standards are listed here:

Program Standard   Problem Solving

Course Standard   Students will learn to use a variety of strategies to solve multistep, nonroutine problem situations (strategies should include using organized charts or lists; seeking patterns; using simulations or diagrams; guess and check; and solving simple problems).

2. *Do the tasks require students to integrate knowledge from different disciplines in a meaningful form?*

It is most appropriate to build tasks around interdisciplinary themes. These themes can be broad so that they include many different disciplines and engage students in looking at questions that bring together their personal concerns with those of the larger society. For example, an interdisciplinary theme built on prejudice might deal with the students' own experiences of prejudice as well as society's need to show respect for all. This theme is more meaningful than, for example, an interdisciplinary theme on the Civil War that has students studying war maps in history class and reading *Across Five Aprils* in English class.

Using broad themes allows you to draw on the different knowledge bases of the disciplines to build the assessment tasks. Language arts includes reading and writing, math has computation and problem solving, science has experiments, art has kinesthetic activity, and so on. The web design of interdisciplinary curriculum described in Chapter 2 will help you develop the disciplines into an interdisciplinary theme. The theme of "environment" shown in the Ossining example illustrates how mathematics, science, language arts, and computers are interwoven in an assessment task. Students are required to use knowledge from different disciplines, integrate them, and produce a product (a computer spreadsheet and graph) to demonstrate their understanding.

3. *Do the tasks mirror real-life tasks, emphasizing depth of knowledge over mere recall?*

Some assessment tasks are well developed and engage students in complex tasks, but their relevance to the real world is questionable. For example, a third-grade teacher had his class read a historical fiction book and then bring costumes from home to reenact the story. The play was fine, and everyone had fun. As a class activity incorporating a multimodal instructional format, it was well implemented. But the teacher could not use it as an alternative assessment because, for the play to be a meaningful assessment task, it would have had to involve those characteristics of performance that students in the real world will need to be successful.

In contrast, the Vermont writing portfolio requires students to write a letter—a task that everyone agrees students between grades 4 and 8 should be able to accomplish. Letter writing is also a skill that every student will need to have to be successful in real life.

4. *Do the tasks allow a student to model, practice, and model the task again so as to gain mastery?*

Most alternative assessments seek the student's best work, best draft, or best attempt to solve a problem. Students are expected to achieve the highest level of excellence or mastery on a task. This level of achievement indicates that students have achieved the standard. Students are not penalized for poor attempts as they are when a teacher deducts credit for a student who retakes a test. The highest level of achievement is considered the student's best work. To get there, students are expected to seek help from teachers and parents, to conduct individual research, and to produce different forms of the task completion before getting it at their best level. An analogy of this is the example of the Olympic diver who tries, receives feedback from the coach, practices again, receives more advice, practices again, and so on until the time of the event, when the diver is expected to give his or her best work performance.

The example titled "Move Over Rosie" shows how students are given time to perfect their television commercial and written product before they are allowed to fix it and show their product to the public. The teacher serves as a coach, helping the students to stretch themselves to meet a high level of achievement. It is crucial here that the task be designed to improve student performance, not just audit it.

5. *Do the tasks require students to research, to produce, and to think?*

In Chapter 2 we discussed how assessment tasks can easily incorporate higher order thinking skills. One of their chief advantages over most standardized tests is that they have room for students to be engaged in thinking tasks. Hafner (1993) reports that mathematics students who are exposed to instruction that uses a bottom-up, constructivist, and problem-solving approach achieve at higher levels than those students who are exposed only to instruction focusing on measurement of basic skills. Incorporating the thinking skills of analysis, synthesis, and evaluation discussed in Chapter 2 involves students in becoming active constructors of their own mathematical reality.

One problem from the Syracuse city schools mathematics test illustrates how students are required to research, produce, and think.

> You plan to paint the walls and ceiling of your bedroom. Draw a diagram showing all four walls with closets, doors, and windows. Write in estimated measurements for each length and width. If one gallon of paint covers 350 square feet, determine how many cans of paint to buy for your room. Label and show your work.

6. *Do the tasks involve the students, at some level, in cooperative learning with other students?*

In the previous chapter I discussed the benefits of having students work together to do a task or solve a problem. There is ample evidence that overall student achievement rises when students work together.

Not all assessment tasks need to involve students working together. The issue of how much of the grade reflects group effort and how much the individual's should be spelled out at the beginning of the task. Students, parents, and other teachers may criticize you for using cooperative work groups. In response, you might note that, in addition to evidence of higher achievement, most major corporations now include in an employee's performance appraisal a measure of how well he or she worked at a team effort. Some writers in the business field (Peters, 1988; Reich, 1987) see the power of the team effort as a key to a company's growth and productivity. Where does one begin to learn to work on a team? Aside from the family, the schools are the chief instructors in team cooperation skills.

The community service assessment task at Glendale High School is a good example of how cooperative groups can be used as part of an assessment. In this case, the student's performance is evaluated by an external agent not associated with the school. The student is judged on, among other things, how well he or she works in the organization.

7. *Are the performance standards clearly articulated?*

Students need to know what is expected of them. There should be little guesswork involved in completing the tasks. Once you have been through a few rounds of the assessment tasks, you should have some models of excellent products, performances, or portfolios that you can share with your students. In this sharing, you should provide examples and reasons that a particular assessment task was judged as excellent. This allows students to compare and contrast their work as they complete the task.

The journal entries at the William Floyd School District suggest that the performance standards are clearly articulated. Explicit directions are given for each journal entry. In addition to the examples and directions, the students should be shown how the scoring mechanism works for the assessment. There should be no surprises. In the next chapter, we will discuss in detail how to articulate the scoring procedures clearly.

8. *Do the tasks have multiple forms of "right" answers?*

In preparing the tasks, you need to realize that you will probably receive as many forms of "right" responses on the assessment tasks as there are students in your school. Because we are asking students to become engaged in the task and to construct their own understanding from the knowledge presented, you need to expect diversity in their answers. There will be no one right answer. Unlike multiple-choice answers, the students' responses often will be "all of the above." Your scoring procedures should be broad enough to allow this creative expression of understanding.

In one fourth-grade class, some students voiced anxiety that there was no one right answer to the test questions. Despite the teacher's explanations, the students could not understand what the teacher wanted. One girl asked if the teacher "could tell us what the right answer would be." The teacher's clever response does the trick in explaining this procedure. To explain the concept, she used the analogy of the diversity of cars on the market today. First, she asked students to tell her what kind of car their parents owned or what kind of car they had seen recently in an ad. Once she had a number of responses, she asked the students if there was any type of car that was more "right" than another. The students understood that the type of car you own is linked with your own personal need.

9. *Do the tasks allow every student access to the task and also to some level of success in task completion?*

Some school districts made initial attempts to create rigorous tasks at world-class levels of performance. As a result, a great many students failed to meet minimum mastery levels. Many feel these demanding task levels are necessary if we want students to work harder and be equal to the high standards set in other parts of the world. Others complain that the standards are set so high that few students can achieve them. If high stakes are involved in meeting a mastery level, such as graduation or entrance to a school or program, then the pressure becomes more intense. Initial attempts by a teacher or school to use performance tasks do not need this kind of pressure.

It is recommended that assessment tasks be designed to be demanding but not impossible for all but a few. The key to achieving high standards is instruction geared to meeting the standards. Once the teacher has a feel for the students' level of proficiency on the performance tasks, he or she can adjust the instruction to ensure that all students can improve on the assessment tasks. As overall student performance improves, the assessment task proficiencies can be increased to demand a higher level of performance. The instruction then adjusts to this new level, and the cycle starts over again. Gradually, the assessment tasks reach the demanding level required by the teacher. The difference is that all the students have come along and have achieved success.

Building Assessment Tasks

As you build your assessment tasks, refer to the following questions to guide you. The questions were discussed in the preceding section. Here you can provide your own answers and/or rationale for the design of your assessment task. As you proceed, you will find that these structured responses will help you.

_____ 1. *Are the tasks linked to the exit standards and/or to the course standards?*

_____

_____

_____

_____ 2. *Do the tasks require students to integrate knowledge from different disciplines in a meaningful form?*

_____

_____

_____

_____ 3. *Do the tasks mirror real-life task expectations, emphasizing depth of knowledge over mere recall?*

_____

_____

_____

_____ 4. *Do the tasks allow a student to model, practice, and model the task again so as to gain mastery?*

_____

_____

_____

_____ **5.** *Do the tasks require students to research, to produce, and to think?*

_____

_____

_____

_____ **6.** *Do the tasks involve the students, at some level, in cooperative learning with other students?*

_____

_____

_____

_____ **7.** *Are the performance standards clearly articulated?*

_____

_____

_____

_____ **8.** *Do the tasks have more than one "right" answer?*

_____

_____

_____

_____ **9.** *Do the tasks give every student access to the task and also to some level of success in task completion?*

_____

_____

_____

Problems in Designing Assessment Tasks

Although there is a high interest and in many cases high stakes involved in the development of alternative assessments, many experts (Linn, Baker, & Dunbar, 1991) believe we have little knowledge of the quality of these assessments. Many problems are reported in the research with the construction of alternative assessment tasks. Most of these can be overcoame with time and a focus on research. An example of the type of current thinking on this matter can be seen in Linn's (1994) discussion of the need to revise the standards for educational and psychological testing. Here are some of the identified problems.

Standardization

This is probably the biggest hurdle facing alternative assessments. The next chapter is devoted to ways of dealing with some of the problems surrounding reliability, validity, and generalizability.

Technical Issues

Those who construct assessment tasks must consider a number of problems if the tasks are to prove adequate to collecting information. First the tasks must be meaningful for students of a given age. Asking high school students to complete a task that does not challenge their creativity is not only not meaningful but an insult. Similarly, asking young elementary students to interview adults about some topic is much too complex, and the results will be meaningless save for those few students who could manage the task at all. Thus, selecting age-appropriate tasks is crucial.

Second, time becomes an issue because most alternative assessment tasks require students to do, demonstrate, or collect things, and this takes time. Unlike the multiple-choice exam, which can be constructed to fit the forty-minute or one-hour period, this type of assessment is more open-ended. Some students will complete their task earlier than others. This does not mean they will get a better grade or are more proficient. It simply means that mastery of a task is not time-bound. Allow for plenty of time when designing assessment tasks.

Third, most assessment tasks require a preassessment activity to help prepare students for the task. A mathematics assessment involving setting up an aquarium requires students to measure and calculate the number and types of fish that can be included. In a preassessment task, the teacher may need to instruct students on what a *school* or *pair* of fish means, or on what different temperatures mean. Preassessment instruction eliminates students' preconceived ideas or lack of information, such as vocabulary. It allows the collection of data on the performance task to entail only those data directly related to the course outcome.

Fourth, sometimes a student's performance or presence outshines the substance of the product. McDonald (1993) refers to these occurrences as *lapses*. Exhibitions involve both substance and presence but often tip in favor of the presence. For example, a student who completed a well-documented, technically smooth video on trash collection in a local community received numerous compliments. Yet the substance of the video had few connections to the concepts in the course outcome.

Fifth, bias still emerges in constructed alternative assessment tasks just as in the standardized tests. The preparer needs to avoid including stereotypes or discriminatory references related to gender, ethnicity, race, and religion.

Sixth, if students are going to feel empowered in this assessment task, they will need to have some choice in how to complete the tasks. The preparer should give students the opportunity to have a say in what products are going into the portfolio, what products will be developed, and how the performance will unfold.

Costs

The testing industry in the United States is a $1 billion a year enterprise. Alternative assessments will not save you a lot of money. In some cases, they may cost more. In other cases, they will replace costs you now have in other tests. Up-front costs include staff development for teachers in the philosophy and techniques of alternative assessments (Guskey, 1994), payment to the individuals who actually construct the tasks, and training costs involved in determining the scoring mechanism and scorer reliability. Madaus and Kellaghan (1993) have tried to calculate the cost and report a price of $135 per student to score an essay exam paper in four or five subjects for 16- and 18-year-olds. However, the costs of administering the tasks can be small, especially if the tasks are part of the classroom instruction process. Extra aides may be needed or shifted around to help the classroom teacher with the logistics of the tasks. The scoring of the finished product, performance, or portfolio needs to be completed by trained teachers, and this can be labor-intensive. Using a sampling matrix like the one used in California for the past fifteen years can cut costs. Popham (1993) discusses this procedure in some detail.

Comparability

Many states are implementing their own assessment tasks. The comparability of these various assessment tasks is difficult to determine. One can see the problems this can pose for a student who moves from state to state. Not only can the data collected be different, but the interpretation of the information by professionals in different states can differ as well. The New Standards Project is attempting to provide an assessment bank of performance tasks and of portfolios, and the Coalition of Essential Schools is trying to provide a hypermedia-based sampler of exhibitions from member schools. In addition, the National Assessment of Educational Progress is reformulating the types of testing it provides on program status to states. These and other national initiatives may solve some of the comparability problems associated with performance assessment tasks.

Importance

The importance of assessment tasks, whether they are high stakes or low stakes, needs to be spelled out early in the construction process. Are students, teachers, schools, or programs being held accountable for positive assessment results? One of the foremost school districts dealing with alternative assessments in a high-stakes arena is Littleton, Colorado (Davis & Felknor, 1994), where, in 1991, the high school based a student's diploma on formal demonstrations of learning rather than on course credits. Over the next three years, it became clear that many students were going to have problems graduating with the new standards. In addition, there seemed to be confusion about what the standards actually measured. In this high-stakes pressure, a new board of education was elected to eliminate the performance-based requirements.

Teachers need to decide if they are going to "count" the alternative assessment tasks with the same importance they now give to other, more traditional test measures. As a corollary, teachers need to determine if the measurement standards are going to be tough from the start or increase gradually over time. We will deal with this issue in the next chapter.

Planning for the Assessment Task

I assume that you have developed well-written and mutually agreed on exit and course standards for your students. Thematic units should be part of these standards. The next phase is to develop assessment tasks for these standards. Standards by themselves mean little if you cannot show some evidence that learning took place. To ensure that an assessment task implementation is successful, there are a number of steps you should follow.

1. *Identify assessment needs.*

Begin with course standards, a natural place for culminating activities to take place and therefore perfect for testing. Later in your planning you may want to test unit standards. First, however, deal with a bigger picture—a quarter, semester, or year-long course standard.

The teachers involved in teaching the previously developed standards first need to determine if any of the standards are currently being tested by traditional assessment means. There may already exist a well-defined test to measure a standard. A language arts teacher, for example, may already use a holistic scoring rubric to assess students' creative stories. There is no need, then, to reinvent the wheel on the first standard reviewed. After reviewing all the standards, determine a few that require the development of alternative assessment procedures. These are standards that have no existing testing associated with them. They also may be standards that cross discipline lines and are truly interdisciplinary. Agree as a group on which standard you will begin with. Prioritize the standards in terms of the one you would like to start working on.

For the first standard on your new list, ask yourself how you could demonstrate to the school community of students, parents, and other teachers that students in your class have developed an understanding level of performance on the subject in your course. What will students need to show, do, or produce for you to assess this?

2. *Identify the purpose of the assessment task.*
Earlier in this chapter, we identified four purposes of assessments:

- Keeping track of what the student has accomplished
- Checking up on where the student is now
- Finding out how the student understands
- Summing up to provide a judgment of the student's work

These purposes are not mutually exclusive but may have a number of common features. It is important, however, to be clear about them at this stage. The kind of information you gain from the task you are about to design will be determined by your purpose. The team of teachers should agree on the purpose. It is not appropriate, for example, for the math teacher to use the information gained from the assessment task to judge a student's performance while the science teacher uses the same information to check up on where the class as a whole is so he can make adjustments in the instruction plan. This can cause confusion for students and parents alike.

3. *Choose the assessment task.*
As mentioned earlier, there are three common types of alternative assessment tasks:

- Products
- Performances
- Portfolios

Discuss with those involved what type of task you would like your students to complete. Consider factors such as time, cost, age of students, and diversity of assessment tasks.

Within these three types of assessments, it has been observed (Jorgensen, 1993) that four different activities emerge:

- *Budgeting:* Time, money, or resources are spent to accomplish a purpose.
- *Communication tasks:* A letter or report is written. A speech or oral report is presented.
- *Scientific problem solving:* The science lab report is an example.
- *Model construction:* A design of a solution or a construction of a situation is undertaken.

You may want to begin your assessment with one of these four activities. They are the easiest to incorporate and can be applied to a host of different situations.

The tasks should include activities that force learning across the disciplines. One way to do this is by taking each discipline to be covered and incorporating a task:

- *Science:* Construct a three-dimensional model of a human cell.
- *Language arts:* Write a brief report on the functions of each part of the cell.
- *Reading:* Read *The Andromeda Strain* by Michael Crichton (New York: Ballantine Books).

A second method is to create a task that accomplishes a number of activities at the same time. The example of the students creating a television commercial for paper towels mentioned in the last chapter ("Move Over Rosie") integrates the various disciplines without differentiating between them. For the students, the tasks are related and contribute to a whole. They rarely are conscious of the interwoven pattern of the different disciplines that exists in the first method.

The tasks need to be given a context that is authentic. Wiggins (1992) reports that the test may be a contrivance but that it need not feel like one for the student. As much as possible, have the task satisfy a real audience and really work. Keep the tasks as efficient as possible in terms of cost and time without robbing them of their meaningful connection to the real world.

4. *Write the assessment task.*

The written form of the assessment task needs to be related directly to the standard, be clear in direction for the student, and provide the teacher with a mental picture of what will be produced. For example, the course standard described here is followed by an assessment task for a high school global studies course.

Course Standard   Students will compare and contrast the European perspective on the benefits of Columbus' landing in the New World with the Native Americans' perspective on the event.

Assessment Task   Students will demonstrate an understanding of this course standard by developing a global studies portfolio including three items: (1) a well-written research paper comparing and contrasting the two perspectives, including at least three themes, such as missionary zeal, trade, exploration, culture, disease, wealth, and or migration; (2) an advertisement in a hypothetical European newspaper of the fifteenth century asking for volunteers to come to the New World and an artistic drawing that could have been done by an Native American explaining the arrival of the Europeans in the New World; and (3) results of an essay test administered at the end of the first quarter.

5. *Prepare the students.*

A new assessment procedure requires that you spend time with the students, regardless of their age, to explain the features, relive the anxiety, and do any preassessment instruction.

a. *Explain the features:* The students need to be familiar with the design of alternative assessments. The meaning of products, performances, or portfolios should be explained. If a model or an old form of alternative test is available, share it with the students. The students should not be baffled by the design or the instructions. Share the scoring measurements as well. Students need to know exactly what each measurement means. If you have an excellent outcome from a previous assessment task, share it with the students. Explain what features of the task completion rendered this outcome excellent.

b. *Relieve anxiety:* Very bright students and those who overachieve will be anxious about a change in assessment form. These students excelled using standardized, multiple-choice, fill-in-the-blanks tests. The new form of test will cause fears that they will not do as well. Certainly, different study habits will emerge from this type of testing. Cramming will be eliminated because coverage and superficial memorization will not produce a superior result. There is every reason to believe that bright students should do equally as well on the new form. The student at the other end of the range will also be anxious. He or she always has trouble with tests. They ask themselves why a new form should be any different. They also may not want to put out the extra work required. Some of these students are content floating along. Others have learning problems that they cannot overcome, perhaps forever. Each student needs to be aware of the purpose of the assessment task and feel comfortable with the procedure to try to do his or her best.

c. *Preassessment instruction:* Students should not be punished on a test for not knowing some basic facts that are part of the assessment. For example, knowing how to operate a video camera for the television commercial or knowing what a school of fish is for an aquarium project are necessary skills and/or knowledge to complete the assessment task. The task is important, not whether or not a student knows these other skills or facts. Teach students what they need to know to complete the task. Remember—you are assessing the student's *understanding* of the knowledge, not *recall.*

6. *Prepare parents, community members, and other teachers.*

Do not assume that because you understand the reasons and even the necessity for alternative assessment, others do as well. Others may oppose your views and try to sabotage your efforts. Explain to parents, community leaders, and other teachers why you are doing what you are doing. Involve them at different stages in the activities. Students may use local business people for research, parents as sources of information and interviews, and other teachers for guidance in completing the task. In the scoring phase of the operation, parents, community members, and other teachers should be invited to be judges and assessors.

One school district used a PTA meeting at an elementary school to demonstrate the power of the new assessment tasks. First they distributed a multiple-choice exam on electricity to the parents. Questions about open and closed circuits and AC and DC power were asked. The parents commented that they could remember studying all this stuff but could not remember it. The second task the parents were given was a box of wires, batteries, light bulbs, and a electric switcher. They were told to get the bulb to light. Every one of the parents successfully illuminated the room. The debriefing involved comparing and contrasting the two forms of assessment. Obviously, parents enjoyed the latter more and reported understanding electricity more from doing this task. Such a demonstration is an example of how to involve parents in the change process.

7. *Pilot the assessment task.*

You will have some "bugs" in your assessment task, guaranteed. Students will take your carefully orchestrated plans and find a different way to interpret the instructions or manipulate the resources available. Testing the test will help you find the bugs that you first missed. Use a small sample of your students to test the assessment task. Ask the students for their feedback. If you are really brave, ask another teacher to administer the assessment task to his or her students. This blind piloting will provide feedback from the teacher on the assessment task's strengths and weaknesses. Once you have collected your feedback, redesign those portions of the task that need additional work.

8. *Administer the assessment task.*

Unlike standardized tests, alternative assessment tasks need not be administered to all students at the same time. The tasks can be spaced out over a quarter, semester, or year to allow ample time for students to complete the work. Portfolios, for instance, take time to assemble. The contents of these may also vary from student to student.

Eight-Step Planning Guide

As you start the process of designing your own assessment tasks, use the following form to guide your efforts. Some of the responses could be completed individually to be shared later among teachers working on the same design task. This form will help guide your thinking and serve as a format to guide discussion among others who may be working with you.

_____ **1.** *Identify assessment needs.*
Which standards need alternative assessment procedures? What will students need to show, do, or produce for you to assess the standard?

_____

_____

_____

_____

_____ 2. *Identify the purpose of the assessment task.*
Do I need the assessment tasks to

keep track: _____

check up: _____

find out: _____

sum up: _____

_____ 3. *Choose the assessment task.*
Which type of activity do I want the students to be engaged in?
What are the advantages and disadvantages of each compared to
the standard chosen?

Product: _____

Performance: _____

Portfolio: _____

_____ 4. *Write the assessment task.*
Finish this statement: The student will demonstrate an understanding of _____

_____

by _____

_____

_____ 5. *Prepare the students.*
What features of the assessment task need to be explained to the
students? _____

_____

Which students will need individual attention in making the transition to an alternative assessment task format?

_____

_____

What items on the assessment task need to be included in a preassessment instruction? _____

_____

_____ 6. *Prepare the parents/community/other teachers.*
How will you inform the parents of the new assessment tasks, and
how they will be used in curriculum and instruction? _____

_____

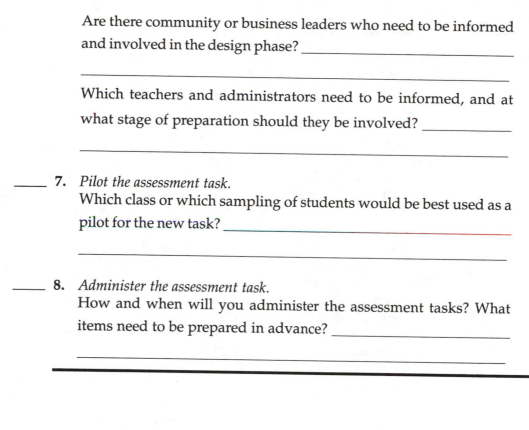

Are there community or business leaders who need to be informed and involved in the design phase? _____

_____

Which teachers and administrators need to be informed, and at what stage of preparation should they be involved? _____

_____

_____ 7. *Pilot the assessment task.*
Which class or which sampling of students would be best used as a pilot for the new task? _____

_____

_____ 8. *Administer the assessment task.*
How and when will you administer the assessment tasks? What items need to be prepared in advance? _____

_____

Summary

This chapter demonstrates how to build alternative assessment tasks, the tasks students will perform to demonstrate an understanding of the interdisciplinary standards developed in the proceeding chapter. The distinction between the terms *assessment, evaluation,* and *reporting* is discussed, with an emphasis on assessment, a collection of information about a student over a period of time. The purposes of assessment are divided into four interrelated areas: (1) keeping track of what a student has accomplished, (2) checking up on where the student is at in the curriculum sequence, (3) finding out how the student understands the curriculum, and (4) summing up so as to provide a judgment of a student's performance. The three types of alternative assessments—products, performances, and portfolios—are discussed and illustrated with actual examples from schools. The qualities of the assessment tasks that form the building blocks of your design are enumerated. Such factors as crafting the tasks to integrate knowledge from other disciplines; requiring the students to research, produce, and think; and clearly articulating the performance standards are discussed. Problems in constructing the tasks are also discussed. Examples are issues of the technical adequacy of the task construction, cost, comparability, and the high-stakes versus low-stakes importance of the tasks. The chapter concludes with an eight-step planning guide to assist you in designing your own assessment tasks.

References

Chittenden, E. (1991). Authentic assessment, evaluation, and documentation of student performance. In V. Perrone (Ed.), *Expanding student assessment*. Alexandria, VA: Association for Supervision and Curriculum Development.

Cronbach, L. J. (1960). *Essentials of psychological testing*, 2nd ed. New York: HarperCollins.

Davis, A., & Felknor, C. (1994, March). The demise of performance-based graduation in Littleton. *Educational Leadership, 51,* 64–65.

Engel, B. (1990). An approach to assessment in early literacy. In P. Kamil (Ed.), *Achievement testing in the early grades: The games adults play*. Washington, DC: National Association for the Education of Young Children.

Feur, M. J., & Fulton, K. (1993). The many faces of performance assessment. *Phi Delta Kappan*.

Gardner, H. (1991a). *The proceedings of the second national conference on assessing thinking: Shared perspectives, December 1990*. Baltimore, MD: National Thinking Assessment Network.

Gardner, H. (1991b). *The unschooled mind: How children think and how schools should teach*. New York: Basic Books.

Glazer, S. M., & Brown, C. S. (1993). *Portfolios and beyond: Collaborative assessment in reading and writing*. Norwood, MA: Christopher-Gordon.

Goodman, K. S., Goodman, Y. M., & Hood, W. J. *The whole language evaluation book*. Portsmouth, NH: Heinemann.

Guskey, T. R. (1994, March). What you assess may not be what you get. *Educational Leadership, 51,* 51–54.

Hafner, A. L. (1993). Teaching-method scales and mathematics-class achievement: What works with different outcomes? *American Educational Research Journal, 36,* 71–94.

Haney, W. (1991). We must take care: Fitting assessments to functions. In V. Perrone (Ed.), *Expanding student assessment*. Alexandria, VA: Association for Supervision and Curriculum Development.

Harp, B. (1993). *Assessment and evaluation in whole language programs*. Norwood, MA: Christopher-Gordon.

Hill, B. C., & Ruptic, C. (1994). *Practical aspects of authentic assessment: Putting the pieces together*. Norwood, MA: Christopher-Gordon.

Jorgensen, M. (1993, December). The promise of alternative assessment. *The School Administrator, 50,* 17–25.

Linn, R. (1994). Revise standards for educational and psychological testing. *Educational Researcher, 23*(9), 4–14.

Linn, R. L., Baker, E. L., & Dunbar, S. B. (1991). Complex, performance-based assessments: Expectations and validation criteria. *Educational Research, 20*(8), 15–21.

McDonald, J. P. (1993, February). Three pictures of an exhibition: Warm, cool, and hard. *Phi Delta Kappan,* 480–485.

Madaus, G. F., & Kellaghan, T. (1993, February). The British experience with "authentic" testing. *Phi Delta Kappan,* 458–469.

Peshkin, A. (1993, March). The goodness of qualitative research. *Educational Researcher*, 23–28.

Peters, T. J. (1988). *Thriving on chaos.* New York: Knopf.

Popham, W. J. (1993, February). Circumventing the high costs of authentic assessment. *Phi Delta Kappan,* 470–473.

Reich, R. B. (1987). Entrepreneurship reconsidered: The team as hero. *Harvard Business Review, 65*(3), 77–83.

Rhoades, J., & McCabe, M. E. (1992). *Outcome-based learning: A teacher's guide to restructuring the classroom.* Sacramento, CA: ITA Publications.

Tierney, R. J., Carter, M. A., & Desai, L. E. (1991). *Portfolio assessment in the reading–writing classroom.* Norwood, MA: Christopher-Gordon.

Tucker, M., & Resnick, L. B. (1990). *Setting a new standard: Toward an examination system for the United States.* Pittsburgh, PA: University of Pittsburgh.

Wiggins, G. (1992, May). Creating tests worth taking. *Educational Leadership, 49,* 26–32.

Wolf, R. M. (1993, November). The National Assessment of Education Progress: The nation's report card. *NASSP Bulletin, 77,* 36–45.

Worthen, B. R., & Sanders, J. R. (1987). *Educational evaluation: Alternative approaches and practical guidelines.* White Plains, NY: Longman.

4 Developing Measurement Criteria

*T*he process of constructing assessment tasks is not complete until a clear system of measurement is established. This chapter will explore different types of measurement that can be used with authentic assessment tasks, show how to build a scoring system, provide examples of actual measurement systems in operation, and conclude by demonstrating how reflection can be built into the process, especially as it relates to ensuring measurement reliability, validity, and generalizability. This chapter covers the last two steps in our four-step design taxonomy:

- Standards
- Assessment tasks
- Measurement*
- Reflection*

Measurement

Determining What You Need to Measure

Probably the best universal example of a measurement system that involves students in an authentic assessment task is the driver's road test. Most of us have gone through this assessment with emotions ranging from delight to fear to dread. The road test is an authentic test of your driving ability. The instructor rates your performance on a number of criteria using a varied range of points. If you gain enough points, you pass. If you do not gain the points, you fail but can try again. Mastery is based not on time but on proficiency.

Measuring an authentic assessment task is not as simple as most other evaluations. There are many ways to demonstrate proficiency. The measurement process must ensure that it can capture the essence of student proficiency and not get bogged down in measuring the details of performance. The measurement must focus on the student's understanding in the performance application and avoid some of the many accompanying variables. In addition, the measurement must choose a limited dimension or aspect of learning to evaluate. It is very difficult to measure a host of different dimensions at one time without losing focus. A long checklist of criteria can involve the evaluator in mere data collection with no analysis of student understanding. This cheats students of an in-depth analysis of their thinking ability.

The road test evaluator knows the criteria that assure society that you can perform at a certain standard. If you pass, you will be allowed on the road. In a similar fashion, the instructor needs to define what he or she will be looking for in the assessment measurement. The focus should be on the academic course standards that were developed in Chapter 2. It can be assumed that, if the instructional process is strong, all students can fulfill the course standards. You should measure the course rather than the exit standards. Exit standards can be too vague to measure with any sense of reliability or even validity. For example, the exit standard

Value mathematics as a tool to solve problems

is one all schools should hope students will achieve. But this is a content-level standard and cannot be measured. How would one begin to measure *value?* However, one can assume with a high degree of confidence that this exit standard can be achieved if all the math course-level standards are met. The course standard

Calculate and design a graph showing the relationship of two types
of home mortgage interest rates over the 25-year life of a loan.

is measurable and can easily be demonstrated by students at different levels of competency.

To start with course-level standards, the best place to begin is to look at the verbs used to describe student activities. These verbs are usually action-oriented and, as discussed in Chapter 3, are aimed at higher order thinking skills. One course standard in mathematics states:

Students will utilize mathematical skills, processes, and concepts
in solving a wide range of problems within a variety of settings.

The assessment task asks students to imagine they are a meeting of the Ice Cream Sales Committee, which must decide kinds of ice cream and how much of each to sell at the next sale. Students are given a chart that lists data from past ice cream sales. The students are to decide whether to sell only chocolate ice cream bars next time.

The verbs in the course standard are *utilize* and *solve.* If we placed them in a grid depicting them as the reasoning process we are measuring, we could construct a system as follows:

Reasoning process
Utilize
Solve

There are, however, other systems to illustrate the learning concept in the course standard. One is the taxonomy of knowledge that Bloom (1956) presented, discussed in Chapter 3. You can determine what to measure on the basis of this six-step process:

Knowledge
Comprehension
Application
Analysis
Synthesis
Evaluation

Another system that is being promoted by the Association for Supervision and Curriculum Development is the Dimensions of Learning Model (Marzano, Pickering, & McTighe, 1993). This model is based on the premise that five types of thinking are essential to the learning process: (1) positive attitudes and perceptions about learning, (2) thinking involved in acquiring and integrating knowledge, (3) thinking involved in extending and refining knowledge, (4) thinking involved in using knowledge meaningfully, and (5) productive habits of the mind. Dimensions 3 and 4 are the most crucial because in these areas students add new distinctions, make connections to previous and other new knowledge, and show understanding through application of knowledge. These are cognitive processes described in the earlier chapters as students understanding knowledge for performance. In extending and refining knowledge, students would be comparing, contrasting, deducing, analyzing, creating, and making abstractions. In using knowledge meaningfully, students would be making decisions, investigating, inquiring through experiment, solving problems, and producing.

A model of learning that involves the psychomotor domain is presented by Simpson (1972). These major categories, from lowest to highest, are: (1) perception or interpreting, (2) set or preparing, (3) guided response or learning, (4) mechanism or habit forming, (5) complex overt response or performing, (6) adaptation or modifying, and (7) origination or creating. Use this model for those course standards that involve students in more hands-on activities.

A common question is: How often should you assess higher order thinking skills used in your curriculum? A common goal is to have 60 percent of your assessments measure higher order thinking or performance skills. To measure learning domains that involve only basic skills will result in a dumbing down of your curriculum. The old saying "what gets measured gets done" can be applied here. If you set out to measure higher order thinking skills like analysis, synthesis, and evaluation, you will instruct students in how to use these skills to solve problems.

Who Should Measure?

There are four sources of evaluations: (1) student self-evaluation, (2) peer evaluation, (3) parent/community evaluation, and (4) formal and informal teacher evaluation.

Self-evaluation

Teaching students to assess their own work is effective at improving overall student performance. It involves self-reflection rather than reliance on an external evaluator. The process itself helps students keep clear the measuring criteria or dimensions of learning that need to be addressed. If students are aware throughout their classroom work of the criteria against which they are being measured, the quality of the work toward meeting these criteria is better. A disadvantage of student self-evaluation is that students may not be truthful and the information they offer can be limited. One way to overcome these disadvantages is to make student self-evaluation only one part of the evaluation process.

An eighth-grade English assessment at the Anne M. Dorner Middle School in Ossining, New York, combines student self-evaluation with the teacher's evaluation. The assignment requires students to write an "Origins of Humans" research report. This is an interdisciplinary study of early humans integrating four disciplines. English, social studies, math, and science. In writing the report, students must use main topics from their previous written outline and include five paragraphs: an introduction, three body paragraphs, and a conclusion. Transition words and clear topic sentences should be used. Listed here is the assessment with the specific points added to each criterion. The student self-assessment must be submitted with the report.

Student Assessment	Teacher Assessment
Topic sentences	20 points
Use of transitional words	10 points
Introduction	10 points
Body paragraph #1	10 points
Body paragraph #2	10 points
Body paragraph #3	10 points
Conclusion	10 points
Mechanics	20 points
Bibliography	30 points
Notes	45 points
Outline	25 points
Total	200 points

Another example comes from a task developed by the Maryland Geographic Alliance. At the end of an extensive analysis of two different types of environments, students are asked to rate their performance. They are instructed to circle the number that shows how easy or difficult it was for them to complete the activities in the task, from the following scale:

1	2	3	4	5
Very easy	Somewhat easy	About average	Somewhat difficult	Very difficult

One example of an indigenous book that directly influenced classroom practice in this area was Nancy Atwell's *In the Middle: Writing, Reading, and Learning with Adolescents* (1987). One of her procedures is to interview each student as a method of including students in the assessment process. Teachers are encouraged to ask such questions as: What was the main thing you hope to learn this grading period? What main thing did you learn? What is one thing you intend to do because of what you learned?

Peer Evaluation

The advantage of peer reviewers is that they also learn along with the student they are helping. They need to keep on task if their help is to mean anything to the other student. One chief difficulty with this process is that the peer reviewers need to be able to actually help. Students with vastly different abilities should not usually be paired. Research supports the belief that all students, regardless of ability, can gain in achievement, parents and other community members still have difficulty accepting this concept. Parents of bright students, in particular, feel that their child is deprived of instruction if the child is involved in extensive cooperative group learning with students of lower achievement levels.

The Croton Harmon Schools (Croton-on-Hudson, New York) and the Tuckahoe Public Schools (Tuckahoe, New York) provide an excellent example of how to use peer reviewers. Seniors at the high schools have the option to choose an internship program for their final six weeks of school. This project includes a full-time experience at a career site, extensive research in the career area, and periodic meetings with mentors. The culminating event of this project is a thirty-minute presentation or exhibition before a review panel made up of teachers, community members, and other seniors. In the Croton schools the other seniors, as members of the evaluation committee, rate the student's exhibition on seven criteria: (1) organization; (2) effective introduction and conclusion; (3) demonstration that the knowledge has personal meaning; (4) connections made between research and experience; (5) appropriate visual aids and props; (6) smooth, polished, well-prepared presentation; and (7) the use of voice to emphasize points and engage audience. It is found that seniors respect each other's evaluations often more than those of adults.

There is strong research to support the use of other students in helping students evaluate their work. Slavin, Madden, and Stevens (1990) describe some of this research. One study on the use of peer feedback on written student work shows that peer help clearly produces higher quality writing at the surface structure level of revisions and substitutions. The overall rhetorical quality between rough and final drafts improved. The use of peer helpers seemed to help improve mechanics: punctuation, capitalization, spelling, and handwriting. The significantly better writing found in the peer review groups may have been due to helping the writer anticipate the audience for the written work as well as helping maintain enthusiasm for the writing task.

Parent/Community Evaluation

Involving parents and community members in evaluation is a powerful method of not only diversifying your evaluation workload but also validating your curriculum. Many community members would love to serve the schools in this fashion. It brings them into contact with kids and with their community schools, and makes them feel they are contributing to the education process. For senior citizens, especially, it is a meaningful way of involving them with another generation. For parents serving as evaluators, it demystifies the educational process. This is especially important nowadays when instructional methods and even curriculum have changed from the parents' school days.

In one middle school, students are required to work in cooperative teams to develop projects to restore environmental, cultural, and historical beauty to the town's neglected riverfront. The students present their ideas for development and restoration in an oral presentation complete with scale models, drawings, and/or photographs. The teacher assembles a panel of community members to evaluate the student work. The mayor, trustees, police chief, superintendent of schools, town engineer, and other community residents evaluate the student presentations. Students dress up for their presentations because they want to impress the evaluators from outside the school. Using outside evaluators in this way adds an authentic feeling to the whole enterprise. Peers, too, can be valuable members of such an evaluation review committee.

Teacher Evaluation

There are really two different tasks involved here: the informal or observational rating and the formal assessment. The observational rating is popular with teachers because it can be done while they are teaching and does not involve designating a separate time or place to evaluate student work. The informal process of rating a student during a "performance" piece of the assessment is illustrated in the observational rating guide used by teachers at the Susan Lindgren Elementary School (St. Louis Park, Minnesota). Students in this school experience a hands-on inquiry approach to their surroundings, performing experiments, and collecting numerical data to depict in charts, form hypotheses, and retest. Because students are constantly assessed on the same criteria, the quantity of assessments creates validity as the teachers share results with the students. The Experiment Observation Checklist is presented here.

Date:

_____ Patience and self-discipline (staying focused)

_____ Craftsmanship (use and care of materials and tools)

_____ Relying on data (observation, collecting evidence)

_____ Understanding (cause and effect, purpose, solution)

_____ Communication (written and oral)

_____ Cooperation (functioning in group)
    E (excellent)
    S (satisfactory)
    N (needs improvement

The formal part of assessment is the most common. Teachers evaluate all the time and are trained for this task. Probably one of the chief drawbacks to implementing performance-based assessment is precisely this fact—it takes more teacher time. Most of the assessment examples described later in this chapter and in Part II of this book involve the teacher actively and heavily as the prime evaluator. For performance evaluation to become more a part of the mainstream curriculum and assessment process, evaluators other than classroom teachers need to be involved.

Perhaps the answer to this dilemma is to combine the four types of evaluation described in this section. This balance provides students with frequent significant feedback in different formats. There are few guidelines on how often to include other evaluators in the process. Currently, teachers are the prime evaluators of performance assessment tasks, whether the assessments are developed for the classroom or at the state level. One challenge to teachers is to develop more opportunities for self-peer, and parent/community involvement in evaluating.

Scoring or Rubrics

Scoring the learning domain that you have established calls for a mechanism that is clear, simple to use, common, and accessible to students and evaluators. *Rubric* means a characteristic mark, the term is taken from Romans custom of placing red *(ruber, rubra, rubrum)* clay on the ground to mark a spot. The rubric sets the essential characteristics and criteria of an intended performance or product and also provides for evaluation data.

Two types of rubrics are commonly used by teachers: holistic and analytic. The holistic rubric considers the performance as a whole; the analytic breaks the performance down into component parts. One or both types of rubrics can be used to score the standard. The following chart illustrates how each can be used.

Comparison of Scoring Rubrics

Holistic

_____ **3.** *Excellent:* The project demonstrates detailed planning and implementation.

_____ **2.** *Proficient:* The project demonstrates basic planning and implementation.

_____ **1.** *Needs improvement:* The project lacks planning and implementation.

This rubric gives the student a summary evaluation of the project. The scoring can be done quickly and has clear criteria. For evaluating the entire curriculum program, it is ideal. Its chief disadvantage is a lack of specificity. The student may wonder what exactly did he or she not do to achieve the level 3 or excellent score.

Analytic

_____ **3.** Responses are complex and demonstrate understanding by integrating one's own experiences, past readings, and discussions with classmates.

_____ **2.** Responses show some understanding by summarizing or retelling the information or linking it with past experiences or readings.

_____ **1.** Responses are not congruent with the text; inaccurate or incomplete information is provided.

This rubric provides a more thorough analysis of specific strengths and areas for improvement. An advantage for pupil evaluation is that it gives the student specific information on his or her performance. Another advantage is that the process involves the evaluator in a more in-depth understanding of the student's attempt to meet the course standard. A chief disadvantage of the use of this type of rubric is that it takes time to do the assessment correctly.

Although these two examples have numerical scales, it is proper to include descriptive scales as well. Numerical rating allows for some statistical operations and provides a quick scale for a student to remember. "I got a '3' " is easier than saying a long descriptive phase. Descriptive scales, however, provide more information. A picture scale could be included, which helps some students visualize better their assessment work. An example of a line scale is shown here:

_____3_____2_____1_____

| Complex integration | Some summarizing, linking | No congruence, incomplete |

For younger children, the use of a symbol is common—for example, a pen for writing. The high end of the scale would receive five pen symbols, the

FIGURE 4–1

end just one pen symbol. Symbols are easy to use. The use of "smile faces" is common. Figure 4–1 shows examples that incorporate a three-point scale using the symbol of a smiling face.

A common question is: How many marks should be included in a measurement scale? There is no right or wrong answer. The more precise question is: How much information do you want to convey to the student through the scoring process, and how much time do you have? If you want students to gain a detailed insight into their work performance and you have the time to construct and score, then a multi-item scoring rubric is desirable. If you are trying to provide a high interrater agreement, a shorter scale will produce higher results.

Two examples of very different scales are illustrated here. The new science textbook *Science Plus: Technology and Society* (Austin, TX: Holt, Rinehart & Winston, 1993) lists scoring scales for evaluating student reports and presentations that run from 5 through 30 points, with five-point intervals at the lower end of the scale and one-point intervals from 15 through 30, the higher end of the scale. Marzano, Pickering, and McTighe (1993) present numerous rubric scales from 4 through 1, with 4 being the high performance end and 1 being the poor performance end.

Another method of developing a scoring scale is to use a modified or two-step rubric scale. This scale may have four or five different measurement criteria, but only the first, last, and midscale description are crucial. The other scales are modifications of these essential three. In this manner, the scorer can make a quick judgment about where the student work is at and then modify this judgment slightly up or down a scale to adjust for performance variations. The Region 15 schools in Middlebury, Connecticut, use this form of scoring with an additional twist. They use a scale of S, T, U, V, W, X, so that evaluators and students do not associate the scale with the traditional A–F sequence.

Rubric for Scoring a Video

S: This work goes beyond the rating of T. It is especially eloquent and effective.

T: The video has a clear theme and purpose. The information contained in the shots provides accurate and appropriate support for the theme. All the shots build solid support for the theme and purpose. It is clear that the student understands the core curriculum related to this project. The flow from shot to shot is so smooth that it is unnoticeable. The whole video has the intended impact on the target audience. The technical quality of the sound and picture is excellent. Music, titles, and special effects, if used, strongly support the theme and purpose.

U: This video is generally as good as one receiving a rating of T but is uneven, with some relatively less well developed aspects.

V: This video is generally like one receiving a rating of W but has one or two areas that are relatively better developed.

W: This video does not have a theme or purpose, or the information contained in the shots does not support the theme or purpose well. The shots seem like a series of "pieces" without a smooth, flowing sequence. It is not clear that the student understands the core curriculum related to this project. The whole video does not achieve its intended impact on the audience. The technical quality of the sound and/or picture is poor. Music, titles, and special effects, if used, do not support the theme and/or purpose and may distract the audience.

X: This video is extremely weak.

In this example, T and W are the anchor points, with S, U, V, and X allowing the scorer to make minor modifications.

A common scoring scale used by teachers is the 0–100 scale, where 0 means no or poor performance and 100 means excellent. A mark of 65 usually means passing at a basic competency level, whereas a mark of 80 is an indication of mastery. One of the chief problems with this type of rubric is that there are usually no descriptions for any of the other points on the scale. For example, if a student scores 35, what does that mean? If 65 is failing, and there are no descriptors for any other marks between 0 and 65, then 35 means the same as 5 or 25 or 50 or even 64. The point is that if a teacher is going to use a 0–100 scale, there need to be descriptions for each of the levels. One method of presenting this is to cluster the points:

90–100	Exemplary response	Demonstrated competence
80–90	Mastery level	
70–80	Minor flaws but satisfactory	Satisfactory responses
60–70	Serious flaws but nearly satisfactory	
40–60	Begins but fails to complete problem	Inadequate responses
20–40	Unable to begin effectively	
0–20	No attempt	

Still another common method for teachers to use in scoring is the assignment of points for a performance. This is commonly referred to as a checklist. The points allocated for each specific subpart of the performance are weighted so that the more complicated or skill portions of the performance are given more credit. The advantage is that a teacher can devise such a rubric quickly, the student knows exactly which parts of the performance are most important, and the feedback the teacher provides is specific to the task. The chief disadvantage is that no scale is involved. There is no 0 and no 100. There are just points assigned. A student can get the maximum allocated or the minimum allocated but does not know if he or she has achieved mastery or is below competency level.

An example of an elementary mathematical problem-solving task called "Travel with Charlie" illustrates how the student gains points for each of the mathematical tasks he or she completes.

Points	Description
2	The student clearly identifies or states the problem presented.
	(What is the greatest distance that Charlie can travel in five days?
	The student identifies or lists known information.
1	Charlie must visit three specific points.
1	The points are within a 1,000-mile radius.
1	Charlie must stop to eat and sleep.
1	Charlie can travel faster on days one and two.
2	The student clearly states the approach or strategy for solving the problem.
3	The student describes the process used to solve the problem.
1	The student uses appropriate graphs, pictures, charts, or other methods to organize or display data correctly.
2	The student solves the problem by showing that Charlie can travel to three specific points in five days.

1	The student states what he or she learned from the problem.
_1_	The student produces a quality report or paper.
18	Total possible points

Another example of this type of rubric is seen in a middle school language arts class. Here students need to complete three tasks: (1) create a colorfully written advertisement for the book *To Kill a Mockingbird*, (2) recreate the last chapter of the novel, and (3) dramatize what the student thinks is the most important scene. The rubric for this project is illustrated here.

Advertisement

Points	Criteria: 18
6	**1.** Clear use of language (proper spelling and syntax)
6	**2.** Clever slogan that interests and catches the reader's eye
6	**3.** Artistic depiction of logo as a reflection of written work

Recreation of Novel Ending

Points	Criteria: 26
6	**1.** Clear, concise language structure
6	**2.** Creativity—student taps imagination to recreate alternative ending
6	**3.** Follows directions with regard to specific requirements (three pages double spaced, neatly presented)

Dramatization

Points	Criteria: 20
6	**1.** Clear rationale for why this scene is important
7	**2.** Obvious preparation in teamwork (knowledge of lines, intonation)
7	**3.** Students display a clear understanding of plot and characterization

How to Develop Scales

Developing scales is not difficult but this task is crucial to making your assessment task authentic. Wiggins (1993) says that scoring rubrics need to be able to discriminate between performances and between performances of different degrees of quality. Researchers commonly use two methods to make salient and educative distinctions on scoring scales. These are described by Lindsay and Norman (1977) as confusion scaling and direct scaling.

Confusion Scaling

Confusion scaling is popular in many forms of psychological testing. This procedure determines the distance needed between two scores or descriptions by the number of times they are confused with each other. The method allows us to equate the differences in intervals between two scale values. For example, we give three technology teachers model rockets designed by middle school students and ask them to rate each rocket on design using the following scale.

> 5 (Exceeds all specifications)
> 4 (Meets the specifications)
> 3 (Meets most of the specifications)
> 2 (Meets some of the specifications)
> 1 (Meets a few of the specifications)
> 0 (Does not meet any specifications)

In our trial, we find that the three raters cannot agree on the difference between a rating of 1 and a rating of 2. The test designer then needs to make the difference sharper in the descriptive scale or else collapse 2 into 1.

Direct Scaling

This procedure is more direct then the previous one. Here we ask the raters to assign numbers to physical attributes in a way that is proportional to the subjective impressions they make. One way to use this procedure is *magnitude estimation.* Here the rater is given an exemplary product—a rocket that exceeds all design specifications, or a product rated 5. The rater is asked to judge other rocket designs on the basis of their distance from this model. For example, you might ask the rater to place the rockets in similar piles based on the differences of design and distance from the exemplary rocket. All those rockets meeting some of the design specifications would be placed in the same pile. Once the different piles have been established, you can place number values on them based on the magnitude of difference from the exemplary model.

Developing rubric scales is an excellent area for parents and community members to become involved. There is no better way to showcase your curriculum than to involve them at this level. In addition, their insights and expertise will help make the scales much more valid.

Types of Measurement

Seven different examples of how measurements can be used are described here, followed by a chart illustrating how the components of measurement—learning domain, evaluator, and scoring—are related.

1. Hot Wheels Track*

This physics assessment project examines students' understanding of the relationship of velocity and time. Equipment includes a velocity versus time graph, plastic tubing, ring stands, clamps, a small steel ball, a stopwatch, a meter stick, and metric graph paper.

   a. You will be given a velocity (speed) versus time graph that describes the motion of a moving car on a track. In one or two sentences, describe the motion of the car (be specific). (5 points)

   b. Arrange the plastic tubular track in such a way that a "car" (actually a small steel ball) traveling on your track will have the same motion as in the graph. Draw a picture of your track setup. (5 points)

   c. Record and graph distance versus time for the "car" running on your track. Arrange your data in a neat, well organized manner and make sure you label everything clearly. (10 points; record data and attach graph). *Note:* You will have to run the "car" on the track several times in order to get enough data points to make a graph.

Each pair of students receives one of the following velocity versus time graphs:

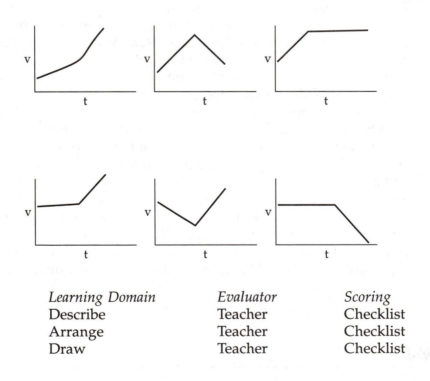

Learning Domain	Evaluator	Scoring
Describe	Teacher	Checklist
Arrange	Teacher	Checklist
Draw	Teacher	Checklist

*Source: Sandy Grindle, Bonita Vista High School, Chula Vista, California, and Rod Ziolkowski, Cerritos High School, Cerritos, California. This work was supported in part by NSF Grant ESI-9254454.

2. Literature Review

Students' responses to literature in this high school English class are rated on the basis of three criteria: main idea, connections, and responses. Each of these categories has a number of descriptors. A sample is provided here. The responses are recorded during the year in the student's literature portfolio.

Rubric			*Criteria*
1	2	3	State main Idea. How well does the student summarize the reading, demonstrate completeness, provide examples from the text?
1	2	3	Make connections. How well does the student make predictions, challenge the author about conclusions, and provide self-insight and/or reflection?
1	2	3	Make responses. How well does the student answer questions posed by the teacher and/or other students and respond to problems in the text?

Rubric Scoring
1   Student demonstrates proficiency in responding to the criteria.
2   Student demonstrates adequate response to the criteria.
3   Student needs to complete responses to specific criteria.

Learning Domain	*Evaluator*	*Scoring*
Read	Teacher	0–3 scale
Produce	Teacher	0–3 scale
Reflect	Teacher	0–3 scale
	Student	Written essays

3. Industrial Development

In this project, middle school students inquire and learn about the effects of various industries and development on a mountain environment. During the four to six weeks that students work on this project, they will investigate the effects of developing industry and/or population growth in a mountain forest or wetlands area. The type of industry suggested includes ski resorts, timber-processing plants, a coal-powered electricity-generating plant, a hydroelectric project, a cattle ranch, a regional airport or condominium community. Information should include effects on water, soil, and air quality; effects on vegetation and wildlife; and economic effects on the community. Each student must present evidence of all scientific, mathematical, and investigative processes used; a scientific explanation of effects on the environment; a recommendation regarding desirability and/or regulations for a specific type of development; and supporting evidence of recommendation.

The scoring is based on three criteria: process, results, and presentation. Each of these criteria has a number of descriptors. Some of these are listed here.*

Process

1. The student chooses an industry or other form of growth for the project.
2. The student gathers and documents information from many sources.
3. The student specifically documents how he or she has applied the scientific process to this project.

Results

2. All mathematical and scientific calculations and formulas used in the investigation are displayed and explained.
5. Technology is applied to organize data in a meaningful way by the use of charts, graphs, and diagrams.

Presentation

1. The student provides a clear oral explanation analyzing the results of the project in a way that demonstrates a high degree of understanding of the information and related processes.

The students are scored on three levels: Excellent, Proficient, and Needs Improvement. Those descriptors listed here are those rated as Excellent. Proficient level means a lesser quality, and Needs Improvement means poor quality.

Learning Domain	Evaluator	Scoring
gather	teacher	holistic
calculation	teacher	holistic
explanation	teacher	holistic
produce	teacher	holistic

*Source: Little Middle School in Littleton, Colorado. Designed by Marc Bacon.

4. Vermont Writing Assessment

The State of Vermont developed a writing assessment for all students, which was piloted in the 1990–1991 school year. The writing portfolio used in grades 4 and 8 included two types of products. (1) a collection of six pieces of writing done by the student during the academic year, and (2) a "uniform writing assessment," a formal writing assignment given by all teachers to all students at the respective grade levels. The analytic assessment guide used for the uniform writing assessment is organized in a grid format. The criteria assessed are: purpose, organization, details, voice/tone, and "GUM" (grammar, mechanics, usage). The rubric to measure these criteria is a holistic one with the scale of Rarely, Sometimes, Frequently, Extensively.

There is also a Nonscorable mark that includes all illegible, incoherent, or blank papers.

Learning Domain	*Evaluator*	*Scoring*
Produce	teacher	holistic
Communicate	teacher	holistic

5. Special Education

Teachers of special education students have been rating student performance for a long time and are familiar with the process. In the following example, students are rated on the criteria of personal care, health, and safety activities. The rubric is a descriptive analytic type.

Completes dressing activity.
Completes hygiene grooming activity.
Completes personal health care activity.
Completes physical fitness activity.
Completes safety or emergency activity.

Each of these criteria is rated on one of the following descriptive scales.

Initiates activity.
Carries out steps.
Conducts self safely/appropriately.
Attempts to modify performance with unanticipated events.
Modifies performance with unanticipated events.

Learning Domain	*Evaluator*	*Scoring*
produces	teacher	descriptive analytic

6. Walden III: ROPE

This program, Rite of Passage Experience (ROPE), in the Racine, Wisconsin, Unified School District, consists of sixteen areas of human knowledge and skills in which students are required to show mastery in presentations before they can graduate. Preparation for these presentations involves three required phases: a written portfolio, a written project, and an oral demonstration. In U.S. history, for example, students are required to present some kind of overview of American history. The student can select the basis for the overview—wars, periods of formal history, national expansion, industrial development, technology, stages in political development, and so on. The point of this requirement is for the student to demonstrate some sense of the progression of U.S. history. The basis for the overview should be clearly explained in the presentation. Finally, as part of the presentation, students should be prepared to field questions on the area of U.S. history in general. Examples of these questions are:

- How can a topic be related to the senior at our high school?
- What types of information are important to remember about a country's history?
- Is history always based on books or other written sources?
- Who fought in the French and Indian war? What were the Articles of Confederation? Where was the Underground Railroad? When was World War II? Why did the South pass Jim Crow Laws? How did George Washington get to be a general? What is your place in history?

Students' presentations are scored on the following rubric. The portfolio and project are not measured with this scale but must be accepted by the teacher and the student's evaluation committee (made up of staff, another student, and an adult from outside the school) before the presentation is given in a particular academic area.

EX = Excellent (superior quality work)
CO = Competent (above average work)
SA = Satisfactory (average work)
SS = Substandard (passing but below average work)
UN = Unacceptable (work not acceptable as passing)

Learning Domain	Evaluator	Scoring
Knowledge	Teachers, peers,	Holistic
Application	community	
Analysis		

7. Socratic Seminars

These are classroom discussions between teacher and student and between student and student. The interactions involve listening, information gathering, analyzing, and supporting statements with facts. The seminars center on the curriculum content, and their purpose is to help students analyze and discuss current issues involved in the content area. The role of the teacher is to facilitate the discussion, make sure thoughts are discussed and not feelings, assist the process so that everyone is heard, and help students stay on the topic. Generally, this seminar lasts a class period. Some teachers use them every four to six weeks as part of a process to have students explore a topic in depth as well as to make interdisciplinary connections. Scoring is based on a four-point rubric: 4 = Excellent, 3 = Good, 2 = Fair, 1 = Unsatisfactory. The criteria for an excellent score are listed here.

   a. *Conduct:* Demonstrates respect for the seminar, shows initiative by asking others for clarification, brings others into the conversation, moves the conversation forward, avoids talking too long and use of inappropriate language.

   b. *Speaking/reasoning:* Understands questions before answering, cites evidence from the text (or elsewhere). Makes logical and insightful comments, makes connections, resolves contradictory ideas, considers all sources.

   c. *Listening:* Pays attention to details, recognizes faulty logic, overcomes distractions.

   d. *Reading:* Prepares thoroughly and comes with notes and questions.

Learning Domain	*Evaluator*	*Scoring*
Reasoning	Teacher	Holistic
Speaking	(has been used	
Listening	with peer)	
Reading		

Benchmarks

All performance assessments should give students models or examples of exemplary performance. Students should be able to see, hear, or touch those examples of excellence. There should be no surprises. The term *benchmark* refers to the practice of making a mark on the craftsman's workbench to ensure that each measurement of the raw material (wood, metal, leather, etc.) has the same level of high-quality consistency.

You will not be able to have benchmarks or models of excellence ready the first time you do performance assessments. These benchmarks will need to be discovered among the first products, performances, or portfolios that students make. Once you have them, you can use them to show future students what you expect in terms of excellence. Some teachers may say that by showing students these models you are encouraging copying and limiting creativity. Teachers who use benchmarks, however, find that they have the opposite experience. Using models of excellence to simulate student work raises students' expectations and generally allows the class as a whole to produce higher quality work.

The procedure of first establishing benchmarks involves a method called *four-corner measurement*. The steps are outlined here for a performance assessment involving a written product. However, the process is similar for performances or exhibitions.

1. Distribute the student's performance assessments among a group of four teachers familiar with the content and the assessment task. If you do not have four teachers who are familiar with the process, you may want to provide some preliminary orientation and training in scoring.
2. Distribute the scoring rubric to the teachers who will be doing the rating. You can use parents, community members, or older students in this process. Ask each one to read the written work and place the ratio mark in the upper right-hand corner of the paper. Ask them then to fold down the corner to hide the rating.
3. Pass the distributed writing samples around. Repeat step 2, but this time have the raters place their mark in the upper left-hand corner and turn the corner down to hide the mark.
4. Repeat steps 2 and 3 using the remaining two bottom corners.
5. When all the papers are rated, turn over the folded corners and discover which papers have received consistently the highest marks. These are the products everyone agrees are of excellent quality.
6. Photocopy these writing samples and mark them as benchmarks for this phase of the performance assessment. The next time you conduct a similar assessment task, use these benchmarks (without student names) to illustrate the high quality of performance you expect.

In designing your own measurement process, you can use the chart provided here to help guide you through the different options you can choose from.

Measurement Design Guide

There are three major components to designing a measurement process: deciding what to measure, who will do the measurement, and what scoring mechanism to use. To determine your needs, a set of questions has been developed here to guide you.

What to Measure

_____ 1. Do you have course standards already established?   YES   NO
If YES, then proceed to the next question. If NO,
then go back and reread Chapter 2.

_____ 2. Have you listed the verbs (learning domains)   YES   NO
used to describe the course standards?

_____ 3. Have you chosen a sample of these learning   YES   NO
domains to assess?
If NO, then review that standards to assure
yourself that you have a manageable number
of learning domains to assess.

_____ 4. Does 60 percent of the list learning domains   YES   NO
represent higher order thinking skills or
performances?

_____ 5. Have you provided instruction in the devel-   YES   NO
opment of each of the learning domains on
your list?
If NO, then reread Chapter 2.

_____ 6. Have you developed assessment tasks to   YES   NO
assess each of the learning domains?
If NO, then reread Chapter 3.

Who Is to Measure?

_____ 1. Have you instructed the students on how   YES   NO
to observe each other?

_____ 2. Is at least one of your assessments a self-   YES   NO
assessment?

_____ 3. Do you have a plan to involve parents and   YES   NO
community members?
If NO, talk to the PTA about a plan.

_____ 4. Are all your assessments done by you?   YES   NO
If YES, then prepare a plan to develop
alternative evaluators.

How Will the Measurement Be Done?

_____ 1. Do you want to provide the students with a   YES   NO
summary evaluation?
If YES, then use holistic scoring.

_____ 2. Do you want to provide students with an analysis   YES   NO
           of specific strengths and areas of improvement?
           If YES, then use analytic scoring.

_____ 3. Do you have time to score many learning domains?   YES   NO
           If YES, then use analytic scoring.

_____ 4. Do you want to calculate class and/or student   YES   NO
           average scores, or do a pre/post assessment
           analysis?
           If YES, then use a numerical rating scale.

_____ 5. Have you shared your scoring system with the   YES   NO
           students prior to the assessment?

_____ 6. Do need to develop a quick assessment of   YES   NO
           student performance?
           If YES, then use a performance checklist.

_____ 7. Is the scoring system clear and simple to use?   YES   NO

Do You Have Benchmarks?

_____ 1. Is it possible to determine models of excellence   YES   NO
           before the assessment task?

_____ 2. Have models of excellence been identified after   YES   NO
           the performance task?

To help you view how the different component are related, fill in the following chart.

Learning Domain   *Evaluator*   *Scoring*

Reflections

This section will take you back to those test and measurement courses you had in school. The difference is that the material you are about to read has direct influence on how you develop your performance assessments. In school, most of the course material was future-oriented or esoteric. You will find this material authentic for the task of building performance assessments.

We call this section "Reflections" because establishing reliability, validity, and generalizability for your assessment tasks will take place after your initial presentation of the tasks to the students. No matter what you hear, you cannot build these three traits into your assessment system without first having students perform them, at least on a pilot basis. Many teachers do not consider reliability, validity, or generalizability either because they don't understand the concepts or they do understand but do not feel they are warranted in performance assessments. In the latter case, consider that if performance assessments are to gain any credibility with students, parents, and the community, they need to be reliable, valid, and generalizable. If we as a profession do not establish these traits, then performance assessments will, in time, come under the same type of attack that standardized tests receive today. In terms of the former case, not understanding, this section will help you use the three traits in your own performance assessments. We will consider each of the three separately, but they are related.

Reliability

The term *reliability* refers to the consistency of the performance assessment scores obtained by the same student when rated by different evaluators and when rated on the same task over time. Every assessment instrument has an error measurement or fluctuation in scores depending on testing conditions, the mood of the student, and even interpretations of the assessment task questions. It is reported (McTighe, 1994) that in recent research performance assessments have about the same error variance as that reported for standardized tests. What you would like to ensure in your scoring system is some level of sameness in scores, or reliability. If Jeannette obtains a rating of 5 or an excellent mark for a dance performance she has just demonstrated, there should be some reassurance that she will receive a 5 rating from another rater who watched the same performance. Variation exists everywhere, and you can expect to find it in rating as well, just as in the Olympics different scores are given by a panel of judges to the same figure skater. We are assured that the method of averaging the scores to produce one rating, when done to all the contestants, does yield reliable results. No skater is cheated by a large error in the rating system. Similarly, reliability should be evidence over time with a student's performance. For example, if Regina can produce a 5 or excellent rating on a charcoal drawing she has completed, we can expect that next week, pending no major changes in the student, Regina will be able to produce a level 5 drawing again. There is, then, a reliable measure for her performance.

How does one obtain this reliability? You are about to discover the process.

Rater Reliability

Train your raters in the scoring mechanism you are using. Provide a copy of the rating sheet with clear directions for each criterion. Benchmarks or models of excellence should be available, as well as samples of student work at each of the mark or rating points. The easiest method is the four-corner technique described earlier in establishing benchmarks. Don't expect complete agreement on levels the first time your panel rates together. After the first round, take time to have participants discuss why they rated a student's work with a particular score. This exchange of information among panel members will lessen any variance or bias between different raters.

Try the four-corner technique a few times until there is agreement. The following chart will help you organize the rating system.

Rater Reliability Development Chart

Listed here is room for three trials to develop interrater reliability. Place the rater's name in the appropriate line. Next to each of the raters' names, place the score he or she gave the student's performance. Compute the average.

Hold discussions after each trial. Complete the process a few more times until the scores among the raters are the same.

Score on
Student Performance

Trial I: Rater name _____   _____

Rater name _____   _____

Rater name _____   _____

Rater name _____   _____

Rater name _____   _____

Average _____

Score on
Student Performance

Trial II: Rater name _____   _____

Rater name _____   _____

Rater name _____   _____

Rater name _____   _____

Rater name _____   _____

Average _____

*Score on
Student Performance*

Trial III: Rater name _____   _____

Rater name _____   _____

Rater name _____   _____

Rater name _____   _____

Rater name _____   _____

Average _____

Test Reliability

It is important to ensure that your performance assessment is capable of producing the same ratings each time a student completes the task. In other words, if Elizabeth plays a piano piece as part of her senior high school exhibition project and receives a rating of "excellent," that next week, pending no changes in the student, the same assessment task will allow Elizabeth to obtain the same high rating. One way of ensuring this is to test and then retest using the same assessment task on a sample of your students. This is time-consuming. One way to do a test–retest is to limit the process to certain subparts of the criteria and rate the student over time using an informal observation method. For example, if you want to check a student's use of mechanics on a written piece, you could walk around the room, pausing occasionally at a student's desk, and observe and record whether there are gross violations in the area of language mechanics. Over time, you would be able to say with a high degree of confidence that based on your instruction and the student's hard work, there is a high reliability that the student's paper will be free of flagrant mechanical errors.

Another method of accomplishing this task is to develop alternative but similar forms of the assessment task, complete with the same scoring rubrics. The student or sample of students can complete both assessment tasks, and you can compare the rating scores. If the assessment tasks involve the same process, then there should be a similarity in ratings. A chart is presented here to assist in the process of using alternative forms of the assessment task.

Test Reliability Development Chart

Record the student's name, the date of the assessment, and the form used. Place the score obtained for each of the alternative forms, and calculate the difference. This chart can be reproduced to provide space for every student enrolled.

Student name _____   *Score*

Performance assessment score on _____   ____

using form _____ .

Performance assessment score on _____   ____

using alternative form _____ .

                                                    Difference   ____

If, in using either of these charts, you find a wide difference in scoring reports, then you need to deal with the poor consistency. In the case of rater reliability, it would be helpful to retrain the individuals and hold more discussions among the participants about how they view the rating descriptions. If test reliability is poor, then you need to redevelop the performance assessment. In general, the longer the assessment, the more reliable it is. You might consider lengthening the task. If an alternative form of the assessment task is used, review each task to make sure there is equality in design.

Validity and Generalizability

We have grouped these two traits together because they are related. If your performance assessment measures the learning domain that you have established, then your assessment has validity. Many assessments are sophisticated and fun to complete but do not measure the concept the teacher wants to measure. Validity is one thing you want for your assessment. A second, related characteristic is generalizability. Is the assessment task related to real-world endeavors? Engaging students in tasks that are creative and fun but do not involve skills that can be transferred to solving problems in real encounters does the students a disservice. Validity and generalizability should be connected when one is measuring performance assessments. The closer the assessment is to the real context of the classroom instruction, the more valid it is. Moreover, the more authentic the instruction is in terms of teaching for understanding, the more generalizability the assessment has to offer. Looking at validity for a moment, we should strive for the following.

Content Validity

A well-designed performance assessment should cover the objectives of instruction not use of the curriculum. Wiggins (1993) provides an excellent argument for the need to link tests to tasks, contexts and the "feel" of real world challenges. The assessment should deal with higher order thinking, such as students applying or interpreting knowledge, not just memorizing facts. One way to ensure content validity is to prepare a chart listing the learning domain you wish students to master and then listing the assessment task you with students to accomplish. A key question to ask after reviewing the chart is: "Does the assessment lend itself to discovering the students' use and function of the specific learning domain?"

Compassion Chart for Content Validity

List the learning domain you are measuring and the specific part of the performance assessment you have constructed. Describe for yourself the relationship between the two. Share your response with a peer. Ask your peer if the relationship between learning domain and assessment task is clear.

Learning Domain   *Performance Task*

Relationship between two items: _____

_____

_____

_____

One limitation of content validity is that the task responses will vary from student to student, as they should. We are teaching for understanding; therefore, each student will make his or her individual connections and transfer of knowledge. This is one of the paradoxes of performance assessments. The closer the assessments come to the context of the instruction in a classroom, the more valid they are, but the less standard the results. In other words, for the student in Ms. Jones' math class a performance test measuring how a computer spreadsheet can be used to solve problems is very valid means of measuring the authentic instruction that occurred in the classroom. Yet with Mr. Smith's students, who were instructed using other problem-solving means, this assessment procedure cannot be transferred successfully to the students and therefore is less valid. Ms. Jones' assessment task cannot easily be standardized.

Face Validity

Does your assessment look as though it should be measuring what it promises to measure? If it does, then it has face validity. It "looks good." There should be a connection between face validity and motivation. A good assessment task must hold students' attention and motivate them as well. Too often students ask us, "Why do we need to do this?" A test simply does not mean anything to students when they cannot see its validity in relation to what they have done in the classroom, let alone to real-life experiences. A good way to keep face validity strong is constantly to ask the students and your peers to review the assessment after it is done. Questions like:

> What part of the assessment was the most interesting?
> What part of the assessment was most difficult?
> What part of the assessment took the longest? Was the time worth it?
> What part of the assessment required you to seek other's help?
> Did parts of the assessment relate to what you were doing in the classroom?
> (For your peers) Does the assessment connect to our grade- or course-level curriculum standards?
> (For your peers) What knowledge do you think this assessment measures?

Predictive Validity

Can you check the student's performance on an assessment against criteria the student will need to know in the real world? In other words, can your assessment predict how well a student will do at the next grade level, in the next course, or in jobs in the real world? Anastasi (1968) refers to this type of validity as the ability to use the student's scores and predict with some degree of accuracy how well the student will do in the future. An excellent way to design predictive validity into your assessment is first to go to employers and ask them what they think an employee at this job needs to know to perform well. If you are a teacher in a younger grade, ask the teacher in the next grade what he or she would expect an incoming student to be able to do well. With this information, you can design assessment tasks that can predict with some validity how well students will do in the future.

Generalizability

Another term for this trait is *authenticity*. Wiggins (1993a) defines authenticity as an obligation to make the student experience questions and tasks under constraints of time and of human and material resources, and with access to the tools that are usually available for solving such problems. He feels that teachers should ask themselves whether student responses would be different if different prompts were used in the assessment task. For example, if students were planning a school dance as part of an assessment task measuring mathematical problem solving, would the same scores be obtained if the task were shifted to running a school store? One would expect that the score obtained in mathematical problem solving on the dance task could be generalizable to all tasks requiring the same mathematical problem-solving abilities. Yet Baker, O'Neil, and Linn (1993) have found that generalizability across topics and tasks is difficult to obtain. A high degree of task specificity will require substantial time for generalizability to occur among tasks. The key factors that make generalizability more likely to happen are the extent to which the tasks share comparable features and the type of instruction received by students.

Reflection is not easy to accomplish. Most of us would prefer just to teach, design a performance assessment, administer the assessment, and gather the scores. The day-to-day teaching job is hard enough without having to spend extra time reflecting on the test items. Yet, if our new assessment tasks are to have any credibility with the public, we need to be able to defend the robustness of their design. This need is more crucial if the tests are going to be used in high-stakes—graduation, for example—decision making. We should be able to tell parents and students with some degree of accuracy that our assessment tasks are reliable. In other words, if I give you this assessment again in a few days or if another trained rater were to score this assessment, you would obtain the same score or close to it. Likewise, we should be able to say that the assessment task is connected to the learning domain we have taught in class; that we can use the assessment task to predict how well the student will do in the next task, grade, or course; and that the task motivates students to do well. Finally, we need to be able to show our students and parents that the scores themselves are related to the tasks and demands of the real world. We should be able to give a parent a comprehensive answer to the following question: Are these performance assessments authentic?

Summary

This chapter discussed the last two steps, measurement and reflection, in our four-step design taxonomy of performance assessments. The chapter began with a model of how to determine what to measure. By linking course standards to learning domains, the salient areas to measure were identified. The teacher need not be the only evaluator of performance assessments. The students should do some self-reflection; peers should be be evaluating; and parents and community members need to be part of rating the performances, products, and portfolios.

Designing the scoring scales is a critical task. Two different means were shown how to do this, confusion scaling and direct scaling. The difference between analytic and holistic scoring scales was described. Seven examples of scoring procedures were illustrated and analyzed. the "reflection" section of this chapter dealt with the issue of how to establish reliability in assessments. Content, face, and predictive validity were described as crucial variables to be built into an assessment design. The chapter concluded with an emphasis on establishing measurement designs that are authentic and can be generalized to real-world situations. Throughout the chapter, there are numerous examples of scoring and measurement designs that can be used to aid in one's own assessment development phase.

References

Anastasi, A. (1968). *Psychological testing*. New York: Macmillan.

Atwell, N. (1987). *In the middle: Writing, reading, and learning with adolescents*. Portsmouth, NH: Boynton/Cook, Heinemann.

Baker, E. L., O'Neil, H. F., & Linn, R. (1993). Policy and validity prospects for performance-based assessment. *American Psychologist, 48*.

Bloom, B. S. (Ed.). (1956). *Taxonomy of educational objectives: The classification of educational goals. Handbook I: Cognitive domain*. White Plains, NY: Longman.

Lindsay, P. H., & Norman, D. A. (1977). *Human information processing: An introduction to psychology*. New York: Academic Press.

Marzano, R. J., Pickering, D., & McTighe, J. (1993). *Assessing student outcomes*. Alexandria, VA: Association for Supervision and Curriculum Development.

McTighe, J. (1994). *Assessing student outcomes with the dimensions of learning model*. Paper presented to the convention of the Association for Supervision and Curriculum Development, Chicago.

Simpson, E. J. (1972). The classification of educational objectives in the psychomotor domain. *The Psychomotor Domain, 3*.

Slavin, R. E., Madden, N. A., Stevens, R. J. (1990). Cooperative learning models for the 3 R's. *Educational Leadership, 48*, 22–28.

Wiggins, G. P. (1993a). *Assessing student performance*. San Francisco: Jossey-Bass.

Wiggins, G. (1993b). Assessment: Authenticity, context, and validity. *Phi Delta Kappan*, 200–214.

Part Two
Interdisciplinary
Assessments

The units described in this section vary considerably in design. Some are fully developed units that state clear standards, a well-described assessment task, and a measurement system. Other units describe only one or two of the major components. All the units provide a rich illustration of the concepts described in Part I.

You will find interdisciplinary approaches to all units. For example, the Wallops Island field study at the Harrisburg Academy integrates biology and English. During their trips to Wallops Island, students are required to conduct research and record their findings in a notebook. Using these notes, the students write about their experiences in both narrative and poem form. In addition, a major research study on an organism found on the trip integrates science and language arts skills in a creative fashion.

Another example of interdisciplinary curriculum is described in the "Diet and Food Facts" unit, where students integrate home economics, science, health, and English skills to study the nutritional value of foods popular with adolescents. Both units meet the criteria previously discussed concerning developing interdisciplinary curriculum. They relate to the students' concerns—the environment in the Wallops Island unit and health in the "Diet and Food Facts" unit. Both units deal with primary principles and have multiple goals associated with the tasks.

Setting standards before you develop the assessment tasks is crucial. In Part I, I discussed how the standards guide students' activities during the curriculum and assessment phases of the instructional program. Holt High School uses Professional Standards for Teaching Mathematics as a guide for developing the assessment tasks in the Algebra II unit. Oak Park High School requires as an exit standard for graduation the completion of the Oak Park 2013 unit. The Certificate of Employability required of students at the Milwaukee Cluster High School is based on standards assuring employers that graduates will have mastered essential skills.

Instructing for high standards requires a plan so that students will use higher order thinking skills and demonstrate skills at working cooperatively. Metro High School prints on the student assessment task form descriptive verbs that require students to engage higher order thinking skills. At Holt High School, the learning journals required in the history classroom unit prompt students to reflect on what they have learned in class. The science thinking journal unit used at the Susan Lindgren Elementary School includes questions requiring students to use metacognition skills. Cooperative working groups are required in a number of the assessments. The Algebra II unit at Holt High School has students working together to solve mathematical problems. The Oak Park 2013 unit has students completing futuristic urban planning projects together.

These descriptions of assessment tasks include examples of projects, performances, and portfolios. Mohave Middle School requires students to create mini-business community. At the Martin Luther King, Jr., Middle School, students complete monthly science projects incorporating the multiple intelligence concept described in Part I. The mini-mural project required in the American society unit at the Bunker Hill elementary School is an example of how students complete a project and then switch roles and complete a performance by teaching younger students what the murals mean. One of the most authentic performances in this collection is the job interview at Aurora High School, where business persons rate students on interview skills taught in class. Examples of portfolios can be seen in the senior honors British literature portfolio at Jefferson High School and in the schoolwide portfolios unit at Metro High School.

The assessment tasks in these illustrated units involve a full range of scoring types. Holistic rubrics can be seen in the schoolwide portfolio unit at Metro High School, where students' writing is rated at one of three levels. Analytic scoring rubrics can be seen in the system used at Bob Jones High School in the "Writing as a Process" unit. Here, students' writing is scored on a numerical system, with certain items weighted more heavily because of their importance. Point allocation is used in Jefferson High School's senior research portfolio unit, where the research notebook is worth 100 points and the artistic performance is worth 25 points. The school–business partnership unit used at Aurora High School integrates a rubric and narrative scoring system.

The use of a wide variety of raters can be seen in many of the units. Jefferson High School, for example, uses a self-evaluation in its senior honors British literature portfolio unit. Community and parent rating is used for Aurora High School's school–business partnership unit; Holt High School's Algebra II unit; and the "Water, Water Everywhere" unit at the Hasting Middle School. In this last unit, parents score the take-home tests and vocabulary word study unit of the assessment task. Peer evaluations can be seen throughout many of the units but are given special importance in the Oak Park 2013 unit required for graduation.

All the units illustrated here use integrated curriculum. However, English and science content areas are used more here than social studies and mathematics subject areas as unifying themes. Except at the elementary-level schools, there are fewer performances illustrated and more use of projects and portfolios as assessment tasks. Perhaps the use of performances require more classroom time and more managerial skills on the part of the teacher, making them less popular as a task choice. In these units, it is clear that the teacher's role is that of an active partner in the students' learning process. Students are clearly the workers who are required to learn skills, connect this new knowledge to past experiences and knowledge, and produce or create new knowledge. One sees the crucial importance of setting standards that incorporate higher order thinking to complete these assessment tasks. It is encouraging to see the large number of secondary schools, particularly high schools, that use alternative assessments, because high schools in the past have been more content and subject area–oriented than schools at the lower grade levels. In the area of measurement, none of the units reported much study of the reliability or validity of the scoring. This is understandable in that the assessments are new and are still being developed, but Reflection on the scoring system is crucial for all these units if they are to be accepted as measures of excellence in the future.

In summary, the units represented here are outstanding examples of alternative assessments and should give you many ideas and models for your own use.

Wallops Island Field Study

Subject Area
High school, ninth-grade English and biology.

School and Contact Person
The Harrisburg Academy
10 Erford Road
Wormleysburg, PA 17011
(717) 763-7811
J. Gregory Morgan, headmaster
Susan Roller and Douglas McNaught

Summary
Students are required to complete three projects during and after their stay on Wallops Island. One will count for the course in biology, one will count for the course in English, and one will count for both courses. Students will complete a notebook and lab reports during a seining trip, during the bog and dune walks, and during a boat trip. For English, students are required to complete a "found art" project or an "elemental poem" similar to the writings of Native American poets and the work of John Steinbeck. The combined course project is a report on an organism found during the field study. An assessment scoring guide for the organism report is described here. In addition, students must maintain a writing portfolio containing an expository essay, a personal essay, creative pieces, a book review, and letters of selection and self-evaluation.

Unit

Wallops Island Projects

Name _____

There are three projects you will complete during and after your stay at Wallops Island. One will count for your course in biology, one will count in both courses, and one will count in your English class. For English, in addition, you will be writing an entry or two in your reader/writer's notebook, so be sure to bring it with you. Finally, there will most likely be a participation grade for both English and biology class.

The assignments and due dates are listed below.

Biology Project #1: Notebook and Lab Report
Your hosts and guest lecturers will be giving you a notebook in which you will write down the lecture information and the discoveries you make on the field trips you expedrience. This *notebook* will be collected and graded for completeness (depending on sections assigned). In addition, you will complete a *lab report* based on one or more of the experiments you perform.

These two items, the notebook and the lab report, must be turned in on Monday, April 26.

English Project #1: Creative Writing

Your major English project will be your choice between two possible assignments; one is called "Found Art," and the other is called "Elemental Poetry."

Choice 1—Found Art This project may be done entirely individually, or in pairs—either planned or matched up randomly.

> *Materials:* You will each need a durable, waterproof, fairly small bag (like a large zip-lock bag), sharp eyes, and a good imagination!
>
> *Preparation:* On your seining trip and your boat trip—and on any other occasion—you should keep your eye out for intriguing and unusual objects that would fit into any type of work of verbal art: a poem, a letter, a story, an essay, a riddle, a song, a skit, etc. (I would consider allowing you to create a collage or other type of tactile/visual art, and then writing an explanation of it.) The objects need not *all* be natural (for example, you may want to include a postcard or other souvenir), but most of them probably should be.
>
> *Requirement:* You will need to find 10 such objects and save them in your bags.
>
> *Completing the project:* Upon our return, you will be asked to create this work of art OR to exchange your bag of "found art" with someone else and use this "foreign" bag to create a work of art. It all depends on whether you have some idea of what you'd like to create—and therefore seek those objects that will help create it—or whether you'd like the challenge of incorporating unexpected material into something meaningful.

Choice 2—Elementary Poetry Medievalists divided the "elements" into earth, air, fire, and water. Native American Indians also studied and worshipped the various aspects of nature such as wind or waves or mountains or trees. After experiencing the seining trip, bog and dune walks, and your stroll on the high-energy beach (and elsewhere) you will have had the chance to notice many such "elements" and aspects of nature. We will provide more details on this at the opportune time.

You will have a Writing Workshop day to develop your project during the week after we return. The final version is *due on Friday, April 23, as your contribution to Publishing Day.*

Combined Biology and English Project #2: Organism Paper

While you are on your trip, you will observe many types of organisms. You will need to select one and make it your subject of special study. In addition to observing the organism, you will have access to reference works both on the island and at home after the trip.

Your report will need to include the following *content* and *form* components:

Content:		Form:	
	Habitat		Cite sources in text
	Life cycles		Use correct form
	Subsistence		A works cited sheet
	Interaction with other		Sound organization
	organisms		Helpful transition
	"A day in the life" of your		Effective style
	organism		Correct mechanics

A grade sheet will be provided, and you will receive points for each component based on the completeness, correctness, and credibility of your paper. The grade will count in both your biology and your English class. *This project is due on Wednesday, April 28.*

Summary of due dates in order: Friday, April 23, Found Art or
    Elemental Poetry
Monday, April 26, Notebook and
    Lab Report
Wednesday, April 28, Organism
    Paper

Policies and Directions for Writing Portfolios

Overview

During the semester, we will expect to cover several "units" of literature, each based on a particular work or genre (a novel, essays, short stories, poetry, or a play). For each unit, in addition to your reader responses and freewriting, you will produce approximately two pieces of writing related to what we are reading, and one or two "free" or personal pieces of writing. In nearly every unit, I will attempt to offer oportunities for you to write in different styles and to develop different skills; topics and formats will include formal argument, personal essays, and creative responses (all of which are described below).

All assigned pieces you write will undergo revision and will be reviewed and discussed with your response group; I will also correct, comment on, and evaluate each last draft, using our holistic evaluation sheet. At the conclusion of a unit—or before the given due dates—it will be your task to select and extyensively revise the piece you feel will best reflect your skills and development as a writer. These final pieces will be graded and will become your formal Writer's Portfolio.

In addition to the semester portfolip pieces, you will write a letter describing your selection process and evaluating your progress as a writer.

Wallops Island Organism Report Grade Sheet

Name _____

Criteria	Comments	Possible Points	Points
Habitat	Complete, credible Interesting, detailed Needs development	6	
Life cycles	Complete, credible Interesting, detailed Needs development	10	
Subsistence	Complete, credible Interesting, detailed Needs development	10	
Interaction with other organisms	Complete, credible Interesting, detailed Needs development	12	
Original framework ("a day in the life of")	Complete, credible Interesting, detailed Original, creative Needs development, not sustained	12	
Sources cited	Where needed, quoted if needed; acknowledged	5	
Correct form	Order, completeness, punctuation	5	
Works cited or consulted	Order, completeness, punctuation	10	
Organization	Logical, sustained	8	
Transition	Effective, between sections between and within paragraphs	5	
Effective style	Strong verbs, precise language, varied sentence structure	10	
Correct mechanics	Punctuation, parallelism, etc.	10	
Other comments			

Directions concerning this letter appear below. The letter will also be considered in the overall assessment of your writing.

Your writing portfolio will count as 30% (for freshmen) or 25% (for sophomores) of your *semester grade*. In addition, your portfolio should be a source of pride and may be used to show your next teacher or your college of choice how you have developed as a writer.

Definitions and Descriptions of Types of Writing

Expository Essay   Expository essays are formal responses to assigned reading or to an outside reading appropriate for the unit and approved after we have discussed your idea. These essays include a thesis which shows an understanding of the work, attention to the language and technique of the author, quoted and correctly cited support, and a works cited page. The topic and thesis will determine length, but you should expect to need a minimum of three or four typed pages.

Personal Essays   Personal essays are nonfiction writings (with minor changes in fact for effect) which reveal your opinions, discoveries, attitudes, beliefs, or personal experiences in a way that is meaningful to others. While the material or subject is based on personal experience, the essay should be directed to a public audience, and the writer should have a clear idea of how he or she wants this audience to respond to the writing. Sources of inspiration could be quotations, other essays, opinions, free responses, or memories.

Creative Pieces   Creative pieces include poetry, short stories, or inventive writings in a form you create yourself. Poetry should include several short poems of different types and styles (or one or two long and a few short!)—your poetry should show your willingness to experiment with various subjects and styles. Fiction pieces should generally be at least five pages long, to allow for sufficient development. An exception to this length expectation could be a series of shorter works, such as vignettes, fables, myths, or other naturally short works.

Book Review   A book review is *not* a book report. It concentrates less on plot and summary and more on what the book means and how it conveys its meaning. This selection is only for those who are active and selective readers since the novel reviewed will be read outside of class. Please discuss this option well ahead of time.

Letter of Selection Process and Self-Evaluation
The final part of your portfolio should be a letter addressed to me, a future teacher, or your college admissions committee. (Portfolio assessment *is* catching on in colleges, since grades and test scores are so "bare" and uninformative.

In the letter you will explain your reasons for selecting each of your pieces of writing. You should point out the strengths of each piece and how each one reflects your overall progress as a writer. Include any background information concerning the process of writing certain pieces, especially if the process illustrates your learning a new skill.

In the conclusion of the letter, summarize your *strengths* and point out one or two goals you have for further development as a writer.

Chart for Averaging Semester Grades

Freshmen		*Sophomores*	
Quarter 1* (tests, quizzes classwork, participation)	25%	Quarter 1	25%
Quarter 2	25%	Quarter 2	25%
Portfolio	30%	Portfolio	25%
Exam	20%	Exam	25%

*The quarter grade includes credit (or lack of credit) for completing all preliminary work on writing on time and with reasonable effort and completeness. Do not fall behind in compiling your writing samples; students who do so risk receiving no credit at all for this major portion of their grade, since I will not have a record of completion if material is lost or destroyed.

School–Business Partnership

Subject Area
   High school English

School and Contact Person
   Aurora High School
   West Pioneer Trail
   Aurora, OH 44202
   (212) 562-3501

   Linda Robertson, principal
   Sally Davenport, Art Geigel, Jeff Black, Dick Doughman, Barb Stroh

Summary
In this unit, cooperating businesses in town send employees into the school to teach job interviewing skills, job application activities, and résumé writing. Ninth-graders work on job interviewing skills in the classroom, with possible visits from area business persons giving tips on the do's and don't's of interviewing. Tenth-graders work on job application skills filling out applications provided by local businesses. Juniors focus on résumés and cover letters. Local business leaders make presentations about successful and unsuccessful résumés and cover letters, proper stationary, formats, and typical errors.

The project's culmination is the senior on-site job interview with area businesses. Local companies provide times and "slots" for interviews. The students sign up for the interview and make all arrangements. The students are rated by the interviewer, and this evaluation is shared with the student immediately after the interview. The evaluation is forwarded to the classroom teacher. At this point, if common areas of concern have been indicated, the teacher will adjust the instruction. For example, if students need to improve their interview skills, the teacher would help them with this. A scoring guide is described here which shows that the student is ranked on a scale of 1 to 5 on eight different criteria. There is room for the interviewer to elaborate on the scores by writing a narrative.

Senior Interview

Interview evaluation for _____ Date _____

Evaluation scale: 1 = Unacceptable, 3 = Satisfactory, 5 = Outstanding

Application form filled out completely and legibly.	1	2	3	4	5
Applicant arrived to interview on time.	1	2	3	4	5
Applicant was dressed appropriately.	1	2	3	4	5
Applicant was prepared to discuss his or her attributes.	1	2	3	4	5
Applicant asked questions about the company and the job.	1	2	3	4	5
Applicant was attentive and courteous.	1	2	3	4	5
Responses were clear and concise.	1	2	3	4	5
Discussion was pertinent and reliable.	1	2	3	4	5

Please use brief statements to describe the applicants:

Interview weakness: _____

_____

Interview strength: _____

_____

Overall comment: _____

_____

_____

_____

_____

_____

Interviewed by _____

Teacher's comments: _____

_____

_____

_____

_____

Algebra II*

Subject Areas
High school math

School and Contact Person
> Holt High School
> 1784 Aurelius Road
> Holt, MI 48842
> (517) 694-0097

> Mr. Thomas D. Davis, principal

Summary
This assessment provides students with three problems, which assess a wide range of questions asked. Working in cooperative groups, the students are required to analyze the situation, solve the mathematics, and then draw conclusions from their solutions. Oral presentations are required. For the oral presentations, evaluators from outside the school are used to assist in the process. The students sit as a group but are questioned one at a time with no help from group members. The assessments are aimed at helping students understand why they are using the mathematics they need to employ to solve problems rather than just to apply a mathematical formula.

I began using group cooperative learning where students worked on mathematical situations. They were to analyze the situation, solve the mathematics, and then draw conclusions from their solutions. They would then give either oral group presentations of their solutions or written analyses of the assignment. My assignments demanded that students reason about mathematics and justify their claims and responses. Discussions in small groups increased in length, frequency, and quality. I heard students say to each other, "That's fine, but why?" or "We need to put this into words the rest of the class will be able to understand."

With all these changes in strategies, I began to wonder about whether my traditional tests were sufficient for assessing student understanding. In trying to think about assessing student understanding differently, I began to focus my attention on what the NCTM's 1991 *Professional Standards for Teaching Mathematics* says about assessment. An important issue raised by the *Standards* is to "align assessment methods with what is taught and how it is taught." Faced with the problem of assessing what I speculated to be a new kind of mathematical understanding for my students, I began altering my tests in both content and form to find out what my students did and did not understand. I wanted less computation required on the

---

*Michael Lehman, the author of this unit, would like to acknowledge both the National Center for Research on Teacher Learning and the Holt Public Schools publication *Alternative Assessments,* from which this unit is taken.

tests and more written explanations about solutions to write suitable problems. I include three problems here illustrative of the range of questions students faced:

1. You and your partner have decided to go looking for a buried treasure described on a scrap of paper found in the basement of an old house. The only clue to the treasure's location is the following:

   "The treasure is buried in a spot that is the same distance from the boulder than it is from the railroad tracks. It is also . . ."

   And the rest of the information is missing. But some other clues you may be wise to consider are:

   a. the distance from the track to the boulder is 11 yards.
   b. consider the tracks as the directrix.
   c. keep all of the units in yards or feet.

   Keep in mind the distance of the treasure from the railroad track is interpreted as being the length of the perpendicular drawn to the tracks from the treasure.

2. Hooke's law states that the force F (weight) required to stretch a spring x units beyond its natural length is directly proportional to x.

   You have a spring hanging from the ceiling in the classroom whose hook is 8 ft. above the floor, and you want to stretch it down to 3 ft. above the floor in order to hook it to Mr. Lehman's belt loop. Devise a plan to determine how much weight would be needed to pull the spring down. What would you need to consider? Be as complete in your strategy as possible. (What steps would be needed?) How would you know if the spring would lift Mr. Lehman or not? When wouldn't it lift him at all?

   Create a set of data to prove your conjecture.

3. Suppose you are a doctor doing research on cancer cells. You have found a type of cancer cell growing as follows:

Weeks	0	1	2	3
Number of Cells	1	4	16	64

   You experiment with different drugs and EUREKA! X13V causes the cancer cells to stop all further growth, and the cells start disappearing at a rate of 10,000,000 per hour with a maximum of 5 doses per day. More than 5 doses per day will destroy the patient's liver and kidneys, and the person will die.

   If you have a patient with this type of cancer and you have estimated that they have about $2.814749767 \times 10^{14}$ cancer cells, how long have they had the cell growth occurring?

How long would you prescribe your patient take X13V in order to make sure that all the cancer cells disappear? How many doses will this take? Give your answer in a reasonable unit of time (i.e., days, weeks, months, or years, whichever seems to be the most useful).

If another patient comes in who has had this cancer for a year and is given only an estimated 5 years to live unless you can get the number of cells in her system below 10,000,000 within the 5 years so her body can start to repair the damage the cancer has done, would you put her on this medication and give her hope for a continued life? Be very clear in your explanation and have appropriate figures to backup your determination.

The students had three class days and one weekend to work in their peer groups to solve the problems and construct explanations that provided support for the solutions. When I first passed out the problems, I expected that students would waste a lot of time in the beginning and get themselves into a time bind toward the end. Yet I was pleasantly surprised. Both the observers and I noticed that students used their time very well during the three days. We also noticed that the conversations went beyond simple computation to talk about why different individuals solved the problems in certain ways and what alternative approaches were possible. The students worked very hard but did not seem to panic or be under this tremendous pressure I was used to seeing in traditional reviews for finals. The class seemed to have an atmosphere of seriousness but also of confidence. Students seemed to believe they could solve these problems in ways they could discuss.

I organized the judges into panels of three people, only one of whom knew mathematics subject matter. The second judge was not a mathematics person and focused on the students' confidence levels and abilities to communicate their results. The third judge came from a pool of university professors, mathematics teachers in my building, building principals, district superintendents, school board members, preservice mathematics teachers, and senior honors students.

Before the actual assessment, I gave the judges guidelines and evaluation forms for their tasks (see Appendixes A and B). I developed my criteria (Appendix C) from similar evaluations I had used during the school year for individual student and group presentations. I believed students would feel comfortable with these evaluation categories because they had seen them during the year. Furthermore, these categories defined what I was trying to assess about my students' mathematical knowledge without being too burdensome to the judges. I also wanted a form that would not get in the way of students' and judges' discussions. I gave each student a copy of the evaluation form when I passed out the exam questions so they would know what they were being judged on as they were preparing for the exam.

I reserved the library for the entire exam period (which was, under our school policy, an hour and a half long). I arranged the furniture into four areas so that four groups could be taking the exam at the same time. Each group had as much privacy as possible during the exam. I circulated around the room in order to handle procedural questions if they arose.

During the actual assessment, students went before the panel of judges as a group, but only one individual presented a problem. The judges picked which problem individuals presented, therefore requiring every student to be able to discuss all the problems and not just the one or two with which they felt most comfortable. After the judges heard an individual discuss a problem, they would open the floor to other students in the group who wanted to add anything or refute what they had heard. I set it up this way because I wanted to know what each individual understood but, at the same time, I did not want the students to feel totally alone (without the peers they'd studied with) before the judges.

I combined the information I received from the judges and the problems the students did while in my classroom for a final exam score. I used the average of the three judges' scores for two-thirds of the total exam score; the in-class problems counted for one-third. These scores were combined to make up 26 percent of the students' semester grade.

The results of this assessment gave me plenty of information to digest about my students, my teaching, and our curriculum. First, I learned that many of my students were still only superficially learning and understanding mathematics. In their groups during the year I overheard excellent discussions about issues we studied in mathematics, and they were also getting better at writing explanations and justifications. However, when it came to explaining the mathematics to the judges, they were only able to tell the steps they took in solving the problem. They fell short when it came to explaining why they approached a particular problem in a certain way. A common response judges heard was, "That's the way we did it in class."

I am still trying to figure out why what we did in class did not transfer into better performances during the final. I suspect that some of the students froze in the testing situation despite all I had done to help them relax. Some of the students seemed to have trouble individually explaining problems. They did not have their partners to provide them with connecting ideas that would have allowed them to give coherent explanations. Finally, I wonder if the students needed more practice throughout the school year with performance assessments since the practice might have helped them better understand what they needed to do to prepare a good discussion of a mathematical problem.

I was surprised that some of the students I expected to do well didn't, and some I *didn't* expect to do well did! I think some prompting from judges helped these students begin to respond to the questions. While several students did well on their own, others gave good explanations after the judges asked several questions to help them focus their thinking. I felt especially pleased about this finding. If these students were taking a traditional final examination and got stuck on a problem, they would probably fail. On a performance assessment I could tap into what they actually understood. I also could sort out more complex misunderstandings from simple computational mistakes common on traditional final exams. The performance judges could help students, through probing, sort out conceptual ideas from mistakes based on mere computations.

I gained information from three different professionals about each of my students. Each judge helped me piece together a picture of my students' understanding that would not have been possible on a typical final. The judges' comments reflected a wide range of observations about what mathematical understanding my students had. Most judges focused on what sense students could make of the mathematics they were doing. Typical of these kinds of comments was this example: "The student was accurate mathematically in solving, but did not manifest very deep understanding of what the problem was about." Said another judge, "Started by stating the sense of the problem—the relation between pressure and volume."

Often judges commented on how explanations and calculations fit together with the problem the student was solving and their understanding of it. Here are three comments about one student:

> He calculated the correct equation for the parabola. The only thing he was unable to do was explain the formula (distance) he used to get his equation for the parabola. Other than that his explanations were very good.

> He did not understand derivation of formula for parabola—could not provide explanation for why formula works; however, set up problem nicely, clearly understood problem.

> This judge addressed the comments to the student: "I hope you continue with your agility and explanation based on the graphical representation of this problem. That's important. Push yourself on why the formula/equation works.?

The judges seemed to agree that this student could perform the calculations correctly. Yet they all pointed to the student's weakness in being able to explain how or why the formula worked. He seemed to be unable to make the connections as to why he would use the distance formula, though he knew it was necessary to solve the problem. As a teacher I learned that this student knew how and when to use the formula, but could not say why it worked—which is what I want my students to be able to do. What I learned about this student I might not have learned on a traditional final exam.

Another set of comments on a different student provided another picture:

> Explained that she is just doing the problems like the book said. (She didn't know why she "logged" things to solve for x). Did not really explain why she did things very well. However, she was able to interpret her results and seemed to understand what they meant.

I asked [her] what a log is, and she said "some number to a power" and could explain nothing more about the concept. Throughout her performance she also kept saying she didn't know if she was "right." All of these comments point to an emphasis on procedures—which for the most part were passable until #3 where she divided instead of multiplied (even after a judge gave her strong prompts).

[She] has an attitude problem. She thinks that she really understands more than the other people in her group and she may be partially right but she has a long way to go. When questioned she seems to think that it doesn't matter if she's wrong if it is her opinion. She doesn't seem to realize that in math everything isn't wide open, that there are more than opinions. She worked on problem four and immediately identified logs. She said she doesn't really know what a log is or what it means to log both sides. Most people don't know. She did most of the problem well and was articulate. I couldn't judge her accuracy not having done the problem. One serious error was finding that the treatment would take 1,172 days and dividing by 5 to find the number of doses. When questioned she didn't revise, and simply said she might be wrong. A judge asked about 10 days and how many doses that would be. She seemed to understand that 2 was unreasonable but didn't want to think about it at this point. She did do a good job explaining why it makes sense that it would take longer to get rid of the disease than it would take for the disease to grow.

These comments give me a lot of information about this student. In class she always offered suggestions and usually could derive a correct answer. Her classroom participation led me to think she understood the concepts very well. However, the judges' comments allow me to see that this student is very capable of doing the computation without having the depth of understanding I had hoped for. On a traditional test she would have made the one mistake with the division, and I would have taken off a few points thinking she had just made a simple mistake. I would never have known the depth of her misconception—that when confronted with it she would stay with it even though she would admit it was unreasonable. If I had this information earlier in the year, I would have been able to address some of these misconceptions and then worked toward further understanding.

This student showed she was able to perform the mathematics and understand most of the concepts in the problem. However, some of the information she chose to use demonstrated that she did not know its origin. In a traditional paper-and-pencil exam, with a few lines of computation to illustrate what a student knows, I might never have known that the student did not really understand the distance formula.

While I was learning about my students' substantive mathematical understanding, I also learned about their affective mathematical views. I learned that students seemed to enjoy this type of assessment. They felt confident they could do it! Afterwards, several students told me that they felt good about the exam and enjoyed taking the final this way instead of working problems for one and a half hours. They felt they demonstrated what they really knew. These responses gave me useful information in answering another question I have wondered about: How can we help our students feel good about themselves in relation to mathematics? During the past two years I have been working with one of our school counselors, Jan Wilson, in trying to find ways to help our students improve their self-efficacy in mathematics. As stated in *Everybody Counts*, "In the long run, it is not the memorizations of mathematical skills that are particularly important—without constant use, skills fade rapidly—but the confidence that one knows how to find and use mathematical tools whenever they become necessary" (National Academy Press, 1989). When we talk about student self-efficacy, it is this level of confidence that we are striving for.

Since only some students volunteered their comments, I cannot generalize about all students in the class; perhaps there were several students who did not like the exam and just did not tell me. However, I have been teaching long enough to know that if students truly dislike something, they usually let you know one way or another. Also, by looking at the expressions on students' faces during and especially after the final was done, I was able to get a sense of how they felt about it. I did not see the strained and dejected looks I usually see during and after finals. Rather, I saw students who felt they had accomplished something. They were congratulating each other with "high fives" and commenting on how they felt they did. They also offered alternative ways of explaining a problem to their peers that they had not used before the judges.

Several students that normally did not do well on exams were pleased with their presentations. One student commented that he was grateful for the judges taking the time to ask questions since he knew the information but had trouble finding the right words to describe it. This was similar to what the judges said about him. For this student to walk away feeling good about himself in relationship to a mathematics assessment was worth all my efforts to plan and organize it. The next day, when he found out he got a "B" on the exam, he literally jumped two feet off the ground and went down the hall screaming to his friends.

During the 1991–1992 school year one of the tasks I set was to take what I learned from this assessment and apply it to improve my students' conceptual understanding of the mathematics I am teaching. To this end I decided that I would need to run at least four assessments a year in order to keep my students and myself updated on how we were progressing. This would also provide my students with plenty of opportunity to improve their oral skills as well as their problem solving skills.

I also changed the general format of the assessment during the end of the semester sessions. Instead of having each group spend half of their time before the judges and the other half in my room solving problems, I had them spend the whole time with the judges. During the one-and-a-half-hour time frame, the students would spend one hour discussing the one-and-a-half-hour time frame, the students would spend one hour discussing the problems they had solved and the other half hour solving a problem presented by the judges while the judges observed this process. This allowed the judges to see the students in action so they could judge them on their ability to solve problems and communicate to other group members their understanding of the mathematics involved. This proved to be a very powerful situation for the students. Some of them, who came across in the first part of the exam as lacking confidence in themselves, were able to demonstrate that they did indeed know the mathematics involved. They were able to sway the judges opinions in their favor.

During the current 1992–93 school year I am working on using a variation of this assessment for my precalculus students. The end result will be a paper describing the situation they worked on, explaining the mathematics they used to solve it, and summarizing the results of their project. I am grading their papers and then returning them with suggestions for improvement. They will rewrite them to get prepared for their semester exam. This exam will be a performance assessment before a panel of judges where they will present their papers.

I have also included a practice assessment for the students before the first actual assessment. I had parents and some teacher volunteers come in and let the students practice explaining their solutions. I did this for the first time this fall and it seemed to have two main benefits. It helped the students see what type of questions they would face; and it gave the students confidence in their ability to explain themselves. It did not remove all the nervousness, but it did help. Some judges said that this group was the best prepared of all the first timers.

I am challenged by some hard questions about my instruction, the curriculum, and general conditions of learning high school mathematics. First, how does a teacher come up with problems that lend themselves to a performance assessment? Since the problems require students to think about something, the problems should reflect something worthwhile to wonder about. How does a classroom teacher create problems that fit this requirement around each issue discussed in the curriculum? These questions surround design problems and invite further discussion.

Another set of questions concerns arranging a performance assessment within the traditional school structure. During a normal school day under normal conditions, I have to find a way to put together panels of judges I will need several times during the year. Where can I locate people? How can I begin to involve the community outside school? Also, without the benefit of the university personnel who work in our building, how does a teacher put together these panels? I am currently exploring the use of community members through our Business/School Alliance Organization as a possible answer.

The kind of information I received about each student and the students' reactions made it clear that this is a much better method of assessing understanding than typical paper and pencil tests. If I can assess my students' understanding in a more realistic situation and increase their confidence in themselves in relation to mathematics, how can I go back to traditional tests?

Algebra II Discussion Final: Judges' Guidelines

Please keep in mind that this is a new experience for the students as well as for us. Give the students plenty of opportunity to explain themselves, but if it is obvious that they are trying to fake it or are unsure of themselves, let them know that it is not what we are after and move on.

Only one student per problem. They have been instructed that they will have to discuss the problem on their own without help from other members of the group. After you feel this student is finished, and you want to ask another student some questions about this problem, that is fine.

If you pick a problem that a student seems unprepared for, let her do what she can and then come back to her with a different problem. Please make note of this on the evaluation form.

Please use the following evaluation sheet in assessing the student's discussions. If you find the categories I have outlined unusable or too constraining, feel free to write comments in the comment section or on the back. In assigning the final points you need to be as specific in your comments as possible. Also remember that I will need these forms to discuss evaluations with students who want to check on their performance. If possible, please inform the students of their score. If you can't, due to time restrictions, I will be available for students to check grades before school and after on Wednesday and Thursday.

Name: _____

Mathematics
1) Making sense of problem   1   2   3   4   5
   (understanding concepts.)

2) Problem-solving strategies   1   2   3   4   5
   (methods used.)

3) Accuracy of results   1   2   3   4   5

4) Interpreting results   1   2   3   4   5
   (what do the results mean?)

Clarity of Explanation
1) Ability to communicate results   1   2   3   4   5
   (Clarity, use of charts/graphs.)

2) Explanation   1   2   3   4   5

Discussion of Group Problems
1) Contributed ideas towards   1   2   3   4   5
   the solution of the problems.

2) Group was able to solve the problem presented with this student's help.

1 2 3 4 5

3) With this student's help, the group was able to explain their method of solution to the judges to understand the mathematics involved.

1 2 3 4 5

_____

Overall Score
Grading Scale:
43–50 = A
36–42 = B
30–35 = C
25–29 = D

Comments: Your comments to the students are very helpful not only to me as I assign grades and assess my students and my teaching, but also to the students. They enjoy reading them and seeing what you felt they were able to demonstrate and what you felt they were unclear about. Therefore, please take a few minutes and write down a few comments. I am sure many of the students will be stopping by to check their grade later. Thank you.

Algebra Performance Assessment: Grading Criteria

Thoughts about Grading   The following are suggestions to help you in your grading of the students. You may use them as guidelines or you may chose to set up your own guidelines.

Suggestions for an "A"   Students receiving an "A" should be able to demonstrate to you that they have a clear understanding of the problem and all the concepts it contained. They should be able to make sense of their results in relationship to the situation given. They should be able to clearly communicate their understanding to you.

Suggestions for a "B"   Students receiving a "B" should be able to demonstrate a good understanding of the problem and the concepts it contained. They should be able to make sense of their results in relationship to the situation given. They should be able to communicate their understanding to you although it may not be as clear as you would like. The difference between an "A" and a "B" would be in the confidence the student shows in their work as well as the level of understanding they demonstrate.

Suggestions for a "C"   Students receiving a "C" should be able to demonstrate an adequate understanding of the problem and the concepts it contained. Their understanding may not be as complete as in an "A" or a "B," but adequate enough to give you confidence that they understand what you feel are the important concepts. They may have some trouble making sense of the results but are able to do so with some probing from you.

Suggestions for a "D"   Students receiving a "D" would demonstrate a lack of understanding of some of the key concepts contained in the problem. They would seem to be able to go through the motions to get the results but are unable to explain why they solved it the way they did, other than to say, "That's how we did it in class." They are also unable to make much sense of their results even with some probing from you.

Suggestions for an "E"   Students receiving an "E" would demonstrate a clear lack of understanding of most of the key concepts contained in the problem. They would be unable to explain their results and why they solved the problem the way they did. They would give you a feeling that they have no understanding of the mathematics involved. The student may appear to have done little preparation for this type of assessment.

Learning Journals in the History Classroom*

Subject Areas
High school, history

School and Contact Person
Holt High School
1784 Aurelius Road
Holt, MI 48842
(517) 694-0097

Mr. Thomas D. Davis, principal

Summary
Students in this history class write in journals each week, and the journals are submitted to the teacher every Monday. The journals are a chronicle of and a reflection on what the students has learned the previous week. Initially the students are asked to think about what went on in the class on a daily basis during the previous week and then to reflect on what went on in the class.

The assessment is based on a three-grade rubric: "C," "B," "A." The teachers give specific instructions on how to improve the assessment score.

Unit

I started all this off with a learning journal handout which said: Learners who are aware of the ways in which they learn are generally more effective learners. We can increase our ability to learn more effectively by increasing our knowledge of how we learn. In other words, if we think carefully about how and what we learn, as well as how this "learned stuff" connects to other "stuff" we know of, we become better learners. In other words, we'll "get smarter."

I then gave students a description of what they should put in their journals and, by the way, we've had to do this several times—four to be exact—over the last three years. Originally, what I asked them to do was:

1. Think about what went on in class on a daily basis during the previous week:
   - What did the teacher do?
   - What did the students do?
   - Describe their behaviors.
   - What were the topics studied?
   - What did you learn?
   - What events went on?

*Peter Kressler is the author of this article, which appeared in the Holt Public School publication, *Alternative Assessments*.

2. Reflect on what went on in class:
   - Connect and associate what you learned with other ideas and other topics already known about.
   - Analyze the meaning of what was learned with respect to topics, events and ideas.
   - Write ideas never thought about before.
   - Write about the impact the idea has had.

After I handed this out, I found it was really difficult for a significant number of students to understand and follow the directions. Those students needed more direction because I wasn't getting what I wanted in their journals. So, I asked them again:

> Okay, write what happened in class—in other words, what were the topics discussed, seen or read about during the time you were in the classroom or in the library? What did you learn? What subject matter? What did you learn about how or why a certain group works? or does not work as we use cooperative learning? What did you know about the subject before? Then, write what was new for you. What did you find out about a particular subject matter? Be specific. Write what you think about what you learned. What did you understand and why did you understand it? What didn't you understand, and why? Connect what you've learned with things you've already heard of

That worked reasonably well, but some students still had a problem with my second effort. So I decided to start graduating it—asking them to do it in terms of a "C" grade, a "B" grade, and an "A" grade. I began to grade the journals because I found out from the students that they wouldn't really put forth much of an effort if their journals weren't being evaluated and graded. I asked the students whether or not they felt the journals should be graded and the students decided that the journals should be. I responded with this:

> For a "C" grade just tell me what went on during the class and what the teacher(s) did and the students did. For a "B" grade, write what topics and subjects were studied and what was learned about those subjects during the previous week. For an "A" grade, connect or associate what has been learned with other ideas that you have learned before in this class or in other classes (or anywhere else for that matter). In addition, you must analyze the topics and ideas you learned as well as relate any new ideas that have occurred to you, and the effect or the impact that the ideas had on you.

Learning journals by their very nature encourage kids to think critically because they have to be introspective about their own learning. This is very different from studying for the traditional objective tests I may have given ten years ago, where students memorized or learned to recognize certain things so they could recall them correctly on an objective multiple-choice test. A week or so later, I might ask them something that was on a test and they had no idea what it was.

I've noticed that when I ask students what they thought about, I get a positive response. Because of their learning journals, students are able to remember various ideas and sets of information that they could not remember before, when they simply studied for a test. Also, when I ask them what they've learned and they have to write down their answers, it's more encouraging than looking up answers from questions at the end of the chapter. Students really have to think about what they've learned and reflect on it, meaning that they need to explain it, be analytical about it, and connect it to other ideas they may have learned elsewhere.

Some students do not seem to have a framework of general knowledge. It's hard for these students to make connections. But through the use of student models and conversations within groups about journals, I've found that these kids develop a sense of their own learning and come up with things they've learned so that they, too, are finally able to make connections. I've found that special education experience have become adept at writing journals. It's something that they can think about, take time over, and, if they're willing to make the effort, do quite well.

I ask students to write a semester journal, a compilation of all the things they have learned during the semester. This is quite a job for them. So I prepare at the beginning of the year by asking students in groups to read last year's semester journals and to give a presentation on what student writers learned or what was written in the journals. I did this at the beginning of the course(s) because I wanted to get kids thinking about journals, especially journals dealing with a whole semester. By asking them to go through the learning journals of other students from the previous years and then giving presentations about the journals, I hoped they would understand what learning journals were about. This seemed to work quite well because this year's learning journals were more reflective than those from the previous year.

A few weeks ago I wrote another handout to the students because a number of them were still having trouble with what the journals were for and what was to be written in the journals. The handout said:

Learning journals are a way in which you can revisit and remind yourself what you studied and discussed in class the previous week. Journals are a way in which you can determine what you have learned in the classroom during a short period of time. The journals will enable you to increase your ability to learn more effectively by making you think about what you have learned and why have you learned it. In this way you can put yourself in a position to make connections between the topics and ideas discussed in this class and in other classes, or anything else, for that matter.

Then I wrote some additional directions leaving the "C" grade out because I wanted everyone to succeed at a higher level. I also noticed that students were very good at describing their learning as long as there was teacher information and class discussion. But students were not very good at describing their learning when they were researching or reading some of the class material, or discussing their work in cooperative learning groups. So, I came up with this:

> In order to get an "A" or a "B," this is what I'd like you to do: Write about the topics and ideas and concepts that were discussed in class. Write about the stuff that's in the handouts, the readings, your group's discussion, and your research. Write what you've learned about with respect to topics and ideas. Connect and associate. Analyze. . . . Write about the ideas that have occurred to you as a result of what went on in class. Write about the effect or the impact the ideas had on you.

So, I had handed out several pieces of information over time that instructed students how to do a journal. I also handed out a lot of models that students had written. I've modeled a journal myself. I think that the students are getting to the point where they can write a reflective journal of reasonable quality. This quality (relating learning and reflection) usually happens for most sometimes around December or January. However, for some students, it may not happen for them until February or March.

The learning journal seems to be something that's generally difficult for a sixteen-year-old high school student to do. Some don't have much trouble with the journal, but many have trouble being introspective, which is what the journal asks them to be. Some students have written in their journals, "I didn't learn anything today." And then when I respond by asking how I can give them credit for learning nothing, they have difficulty, saying, "Well, why can't I get credit for that?" Students have trouble understanding that they are responsible for their own learning, which is what the journal demands they be. Some of the things that I'm interested in are that learning journals help kids develop a sense of their own learning and a sense of the control they have over their own learning, a sense of their own way of thinking. Students can control these things themselves, not the teacher controlling learning and thinking, or the school controlling them, but students, themselves, controlling their own learning and being responsible for it.

Students generally don't remember what went on in class the day before, much less the week or the month before. They have trouble remembering what is learned, and they have trouble connecting one particular unit to another. The learning journal helps students do that. It puts them in the position where they have to think about what they are learning, and also what they have learned in the past, and how the present learning connects with the past.

I noticed that most students first wrote about "What I learned," and then, later, they began to write about *we*, seeing themselves as a part of the group that is learning together. This sense of community happens when students become acutely aware of one another, when they feel free to comment about one another and their respective learning.

One of the things I learned by accident at parent–teacher conferences was that the learning journal was a written record of what students had learned in my course and much more telling than a series of grades in a grade book. I told parents that if they wanted to know what their kids were learning in class, then they ought to read their kids' learning journals. Some parents said that they had already done just that and had found it to be quite enlightening.

Reading the journals reminds me of what we did in class and what kids have supposedly learned. It also serves as a check on what we were doing in class, why we were doing it, and what I wanted kids to get out of their lessons and assignments. Because they're writing to me in their journals about their learning, I can also check for errors or inaccuracies in subject matter learning.

One of the things I notice as I read the students' journals is that they become more and more interesting. They can't be merely skimmed over. The skimming doesn't work because the journals become something interesting to read, interesting because it's exciting for me to find out what students have really learned, what they think about what they've learned, what kinds of connections they've made, and what sorts of insights they came up with that I may never have thought of. And the new insights happen quite often.

The next day debriefing session also allows me to correct the inaccuracies that students have concerning content. Reading the journals is also valuable because sometimes I don't realize what sorts of backgrounds these kids have. The journals allow me to find out about them as individuals, and to be aware of where kids are when I set the lessons up.

It has become invaluable for me to think about what kids have learned the previous week because I read and evaluate all of the journals on Monday evening. Then I can respond to the journals the next day in order to give immediate feedback. It is a large chore and I understand that, but it's critical that I get them back quickly. I can then make comments in class about what students say they've learned and illustrate some of the connections they've made. This also allows me to copy student models and share them if I think that something was particularly well written or particularly reflective and interesting.

When I have a student teacher I have to leave the room from time to time because it is the student teacher's responsibility to do the teaching, and that student teacher needs to be alone with the students; otherwise, it's not a real-world situation. When I read the journals I am able to find out what's going on in class during the time I'm not there. I am able to find out what my student teacher is doing, what she is saying, what kinds of things she is emphasizing and, more importantly, what the students are actually doing. The reading allows me to have conversations with her about what is going on because, of course, she reads the journals as well. The journal helps her think about adjusting what she is having kids do with their assignments.

Students are constantly working in groups, doing group work or cooperative learning. One of the things I'm doing currently in a class has to do with some "government and economics stuff" as we call it. It's really some resource material that describes democracy, capitalism, socialism, communism, and fascism along with some essay questions the students must answer. In addition to writing essays, students must, in groups, make presentations to the rest of the class of one of their answers to the essay questions. Each group must make a presentation and all members in the groups must participate.

The journal allows me to find out what's going on in the groups, because students often write about what they learned as a result of their group interaction. Students tend to write about who's doing the work and who isn't doing the work, and what they're finding out in the group and how the group operates. The journals show me that if the group is functioning well, all are participating and it is a cooperative learning group in the purest sense: They are learning from one another and are producing products, making presentations, accomplishing things together, and having conversations with one another.

Students tend to write more about the groups and not the content when the groups are dysfunctional: when someone isn't doing the job, when people aren't getting along, when they're not learning very much, etc.

This is valuable information because it allows me to think about how I could structure activities so that group members have to cooperate with one another and have conversations with one another about what they're learning.

Also, when students write about what's going on in their groups, it allows me to think about which students might work together in a more positive, productive way. Then I might redo the groups so they can work more effectively.

It is difficult for social studies, American History in my case, to figure out exactly how to use current events. How should we do current events in a more meaningful way, a less artificial way, a way that doesn't involve all kinds of tests and the sort of teacher-manufactured or textbook-manufactured things that don't promote active engagement in current events? These artificial methods generally don't encourage kids to watch the news or read the newspaper. Journals tend to help with this. If there is something going on, I can ask students to write what they learned about a particular event, such as the Senate hearings for Justice Thomas and sexual harassment. That was one of the issues that came up in class. Students wrote a great deal about that. They thought about the issues involved in the hearings and, later on, throughout their successive journals, referred to those Senate hearings.

Learning journals by their very nature encourage kids to think critically because they have to be introspective about their own learning. This is very different than studying for traditional, objective tests that I may have given ten years ago, where students memorized or learned to recognize certain things so they could recall them correctly on an objective multiple-choice test. Then a week or so later I might ask them something that was on a test and they had no idea what it was.

I have noticed that when I ask students what they thought about, I get a positive response. Because of their learning journals, students are able to remember various ideas and sets of information that they could not remember before, when they had simply studied for a test. Also, when I ask them what they've learned and they have to write down what they've learned, it's more engaging than looking up answers from questions at the end of the chapter. Students have to really think about what they've learned and they have to reflect on what they've learned, meaning that they need to explain it and be analytical about it, and connect it to a lot of other ideas they may have learned elsewhere.

Some students do not seem to have a framework of general knowledge. It's hard for these students to make connections. But through the use of student models and conversations within groups about journals, I've found that these kids develop a sense of their own learning and come up with things they've learned so that they, too, are finally able to make connections. I've found that special education students who have had, in the past, very little writing and thinking experience, have become quite adept and quite good at writing journals. It's something that they can think about, take time over, and, if they're willing to make the effort, do quite well.

I ask students to write a semester journal, which is a compilation of all the things they have learned during the semester. This is quite a job for them. So I prepare at the beginning of the year by asking students in groups to read last year's semester journals and to give a presentation on what student writers learned or what was written in the journals. I did this at the beginning of the course(s) because I wanted to get kids thinking about journals, especially journals dealing with a whole semester. By asking them to go through the learning journals of other students from the previous years and then giving presentations about the journals, I hoped they would understand what learning journals were about. This seemed to work quite well because this year's learning journals were more reflective than those from the previous year.

Senior Honors British Literature Portfolio

Subject Area
High school English

School and Contact Person
Jefferson High School
1801 South 18th Street
Lafayette, IN 47905
(317) 449-3400

Dennis C. Blind, principal
Joy Seybold, department specialist who designed the unit
All English teachers

Summary
Students who take this course are required to produce a portfolio containing six items: (1) a table of contents, (2) a letter to the reader, (3) a revision of the first semester's paper, (4) works-in-progress, from two to five ready-to-publish pieces, and (6) wild-card writing.

General Information

1. All writings must be typed. All prose must be double-spaced.
2. The portfolio must be neatly done.
3. You must design a cover or a container for your portfolio. It should reflect you as a writer and a reader.
4. The portfolio must contain all the required contents described below. If you wish to include additional pieces, please talk to me about possibilities.
5. Due date: _____

Contents

1. Table of contents
2. Introduction or letter-to-the-reader in which you provide the necessary background information and tie together the contents of the portfolio. You also may choose to explain why you designed the container you created. You may decide to discuss your container in this piece or on the profile.
3. Revision of first semester's descriptive paper (include the graded draft as well). You may discuss your reasons for making your revisions in either your letter or your profile, depending on where it seems to fit.
4. Works-in-progress: Select two or three journal pieces or writings from this year. Revise these to the point at which you are

ready to share them even though you may not be completely finished with them.

5. Ready-to-publish pieces: Select any two to five of the following works. These should be polished pieces. You may polish drafts of papers that you produced in other courses, but you need to submit work that reflects your "best efforts" now rather than your best efforts at an earlier age.
    a. Poetry (minimum of 50 lines)
    b. Short story (minimum 1½ pages)
    c. Personal narrative (minimum 1½ pages)
    d. Short dialogue piece (one-act play, conversation that stands by itself, etc.)
    e. Artwork or photograph with an accompanying creative response
    f. Literary analysis essay (minimum 1½ pages)
    g. Reflective essay (minimum 1½ pages)
    h. Descriptive piece (other than your descriptive paper, minimum 1½ pages)
    i. Character sketch (minimum 1½ pages)

6. Wild-card writing
7. Profile: See the profile description that follows. The profile may be included at any point in your portfolio.

Total pieces: 300 points total
                200 points for the portfolio
                 50 points for the container (remember to discuss it in your letter)
                 50 points for turning in your writing journal along with the portfolio

Profile Description

Use the following questions to develop a profile of yourself as a writer and a reader. In this profile, examine how you have progressed as a writer and a reader during this year. Although you may refer to each piece of writing, your emphasis should be on your writing style, voice and strengths, experiments, areas of improvement, areas of dissatisfaction, and the like rather than on any background information about the piece itself. That type of information may be included in the introduction or the letter-to-the-reader, or it may be inserted either before or after each work.

Although the emphasis of the portfolio is on your writings, the collection needs to include discussions of your "reader self" as well. You may choose to discuss your strengths and weaknesses as a reader in relation to one or more individual pieces included in your portfolio; you may wish to create an essay that comments on your "reader self"; or you may tie your reader self to your "writer self" in the profile. Regardless of how you decide to discuss yourself as a reader, you need to explain your decision in the profile.

At some point, either in the profile or in the introduction, you may wish to discuss some of your revisions. How did you revise? How did you make decisions about how to revise? How did you know when you were finished revising? How did you make yourself stop?

Also, you need to consider how to arrange the items in your portfolio. If you arrange them in an order that is intended to reveal something about how you evolved into the writer you are today, you should discuss this in the profile. If your arrangement is designed to reveal something else, the explanation may more appropriately belong in the introduction.

Remember that the profile involves self-assessment. Although you won't be able to complete it until you made your final selections for the contents, you may wish to keep "self-assessment" notes as you begin the process of compiling your portfolio.

Also remember to *have fun* with this project. Serious, significant work involves a great deal of play and fun. I want you to engage yourself in this work, and I want to be engaged as I look at and read about the writer (and reader) you have created as yourself.

Suggested Questions to Consider and Strategies to Employ

1. How have you developed as a writer this year? Think about your writing goals at the beginning of the year. Have you accomplished them?
2. Reread your journal entries from the beginning of the year and any papers that you have saved from previous years. How do you feel about them and about your progress since you wrote them?
3. As you reread your journal entries, research portfolio pieces, descriptive paper, and any other of your writings available to you, do you recognize any patterns in your writing style, form, voice, development, and the like.
4. How well have you developed your grammar and mechanics skills?
5. How have you developed as a giver and receiver of criticism?
6. How has your approach to writing changed? Do you feel more comfortable? Do you write more frequently just for fun? Do you use the entire writing process whenever you have a writing task?
7. How have your organizational skills, time management skills, cooperative learning skills, and independent learning skills developed this year? How do these relate to your reading and writing?
8. How have your critical thinking, creative problem-solving, and risk-taking skills developed this year? How do these relate to your reading and writing abilities?
9. How have your reading and literary analysis skills influenced your writing? How has your writing development influenced your reading abilities?
10. How do the selections you included in this portfolio reflect you as a writer? Remember to consider both the forms and the content that you chose?
11. What is an area of improvement that you wish to work on as you enter college next year? In what area (areas) do you feel strongest? If you have the opportunity to form a writing group, what areas of expertise will you bring to your colleagues?
12. What risks have you taken this year that have enhanced your reading and/or writing abilities?
13. What changes in attitude, behavior, and/or point of view have you experienced? Have these influenced (or been influenced by) your reading and writing experiences?
14. Have your "favorites" in terms of reading and writing changed this year?
15. How have you incorporated the themes, concepts, and viewpoints that have been part of our experiences this year into your own reader/writer self?
16. Consult your colleagues for suggestions. They know you well and might provide insights.

Senior Honors British Literature Portfolio Evaluation Sheet

Name _____

Components of portfolio project:

_____ **1.** Table of contents
_____ **2.** Introduction or letter-to-the-reader
_____ **3.** Descriptive paper—graded draft plus revisions
_____ **4.** Works-in-progress pieces—at least
_____ **5.** Ready-to-publish pieces—at least two
     poetry (50 lines)
     short story (1½ pages)
     personal narrative (1½ pages)
     short dialogue piece (1½ pages)
     literary analysis essay (1½ pages)
     artwork plus response
     reflective essay (1½ pages)
     descriptive piece (1½ pages)
     character sketch (1½ pages)
_____ **6.** Inclusion of all stages of the writing process for at least one piece. In most cases, the descriptive paper drafts will be used.
_____ **7.** Wild-card writing
_____ **8.** Profile: This essay needs to incorporate the questions and guidelines discussed in the profile description.
_____ **9.** Additional pieces and/or research portfolio (optional)
_____ **10.** Neatness of submitted works—typed (or neatly written when appropriate), collected, and displayed with care
_____ **11.** Correctness: Grammar/mechanics
_____ **12.** Creative container that reflects the writer
_____ **13.** Writing journal from senior year (add minimum number of journal entries)

General Grade Breakdown: 300 Points Possible _____

_____ Portfolio writings: Inclusion of required writings and appropriateness for selection (100 points)
_____ Neatness and correctness (50 points)
_____ Quality of profile (50 points)
_____ Quality of creative container and discussion of it in the introduction, letter-to-the-reader or profile (50 points)
_____ Completion of journal writing requirements

Senior Research Portfolio

Subject Area
High school, English who designed this unit.

School and Contact Person
Jefferson High School
1801 South 18th Street
Lafayette, IN 47905
(317) 449-3400

Dennis C. Blind, Principal
Joy Seybold, Department specialist
All English teachers

Summary
Seniors are required to complete a major research project containing six separate pieces: (1) a bibliography of sources; (2) a research notebook (including prewritings, mini due dates, early plans, etc.); (3) peer and self-editing rating sheets; (4) seven original writings covering four areas of information; (5) an original artistic performance; and (6) a letter to the reader.

Assessment is based on a rating system of points designed to weigh the seven different pieces in the portfolio differentially.

Unit

Calendar for Senior Honors Research Portfolio Project

Due Dates

October 21—Selection of writer, work, and era
October 30—Prewriting activities and notebook check
November 8—Tentative project plan and working bibliography
November 20—More detailed project plan
November 20—Initial peer assessment sheet
December 1–4—Final peer editing workshop
December 11—Due date for entire portfolio
January 11–15—Final assessment week. We will use some of these days to share portfolios, assess individual and peer progress, and bring closure to this activity. Your research portfolio will be a central portion of your assessment for this semester.

There will be ten writer's workshop days during the semester.

Tentative evaluation points for research portfolio contents

1. Bibliography of sources (25 points)
2. Research notebook (prewritings, mini–due dates, early plans, etc.) (100 points)
3. Peer and self editing sheets (25 points)
4. Seven original writings covering four areas of information (175 points)
5. Original artistic performance (50 points)
7. Letter to the reader (guideline will be given later), including explanations of your project and your self assessment pieces.

Total points: 425

Summary of Expectations

1. You will work diligently and seriously (though not always solemnly) during Friday workshop periods and your independent study time.
2. You will meet the posted due dates.
3. You will conduct literary research that focuses on your interactions with a British writer, specific works, and a time period.
4. You will compose a portfolio of pieces that reflects:
   • Your knowledge and appreciation of your subject
   • Your talents and abilities as a writer
   • Your talents and abilities as an artist, performer, or presenter
   • Your attempts to create a lively, diverse collection of pieces that combine research with personal expression

5. You will work in various peer groupings to read each others' works, discuss struggles and goals, revise, edit, and celebrate successes. It is expected that you will be a contributing participant.
6. You will write often. You will reflect even more often. And you will assess yourself on progress based on your own goals and those that I established for you and/or for everyone. (Yes, I will assess too!)
7. You will read original sources.
8. You will not read *Cliff Notes.*
9. You will keep up with your reading and writing so that the final product is a true reflection of your best efforts.
10. You will share your final portfolio with the class.

Requirements: To Be Turned in for Evaluation

1. Complete bibliography of sources. See the reading requirements listed earlier.
2. *Research notebook:* Notes, progress checks, various teacher-designed writing tasks, student-designed writing tasks, and other research related "stuff"
3. Peer and self-editing sheets
4. At least seven pieces of original writing that show your experimentation with different genres and styles and contain the following types of information:
   - Biographical information
   - Historical information
   - Analytical/critical information
   - Content of work

5. One original piece other than a written work that reflects your own artistic performance in another area (e.g., painting, theatrical performance, musical composition, etc.) and relates to the subjects of your research portfolio
6. *Project plan:* This will be developed by you, working with me, and will explain what you are trying to do with each piece and why you included it in your portfolio
7. *Self-assessment piece:* This will describe to the reader what you have learned about yourself in the process of completing this portfolio

Writing as a Process

Subject Area
High school, all subjects.

School and Contact Person
Bob Jones High School
1304 Hughes
Madison, AL 35758
(205) 837-8780

Billy Broadway, principal
Linda Pierce

Summary
This unit evaluates student writing as a performance in process. There is a detailed list of expected outcomes for each of the five categories in the writing process. The assessment allows the teacher to rate student performance in multiples of certain factors rather than on a simple scale from 1 through 3. This allows certain categories to be given more weight than others. A conversion table allows the teacher to convert the scores to the regular "D" through "A" grades.

Source: This unit was adapted from the Analytic Scale Model developed by Nancy C. Millet and Helen J. Throckmorton, which is based on the Diederick Scale originally developed by Paul Diederick and his colleagues at Educational Testing Service to use in scoring SAT essay exams.

Evaluation of Process Analysis

Writer _____

Quality and Development of Ideas: Explains a useful and appropriate process or procedure in a logical, easily understood manner, keeping in mind an intended audience.	7	14	21	28	35
Organization: Effectively introduces the subject in title and lead. Organizes chronologically or in other orderly fashion the steps of the process or procedure. Conclusion summarizes or discusses results and ends well.	5	10	15	20	25
Individuality: Reveals understanding of the process in a unique, individual voice.	1	2	3	4	5
Wording and Phrasing: Uses clear directions and vivid detail and description to present and explain the process or procedure.	4	8	12	16	20
Mechanics: Manages mechanics adequately (9), competently (12), or skillfully (15). Mechanics includes: a. spelling b. punctuation c. grammar	3	6	9	12	15

Conversion Table: 20   40   60   80   100

95–100	A
90–94	A–
83–89	B+
77–82	B
70–76	B–
63–69	C+
57–62	C
50–56	C–
43–49	D+
37–42	D
30–36	D–

Score _____

Grade _____

Diet and Food Facts

Subject Area
High school science, grades 11 and 12

School and Contact Person
North Allegheny School District
10375 Perrysville Avenue
Wextford, PA 15090
(412) 935-5767

Lawrence Butterini, principal
Mary Stiney, assistant principal
Dorothy Drazenovich
Jane Young

Summary
Two activities make up this unit. The first is a hands-on experiment in which students determine the approximate amount of fat in ground beef. The second is a hands-on experiment to determine the amount of fat in French fries. Since both of these food items are popular with American teenagers, the unit has high interest in addition to helping students obtain the problem-solving skills to perform necessary calculations about food and nutrition. Teachers use a point system for activities and quizzes, which is converted into a traditional 0–100 grading system.

Lesson Plan for Interdisciplinary Curriculum

Subject:	Science
Grade level:	11–12
Issue:	Diet and food facts
Lesson title:	The Stoichiometry of Food and Diet
Duration:	3 days minimum
Terminal competencies:	The learner will obtain the problem-solving skills and methods to perform necessary calculations about food and nutrition.

Specific lesson objectives:

The learner will:
1. use stoichiometric calculations to determine food and diet facts.
2. extract the fat from several brands of fast food French fries and compare the fat amounts.
3. determine the amount of fat in ground beef and determine the percentage composition (meat, fat).

Content:
1. Stoichiometry
2. Percentage composition and ppm
3. Food and diet facts
4. Unit conversions

Materials:
1. See lab materials section (attached)
2. Problems on handout (attached)
3. *Modern Chemistry* textbook for problems

Activities:
1. Lab: "Are your French Fries Greasy?"
2. Lab: "How Much Fat Is in Ground Beef?"
3. In-class discussion of lab results
4. Cooperative grouping to solve stoichiometry food problems

Resources:
1. Borgford, C., & Summerlin, L. (1988). *Chemical activities.* Washington, DC: American Chemical Society, pp. 246–250.
2. Castka, J., Metcalfe, C., Tzimopoulos, N., & Williams, J. (1990). *Modern chemistry.* New York: Holt, Rinehart and Winston.
3. Chamizo, J. (1982). How much cholesterol is in your body? *Journal of chemical education,* pp. 59, 151. (1990), February). Milk intake down. *Chem 13 News.* p. 14.

How Much Fat Is in Ground Beef?

In this experiment we will determine the approximate amount of fat in ground beef. Grocery stores and meat markets usually mark the fat content on their packages of ground beef. The law requires that they provide this information. The law also permits no more than 30% in ground beef and 1% fat in lean ground beef.

Materials

1. Several samples of ground beef: ground beef (hamburger), ground lean beef, and ground chuck.
2. Balances.
3. Beakers, 600 mL.
4. Graduated cylinders, 100 mL.
5. Burners.

Procedure

1. Weigh a 100-g sample of your ground beef on a balance.
2. Place the beef sample in a 600-mL beaker.
3. Add 400 mL of water and stir it into the beef sample.
4. Place the beaker on a ring stand and carefully heat it until the water boils gently.
5. Continue to boil the meat for about 10 min.
6. Remove the beaker from the heat and allow it to cool. What happens to the meat? What happens to the fat?
7. Carefully pour off the top fat layer into a clean 100-mL graduated cylinder. If necessary, remove the last traces of fat with a dropper.
8. Measure and record the volume of fat in the cylinder.
9. Because 1 mL of fat has a mass of about 1 g and because your original sample was 100 g, the volume of fat in the graduated cylinder is the approximate percentage of fat in the ground beef.
10. Record your data and repeat the experiment with another ground beef sample.

Questions

1. What effect does heat have on fat?
2. What effect does heat have on protein?
3. What assumptions must you make if you read the volume of fat as the percentage of fat in the 100-g sample of ground beef?
4. What property of fat makes this activity possible?

Notes for the Teacher

Background

This activity is a simple way to give students experience in making measurements and recording and interpreting data. Ground beef (hamburger), lean ground beef, and ground chuck all contain different amounts of fat. The average amount of fat is usually stampled on the package. In this activity we will simply boil the meat to separate the fat. It will float to the top of the liquid where it can be easily removed.

Teaching Tips

1. Samples of 100 g are used to make the percentage calculation easier. However, any mass can be used.

$$\frac{\text{grams of fat}}{\text{grams of sample}} \times 100 = \text{percent fat}$$

2. We read the percentage of fat directly from the cylinder if we assume that the mass of 1 g of fat is equal to 1 mL. This value is a good approximation.
3. Notice that some of the fat may solidify and be mixed with the cooked meat. Point this situation out to students as a possible source of error in the calculations. (Does it make the calculated percentage lower or higher than it should be?)
4. Have students record their data on the board to allow a comparison and discussion of class results.
5. Do not allow the students to eat any of the food in this activity.

Answers to the Questions

1. It melts the fat and separates it from the meat.
2. It coagulates the protein (cooks it).
3. We assume that 1 mL of fat has a mass of 1 g.
4. Fat is not soluble in water; therefore, it separates and can easily be poured off.

Are Your French Fries Greasy?

You have probably noticed that paper in which oily or greasy goods have been wrapped has transparent grease spots. You might obtain the same effect if you drop French fries on your homework. This spot is actually used as a simple test for the presence of fat. In this experiment you will extract the fat from a food sample by dissolving the fat in a fat-soluble solvent. the technique will also be used to compare the amount of fat in several different samples of French fries.

Materials

1. Plain paper, two sheets.
2. Solvent such as trichlorotrifluoroethane (TTE).
3. Vegetable oil.
4. Several brands of French fried potatoes, cooked.
5. Small test tube.
6. Conical flash (or any glass container), 250 mL.
7. Graduated cylinder, 25 or 50 mL.
8. Balance.

Procedure

Part A: Identify the Fat

1. Select about six French fries and place them on one sheet of paper.
2. Observe the appearance of the paper as a result of the fat.
3. Obtain a 2-mL sample of the solvent you will use in a small test tube.
4. Add 2 mL of water to the test tube. Observe. Do the liquids mix?
5. Add a dropper full of vegetable oil. Does it dissolve in the water?
6. Cover and carefully shake the tube. Does the vegetable oil dissolve in the solvent?
7. Carefully record all observations from procedures 2–6. Pour contents of tubes into the waste jar in the fume hood.

Part B: Determine the Amount of Fat

8. Prepare a data table to record the masses before and after the extraction, your calculated mass difference, and your calculated percentage of fat in the sample.
9. Find the mass of the sample of French fries.
10. Place the French fries in the flask. In the fume hood, add just enough solvent to cover the French fries, about 25 mL. Stopper the flask. Avoid breathing the vapors.
11. Swirl the flask for several minutes to dissolve fat in the solvent.
12. Remove 2 drops of solvent from the flask to a piece of paper. Place 2 drops of pure solvent next to these drops.
13. Compare these spots before and after evaporation.
14. Pour off the solvent into the waste jar in the fume hood.

BE
CAREFUL
!!!

15. Place the French fries on a piece of paper in the fume hood so that the rest of the solvent can evaporate.
16. Determine the mass of the French fries. Why is the mass less than the original mass?
17. Determine the amount of fat that dissolved in the solvent and the percentage of fat in your sample of French fries.

Reaction

The organic solvent is only slightly polar because the electrons of each molecule are distributed almost evenly. A water molecule, however, is polar because the electrons are frequently more concentrated at one end of the molecule than at the other. Thus, one end is a little bit negative, and the other end is a little bit positive. The slightly polar and polar molecules will not mix. The fat is only slightly polar, like the organic solvent, so the fat will dissolve in the slightly polar solvent. Slightly polar solvents are also used to remove grease spots on clothing.

Questions

1. What mass of substance left the French fries in ths activity?
2. What percentage of the French fries is assumed to be fat?
3. Compare the fat contents of the various brands of French fries. Compare the appearance of the various brands of French fries.
4. What variables of the various brands of French fries seem to be associated with the amount of fat (e.g., size, shape, surface area, and density)?
5. Describe two tests you did to find out whether or not fat dissolves in the solvent.

Teaching Tips

1. The word "solvent" is used here to refer to the organic solvent, TTE. Water is also technically a solvent for solutions in which polar substances are dissolved. Other slightly polar solvents may be used. TTE is good because it is more dense than water. Thus, in Procedure 5, three layers are observed in the tube. Upon shaking, the top oil layer will dissolve in the lower TTE layer. Then, two layers will be observed with water on top of the TTE.
2. Many organic solvents are flammable. Be sure that no flames are present. Good ventilation, as in a fume hood, is necessary. TTE is toxic to breathe.
3. Any salt on the French fries will not dissolve in the solvent. However, have students try to remove all material from the flask during the final drying period.
4. Some students may want to repeat the extraction to be sure that all of the fat is removed. Compare masses before and after.
5. This activity is ideal for allowing students some practice with the preparation and use of a data table.
6. The more brands available, the more interesting this activity is. Students should be able to bring in French fries from as many sources (including the school cafeteria) as you have student teams. The French fries can be frozen in plastic bags until ready for use.

7. You might want to prepare some French fries at school to include in the study.
8. The most significant variable will be surface area.
9. You might discuss the assumption that all mass lost by the French fries is fat.
10. Do not allow students to consume any materials in the laboratory.

Answers to the Questions

1. Subtract final mass from initial mass. One gram of fat in the diet provides 9 kcal of energy. One kcal is equal to one nutritionist's Calorie.
2. The percentage will be small.
3. Answers will vary.
4. Answers will vary.
5. Oil in the test tube dissolved in the solvent. Fat from the French fries dissolved and remained on the paper after evaporation.

Oak Park 2013

Subject Area
High school, ninth grade

School and Contact Person
Oak Park High School
899 North Kanan Road
Agoura, CA 91301
(818) 707-7926

Jeff Chancer, principal

Summary
This project is based on exit standards that the school has established for ninth-graders. These standards are: students should be effective communicators; self-directed learners; quality producers and performers; community contributors; and creative, complex, and perceptive thinkers. Students will produce a newspaper of the future illustrating what the Oak Park area will be like in the year 2013. Students are encouraged to submit their articles to the local newspaper for publication.

The assessment requires the students to rate themselves, the peer group to rate the student, and the teacher to rate the student on the basis of four main areas: layout, mechanics (including spelling and punctuation), elements (15 items are needed for the paper), and areas covered (geography, geology, demographics, culture, politics, economics).

Oak Park 2013 (Duration: Six Weeks): Culminating Transformational Demonstration for the Global Sphere

Students will investigate, both in groups and as individuals, past, present, and future trends in the Oak Park area. Using this research, students will compose articles on the geography, geology, culture, politics, development, the economy, and the quality of life, and write an editorial proposing a solution to a major concern of the area. Using these writings and accompanying appropriate graphics, students will produce an issue of *The Acorn* dated for the year 2013. Students will draw, graph, and scan graphics necessary to communicate information from the text to be used in their newspaper. Students will submit articles and newspaper issues for publication to local newspapers for publication.

Learner Outcomes and Descriptors

Students who successfully complete required demonstrations and exhibitions in Oak Park's Ninth-Grade Academy will be:

Oak Park 2013: Culminating Transformational Demonstration Rubric for the Global Sphere

Oak Park High School
Ninth Grade Academy

Student: _____
Teacher: _____

	Self	Group	Teacher
• The overall newspaper presents a broad picture of the community in 2013.	____	____	____

Layout

	Self	Group	Teacher
• Masthead is correctly formatted.	____	____	____
• Headlines are effectively written and displayed.	____	____	____
• The overall layout of the newspaper is attractive and eye-catching.	____	____	____

Mechanics

	Self	Group	Teacher
• No misspelled words or incorrect punctuation.	____	____	____
• All stories are consistent with good journalistic style.	____	____	____
• Opinions and editorials are identified as such and are clear, persuasive, supported by facts, and propose a solution if applicable.	____	____	____

Elements

	Self	Group	Teacher
• Feature story 1	____	____	____
• News story 1	____	____	____
• News story 2	____	____	____
• News story 3	____	____	____
• Opinion editorial	____	____	____
• Political cartoon	____	____	____
• Map to support story	____	____	____
• Chart or graph to support story	____	____	____
• Weather map	____	____	____
• Sports	____	____	____
• Entertainment	____	____	____
• Classified	____	____	____
Three elements of group choice:			
• _____	____	____	____
• _____	____	____	____
• _____	____	____	____

Areas Covered	Self	Group	Teacher
• Local geography			
• Local geology	____	____	____
• Changes in demogrpahics	____	____	____
• Changes in culture	____	____	____
• Local politics	____	____	____
• Economics	____	____	____
• Quality of life	____	____	____

Group Evaluation

	Self	Group	Teacher
• Group used time wisely.	____	____	____
• Group met deadlines.	____	____	____
• Individuals in the group shared the workload.	____	____	____
• Group decisions were arrived at democratically and fairly.	____	____	____

Self-Evaluation

This will be written by each student, attached to this form, and added to the student folders.

	Self	Group	Teacher
• Did I do everything I was supposed to?	____	____	____
• Description of what I did	____	____	____
• Description of what I learned	____	____	____
• What could I have done better?	____	____	____
• What was the most valuable thing I did?	____	____	____

1. Effective communicators who:
   a. demonstrate listening and appropriate reactions to others;
   b. express appropriate thoughts, concepts, feelings, and beliefs to others;
   c. convey thoughts, feelings, and/or beliefs through a variety of methods.

2. Self-directed learners who:
   a. seek, identify, and use necessary resources;
   b. identify what they need or want to learn;
   c. apply learning to new situations on their own;
   d. ask *why* and *what if* of self and others;
   e. assess themselves and adjust necessary conditions for self-learning;
   f. set priorities and achievable goals;
   g. assume responsibility for their actions;
   h. develop and implement plans for self-improvement and learning.

3. Quality producers and performers who:
   a. maintain high standards;
   b. create products and performances that achieve their intended purpose;
   c. initiate and follow through;
   d. apply all resources needed to complete the task;
   e. continually assess, evaluate, and adjust to maintain excellence;
   f. consistently produce quality.

4. Community Contributors who:
   a. use effective leadership and interactive skills which develop and sustain supportive relationships;
   b. evaluate and manage their own behavior as group members;
   c. work cooperatively with people different from themselves;
   d. identify problems and persist to consensus and solution;
   e. provide time, energy, and ideas to group efforts.

5. Creative, Complex, and Perceptive Thinkers who:
   a. can successfully anticipate, explore, investigate, analyze and resolve problems;
   b. effectively access, evaluate and integrate information from a variety of resources;
   c. use a wide variety of thinking processes with accuracy to resolve complex issues.

The Theme of the Academy: What Is My Place?

The theme of the academy will be the focus for the coordination of curriculum and will tie it to an immediate, relevant matrix for the student. We recognize the ninth grade as the time when students begin serious planning for their futures. It is imperative that students bound for four-year colleges accumulate the skills and courses that will grant them admission and succeed. Likewise, those students not planning to attend universities need direction to accomplish their high school and postsecondary goals.

Demonstrations and Performances

Demonstrations and performances are designed to direct efforts at enabling students to achieve the outcomes previously described. Performances and demonstrations not only set goals for student achievement, they also serve to certify that students are working toward the academy's outcomes, that they are becoming effective communicators; self-directed learners; quality producers and performers; community contributors; and creative, complex and perceptive thinkers.

Demonstrations and performances will be based on the preceding elements, relating them to the following spheres: work, civic, global, culture, relationships, learning, and personal areas. Demonstrations completed at an established qualitative level will determine proficiency and be a major contributor to the grade in a "subject." Demonstrations and performances may take many forms: a debate, a videotape, an oral presentation, a written piece, and so on. Each of these, however, will be used in the assessment of a student's mastery of student outcomes, specific spheres, and subject areas.

We intend to aim high, to establish performances and demonstrations that challenge all students to achieve their best. As much as possible, demonstrations will emulate re-world situations that will engage the student and illustrate the immediacy and relevancy of skills and traditional subjects. The demonstrations will also encourage the student to become an active learner, interested in his or her environment, confident of accomplished skills, and engaged with his or her life.

Schoolwide Portfolios

Subject Area
High school, all subjects

School and Contact Person
Metro High School
1212 7th Street S.E.
Cedar Rapids, IA 52401
(319) 398-2193

Mary Wilcynski, principal
Don Daws, Mary Vasey, Jane Bolgate, Barb Coates, Rod Kelly,
Joyce Jeanblanc

Summary
The school defines portfolios as a record of learning that focuses on the student's work and her or his reflections on that work. The portfolio includes all curriculum areas and all modes of learning, from writing samples to audio cassettes to hands-on projects. The school has been part of the Coalition of Essential Schools since 1986 and has developed a process of implementing portfolios on a schoolwide basis.

Writing Workshop

Description
This class addresses a variety of writing forms, styles, and genres through reading, writing, and responding to one another's writing. The workshop format encourages students to experiment with new ideas in a supportive environment.

Graduation Expectations Addressed
The student will:

- Communicate, explain process
- Be flexible and set priorities
- Collaborate and cooperate
- Use senses in appreciation and celebration, show ingenuity, show wonderment, curiosity, and enjoyment of learning.

Demonstration

1. At the end of the term, students will put a collection of writing samples together in a booklet.
2. During the last several weeks, students will complete a demonstration based on writing experiences, practice, and presentations throughout the term. They will prewrite, write a rough

draft, work with a writing partner, write a reflection on the demonstration, and submit the final copy for publication.

Criteria/Standards

1. The booklet will have a cover and a table of contents.
2. The collection will include a minimum of twelve samples (six may be class exercises, such as lists, clusters, and sentence work).
3. The final written demonstration will be typewritten and edited for spelling and other mechanics.
4. Writing partners' comments, prewriting, and rough drafts will be included.
5. The final copy will be published or displayed.
6. Students will place work and reflections in their portfolio.

Rubrics/Assessment

Level 1   Look at the following list. If anything is checked, it means you need to rework it or that it is missing and needs to be done. As soon as you take care of it, you will move to level 2 or level 3.

Level 2   This means you did proficient work on all of the items with an *. Good work!

Level 3   This means you not only did the items with an *, but you also did those with **. Your work shows that you spent a great deal of time and effort. Excellent work!

Here's the list:

For your booklet you have:

*   A cover
**   A cover with artwork or decoration
*   Table of contents
*   Twelve examples of your work:
    —Six class exercises—brainstorming list, journal entry, sentences, cluster, mood picture and explanation, flow writing, others _____ , _____ , _____ .
    —Six writings—descriptive, narrative, expository, character sketch, reworked journal entry or flow write, personal essay, short fiction, others _____ , _____ , _____ .
**   Twenty examples of your work. Add the eight additional below.
*   Partner's comments
*   Student reflection

Final Written Demonstration

*   Final copy typewritten on computer
*   Final copy edited for spelling and mechanics
*   Prewriting
*   Partner's comments
*   Student reflection
** Self-evaluation and explanation of the process
** Student showed flexibility in choice of materials.
** Student showed flexibility in willingness to edit and work with others.
** Student set priorities in scheduling time to work and picking projects and material.

Metro High School Portfolio Response Sheet

Name: _____ Advisor: _____ Date: _____
Class: _____ Teacher: _____

Please describe your project. What did you do? Please be *specific*.

_____
_____
_____
_____
_____

Where did you get your ideas? (Did you read about it? ask someone?
use your own imagination?)

_____
_____
_____

What did you like most about doing this project? _____

_____
_____
_____

What frustrated you most? _____

_____
_____

What do you wish you had done differently? _____

_____
_____
_____

Teacher comments: _____

_____
_____
_____

Did you . . .
write
organize
observe
investigate
question
explain
perceive
understand
describe
envision
edit
construct
relate
put in your own words
identify
solve
outline
plan
eliminate
forecast
summarize
shape
generalize
think
demonstrate
practice
compare
classify
analyze
contrast
specify
interview
video
survey
experiment
invent
draw
photograph
present
share
express
create
list
choreograph
report
respond
learn
brainstorm
support
draft
sketch
finish

Career Certificate Program (CCP)

Subject Area
High school, English, math, social studies, and technical education

School and Contact Person
Milwaukee Custer High School
5075 North Sherman Boulevard
Milwaukee, WI 53209
(414) 461-6600

Robert Peters, principal

Summary
This program is designed to increase the number of students who remain in school, increase the number of students who secure a traditional high school diploma and a newly developed career certificate, and increase the options for the graduates to include: direct employment, enrollment in a vocational program, apprenticeship program, and or a baccalaureate degree program. At the end of the program, students are awarded a Certificate of Employability.

Assessment is based on a portfolio that the student develops from grade 9 through grade 12. In addition to traditional grades, the CCP allows students to be rated in alternative measures.

Unit

Career Certificate Program at Custer High School

Description
Custer High School, located on the northwest side of Milwaukee, is undergoing major changes in its curriculum and methods used to deliver instruction to students. The impetus for these reform efforts stemmed from administrators and teachers recognizing that students leaving Custer were not academically or technically prepared to meet workplace demands. Because of the urban setting of the school, the first reform was to create a safe environment for students and staff members. Having accomplished this by the beginning of the 1989–90 school year, teachers moved toward improving the curriculum to foster students' long-term growth and success.

This emphasis on curriculum resulted in the development of the Career Certificate Program (CCP) to meet the needs of students who do not achieve in the regular school setting. Unlike its counterpart, the AMIGO program, it is not a program for at-risk youth. Rather, in the fall of 1992 the CCP enrolled 100 ninth-grade students who have unclear career and/or future schooling goals. Through team teaching, flexible scheduling and the integration of construction technology compwetencies into academic courses, the CCP program has three sequential objectives:

1. Increase the number of students who remain in school.
2. Increase the number of students who secure a traditional high school diploma and/or a newly developed career diploma.
3. Increase the number of students who can compewte for careers through four options: direct employment after graduation, enrollment in a vocational diploma or associate degree program, enrollment in a baccalaureate degree program or acceptance into an apprenticeship.

Students completing two years of the program will earn a "Certificate of Employability" listing employability competency levels attained (see "Identification of Essential Employability Skills" accompanying this practice). Ultimately, students will be better prepared for real-world activities, ehether they include employment or future schooling.

Implementation

Design of this program did not start with curricular outcomes for students. Rather, the originators of the CCP program considered the finished product (or the student who was adequately prepared for the workplace or future schooling) and then "retrofitted" the curriculum to produce that product. This initiative was not "piecemeal restructuring," but involved a total school philosophy and commitment that students should be college-bound or workplace-ready.

The subject areas included in the CCP program are mathematics/science, social studies/English, career specialty areas and electives. Construction technology education is integrated into each of the four academic areas. The competency based program is as rigorous as other high school programs, but with the incorporation of employability, life and interpersonal skills that help students make sound career and/or future schooling decisions. The full-day CCP program functions between 7:35 A.M. and 2:30 P.M. Academic subjects are paired in two hour blocks of time to allow flexibility in instructional delivery and curriculum integration.

Of the 325 students in the current freshman class, many have experienced problems with truancy, tardiness, low academic achievement, or below-grade-level attainment due to lack of motivation, study skills, or poor interpersonal skills. Therefore, students in the CCP have a variety of skill and motivational levels, as well as varied levels of self-esteem. This diversity is utilized by the CCP to enhance learning. the CCP staff has found this diversity to be essential in truly integrating its educational goals.

The CCP attempts to enhance the value of traditional letter grades by focusing students' attainment of employability competencies on the Certificate of Employability. The certificate lists only those competencies that students have achieved, not ones at which they have been unsuccessful. The certificate is certified by Custer High School and the business community, and is provided to employers or admissions personnel to describe specific competencies that students have mastered.

The curriculum has also been expanded. Central to all the individual subject areas are predetermined "thematic units." The units selected for this year are the environment, community service, multiculturalism, and career goals. These nine-week units were selected to make classroom work tangible to the world outside of the classroom.

The CCP teachers begin each unit with a kick-off event presented by outside agencies. The format consists of a keynote speaker followed by presentations to smaller groups of students. Field trips and class technology projects are planned to enhance the thematic units and to extend the classroom walls.

Staff Development   To plan the program, CCP teachers received one hour release time per day in the semester prior to the start of the program. During this time, the staff developed implementation strategies, identified thematic units, integrated the curriculum, and established a time frame for the kick off events. In addition to the planning stage, the teachers were released to attend conferences and workshops. Topics included Tech Prep, Gardner's "Seven Intelligences," assessment strategies, and group dynamics.

During the first year of the CCP, the teachers were assigned a common preparation hour. This enabled them to plan lessons, organize events, contact parents, coordinate activities and resources of outside agencies, customize strategies to meet students' special needs, and to assess goals and outcomes.

Planning   In order to better coordinate program implementation, staff and student programming errors must be corrected before school starts. It is necessary to start the activities on the very first day of school. The time frame of the CCP is very tight and time spent waiting for schedules to be changed is wasted.

Educating all counselors is also essential. There is a temptation to program a student only partially into CCP because it is easier to schedule. This creates confusion and lack of continuity in the delivery of some modules of employability skills.

Evidence of Effectiveness

Continuous evaluation is a major component of the CCP program. The construction technology curriculum has been developed specifically for this program and will serve as a model in developing curriculum in other vocational areas after field-testing during the 1992–93 school year. Potential employers serve on the program's advisory committee and validate curriculum for occupational relevancy and comprehensiveness. CCP staff members collected baseline data at the beginning of the 1992 school year for each of the program's objectives; progress will be measured against these objectives in June 1993.

Identification of Essential Employability Skills

Career Certificate Program (CCP)

Job Seeking–Career Development Skills	*K–12 Goals*
1. Knows sources of information	4, 6
2. Knows own abilities, aptitudes, interests	10
3. Knows occupational characteristics	10
4. Identifies career/occupational goals	10
5. Develops a career plan	10
6. Identifies and researches potential employers	10
7. Knows employment position(s) desired	10
8. Accurately completes	8, 10
a. Inquiry letter	
b. Résumé	
c. Follow-up letter	
9. Accurately completes job application	8, 10
10. Handles interview without errors	8, 10
a. Dress appropriately for a job interview	
11. Seeks information about future education/training	10

Math Skills

1. Understands importance of math in jobs	/
2. Performs basic calculation (=, −, +, x)	7
a. Select appropriate math function	
3. Performs calculations in:	
a. Fractions	
b. Percentages	
c. Proportions/ratios	
4. Makes reasonable estimates	4, 7
5. Uses values from graphs, maps, tables	4, 7
6. Uses English/metric measurement	4, 7, 8
7. Compares numerical values	4, 7
8. Applies geometric principles	4, 7
9. Uses formulas correctly	4, 7
10. Constructs diagrams, table, records	8
11. Uses elementary statistics	7, 8
12. Uses instruments to solve problems:	6, 7, 8
a. Gauges, meters, scales	
b. Calculators	
c. Computers	

Computer Skills—IBM or Apple-Driven	*K–12 Goals*
1. Becomes aware of computer functions	6, 7
2. Inputs and accesses data from computer	6
3. Has experience with computer programs	6, 8, 10
a. Business aplications	
b. Data management	
c. Simple programming	
d. Word processing	
e. Spread sheet	
4. Understands issues associated with computer use	6

Reading Skills

1. Understands the importance of reading in jobs	4, 10
2. Develops vocabulary related to careers and occupations	8, 10
3. Reads for details and special information	4
4. Interprets pictures, graphs, and symbols	4, 2
5. Locates information in reference materials	4
6. Follows intent of written directions/instructions	4
7. Interprets ideas and concepts (comprehension)	4
8. Reads accurately at appropriate rate	4

Writing Skills (whole language newsletters and projects will be used)

1. Understands the importance of writing of jobs	10
2. Develops handwriting legibility	8
3. Composes formal letters	8
4. Fills out forms	8
5. Records messages	8
6. Writes memorandums	8
7. Composes ads/telegrams	8
8. Writes instructions and directions	4, 8
9. Writes reports	4, 8
10. Develops summaries	4, 8
11. Takes notes and/or outlines	4, 8
12. Revises and edits written materials	4, 8

Communication Skills

1. Reports accurately/concisely	8
2. Follows intent of oral directions/instructions	8
3. Speaks distinctly	8
4. Formulates questions	4, 8
5. Answers questions accurately	4, 8
6. Explains activities and ideas clearly	4, 8

7. Uses appropriate vocabulary/grammar	4, 8
8. Gives clear instructions and directions	4, 8
9. Stays on topic	8
10. Uses nonverbal signs appropriately	8
11. Develops oral presentations	8
12. Presents information effectively to groups	1, 8

Interpersonal Skills

1. Functions cooperatively with fellow students	1, 3
2. Functions cooperatively in team efforts	1, 3
3. Functions cooperatively with adult outside school	10
4. Exhibits openness and flexibility	1, 3
5. Seeks clarification of instructions	4
6. Exercises patience and tolerance	1, 3
7. Utilizes suggestions about improving skills	3, 8
8. Uses initiative in getting work done	4
9. Expresses opinions with tact	1, 3
10. Demonstrates ability to negotiate differences with others	1, 3, 4

Business Economic Skills

1. Understands business organization	4, 10
2. Understands business competition	4, 10
3. Knows about processes of marketing	4, 10
4. Knows about processes of production	4, 10
5. Understands business costs	4, 10
6. Understands factors affecting profits	4, 10

Personal Economic Skills

1. Knows how to evaluate products and services	4
2. Knows how to access community resources/services	4, 5
3. Can compute working hours/wages	7
4. Knows how to handle financial affairs	7
5. Can handle records of income and expenses	7
6. Knows how to make price-quality comparisons	7
7. Knows how to prepare state/federal tax forms	5, 7
8. Can evaluate insurance programs	5, 7
9. Knows how to determine credit costs	7
10. Understands legal rights in agreements	5, 7
11. Maintains and utilizes various forms of transportation	9

Manual Perceptual Skills	*K–12 Goals*
1. Constructs/assembles materials	6
2. Uses specific hand tools and instruments	6
3. Develops visual presentations	2, 8
4. Masters keyboard skills	6
5. Operates power equipment	6

Work Activity Skills	
1. Produces types/amount of work required	1
2. Maintains punctuality	5, 10
3. Meets attendance requirements	5, 10
4. Accepts assignments/responsibilities	3
5. Takes responsibility for own actions	3
6. Maintains consistent effort	4
7. Works independently	7
8. Manages time effectively	7
9. Respects rights and property of others	1, 3
10. Adheres to policies and regulations	5, 9
a. Health	

Problem-Solving/Reasoning Skills	
1. Recognizes problems that need solution	4
2. Identifies procedures	4
3. Obtains resources	4, 6
4. Prepares or sets up materials/equipment	4, 6
5. Collects information	4
6. Organizes information	4
7. Interprets information	4
8. Formulates alternative approaches	4
9. Selects efficient approaches	4
10. Reviews progress	4
11. Evaluates activities	4
12. Corrects errors	4
13. Makes conclusions	4
14. Summarizes and communicates results	4
15. Uses results to develop new ideas	4

Expressive Arts

Subject Involved
Middle school, fine and practical arts

School and Contact Person
Fort Couch Middle School
515 Fort Couch Road
Upper St. Clair, PA 15241
(412) 854-3046

Thomas H. Harshman, principal
Ruth Ann Matyuf, associate principal

Summary
An expressive arts program that consists of the integration of five subject areas: art, music, industrial technologies, home economics, and creative expression. The program is a two-year model, with seventh-graders rotating through seven weeks of basic instruction in each of the expressive art areas. In the eighth grade, students can choose from over 40 electives in fine, practical, and performing arts, each ranging in duration from three to six weeks. The program is designed to help students develop life skills, vocational, and avocational interests. The program serves as an interdisciplinary link with the academic subjects. Portfolios are being developed to assess this unit.

Units

In meeting schoolwide curriculum goals, a major component of the middle school curriculum model is the Expressive Arts component. The Expressive Arts department is designed to incorporate the areas of the practical, fine, and performing arts in one program. The model includes art, creative expression, home economics, industrial technologies, and music. It blends subject content in each area with required levels of student activities in the form of product and personal performance.

The addition of a performing arts component (creative expression) provides unique instructional experiences for the students not usually found in traditional or unified arts configurations at the middle school level. Creative expression not only broadens the arts offerings to students, but provides additional instructional support to strengthen and reinforce content objectives introduced in social studies, language arts and foreign language including reporting skills, research skills, public speaking, and cultural enrichment.

Perhaps the most unique feature of the expressive arts program is the development and implementation of an arts elective program at the 8th level. Students can select from 29 expressive arts electives in five content areas.

Acting
Ad Art
Advanced Makeup
Architecture
Broadway
Cake Decorating
Calligraphy
Computer Graphics
Computer Scripting
Crafts

Eating Right
Foreign Foods
Foundry
Furniture Design
Furry Critters
General Shop
Guitar
Holiday Cakes
Jazzercise
Metal Working

Painting and Drawing
Plastics
Plays and Screen
Printmaking
Radio Plays
Rock of Ages
Soft Sculpture
Star Search
Woodworking

Each selective is age-appropriate and reflects student interest. Each is designed to foster life skills and vocational and avocational interests, and to encourage those students with special interests. Students must select one elective in each area during the eighth level. This leaves room for exploration in areas of particular interest which can be 3, 4, 6, 9, or 12 weeks in length, depending on team decisions.

The duration of the electives creates another feature that makes the expressive arts model unique, namely scheduling flexibility. Within the framework of the time allotted in the overall school schedule, the expressive arts team can determine how instructional time will be scheduled at both seventh and eighth levels. This provides flexibility in the scheduling to include correlated electives such as Soft Sculpture (art–home economics), Architecture (art–industrial technologies), Star Search (music and creative expression), and Advertising (art–creative expression).

This flexibility also allows for preschooling and planning for interdisciplinary instruction; integrated units of study with the academics, e.g., seventh-level Nationality Fair (social studies, foreign language, and expressive arts); seventh- and eighth-level colonial units, and eighth-level Greek Week (language arts, social studies, and expressive arts). These are subject to change as new units of instruction are designed and implemented.

A final unique feature of the expressive arts model is the team itself. The team is staffed by teachers who fully understand the importance of the arts curriculum, the needs of the middle school child, and how to meet those needs through the expressive arts model

Mini–Business Community

Subject Areas
Middle school, all areas

School and Contact Person
Mohave Middle School
5520 North 86th Street
Scottsdale, AZ 85250
(602) 423-3700

Carol Erikson, Ed.D., principal
Peggy Eischen, Rudy Swatzell, Mark Norris, Jay Arnsmeyer,
Cheryl Seiler

Summary
Students will develop a mini-community. Each student will have a job, have a bank account, and receive checks and monthly statements. All services will be channeled through this account. Students will learn real-world skills, such as how to balance bank accounts, and will demonstrate how to use bank accounts to make purchases. These tasks are directed at helping students become self-directed learners, problem solvers, community contributors, quality producers, and collaborative leaders.

Students will produce portfolios consisting of student selected work, such as projects, writing assignments, graphs, tests, videos, etc. Parents also will judge student work. Students will be scored on a rubric for each job. The scale has three categories: "Exceeds Standards," "Meets Standards," "Change Needed." The quarterly report home to parents reflects this assessment pattern.

Unit

Skills Contract

The next three weeks will be spent working on basic skills. Each teacher will present a section of basic skills. Each student is expected to keep his or her agenda book up to date concerning the activities in each class. In addition, each student is expected to complete other activities outlined on this sheet.

Required Activities

1. List the activities for each section on the back of this sheet. When all activities are completed in each section, a teacher will initial below.

   _____   _____

   _____   _____

2. Write a book review on book read during seventh-hour TRIP.
   _____

3. Start an individualized vocabulary list. _____
4. Start an individualized spelling list. _____
5. Conduct a survey and graph results. _____

Choice of Activities

Complete as many of the following as time allow. **Remember to be a quality producer.** One quality project is better than three hastily constructed ones.

1. Choose any skill or set of skills and develop a teaching aid.
   a. Make a poster.
   b. Draw a cartoon strip illustrating the skills.
   c. Tape a jingle to help learn the skills.
   d. Construct a game complete with rules on a set of skills.
   Teacher responsible for skill will initial. _____
2. Write a short story. _____
3. Clip a comic strip and write a paragraph about it using transition words that show sequence of events. _____
4. Clip a magazine picture and write a paragraph about it using transition words that show spatial organization. _____
5. Make a reference poster on English measurements/metric system. _____
6. Prepare and deliver a book talk. (seventh-hour teacher or prime. _____
7. Collect five political cartoons and analyze. _____
8. Collect and label ten graphs. _____
9. Choose a short story and write a different ending. _____

Making a Difference

Design for Living

Effective citizens understand the basic beliefs and values of the community, how these beliefs influence that community, and the daily lives of its citizens.

Required Activities

1. _____ Attend all teacher seminars. Instruction and directions will be given in teacher seminars for required activities. Use your agenda book to plan daily work. *Contract ends November 24.*

2. _____ Design a city.

3. _____ Complete pretest. _____ Complete post-test.

4. _____ Keep and balance checkbook.

5. _____ Design your House Four budget.

6. _____ Research and present a social issue.

7. _____ Continue vocabulary list, add definitions.

8. _____ Continue spelling list, each three times and a sentence.

9. _____ Keep notes on the Constitution.

10. _____ Draw a diagram of the organization of the U.S. government, then write a paragraph explaining it.

11. _____ Complete civil protest packet.

12. _____ Nov. 8 _____ Nov. 17. Return permission slips and fee *on time*. Prime Time.

13. _____ Nov. 10 _____ Nov. 19. Participate in activities for two field trips. Prime Time.

14. _____ Nov. 10 _____ Nov. 19. *Wear House Shirt on trip*. Prime Time.

15. _____ Participate on Shadow Day _____ Observation sheet. Second Period Teacher.

16. _____ Prepare a summary project/presentation. Second Period Teacher.

17. _____ Write an evaluation of Shadow Day.

18. _____ Performance of House Four job. Supervisor.

19. _____ Nov. 8. Go over contract with parent. Parent Initial.

20. _____ Nov. 24. Return completed signed contract during Prime time. Prime Teacher.

Turn sheet over for Choice Activities.

Choice Activities

Look over the following activities and choose the ones, which you wish to complete. These are in addition to the required activities. Complete a minumum of *three* choice activities, more if time allows. In addition to math, much of the work on this section will be considered *homework*. Use your Agenda Book! Plan your work, then work your plan.* *Hand in work as it is finished, not all Nov. 24.*

1. _____ Design a personal budget.
2. _____ Plot a supply curve and a demand curve based on a supply schedule.
3. _____ Prepare a display or poster of currency comparison of U.S. and five countries.
4. _____ Use an interview form and interview a business manager.
5. _____ Write an essay on the advantages *or* disadvantages of business competition.
6. _____ Clip and summarize seven news articles about the U.S. economy.
7. _____ Clip and display the market for three stocks for a week. Write summary of action and give several possible explanations.
8. _____ Compile a scrapbook from sales flyers picturing the wardrobe needed for starting a new job. Include a clothing budget and a job description.
9. _____ Research the cost of living and design a poster showing earnings needed for family living in your ideal community.
10. _____ Design a teen recreation center. Include the floor plan, with descriptions of equipment and activities.
11. _____ Compile a ten-page scrapbook of political cartoons and pictures highlighting a social issue. Write an explanation of each.
12. _____ Compose a song making a social statement. (perform)
13. _____ Create a crossword puzzle using vocabulary and/or spelling words.
14. _____ Research and diagram two types of city governments (model, poster).
15. _____ Design and implement a lightbulb project on a present social issue.
16. _____ Analyze a piece of music making a social statement (essay, tape).
17. _____ Create a timeline of social protest/reforms in America's past.
18. _____ Create a wall mural on a social issue.
19. _____ Deliver a 5- to 10-minute speech on a social issue.
20. _____ Send a letter requesting information. Summarize the results of your request.
21. _____ Compile a list of Scottsdale agencies and the services rendered.
22. _____ Conduct a survey on a social issue and present the results.
23. _____ Clip three news items on chosen social issue, label, and summarize.
24. _____ Conduct a family discussion on social issue. Parent.
25. _____ Conduct a family discussion on ways citizens can provide community service. Parent.
26. _____ Any idea you might like to implement as a project? Get teacher approval.
_____ .

Remember

Quality is more important than quantity. Plan your work. Make good use of Community Day work time. Visualize Mr. McKenzie in a tub of jello. Read Read Read. We're House Four Say No More.

House Four: Special Needs Modifications and Instructional Strategies

Exam Modifications

- Substitute a project for a test.
- Read test items to student.
- Allow adjusted time.
- Rewrite/simplify tests.
- Allow student to retest to reach competency.

Assignment Modifications

- Use individual feedback interviews/conferences.
- Use progress charts/monitoring charts.
- Provide instruction using different learning modalities.
- Allow additional time.
- Reduce number of problems assigned.
- Reduce number of problems assigned.
- Allow different formats to teach content:
  —"Hands-on" activities
  —Video, audio tapes
  —Games/experiments
  —Art/visual products
  —Oral presentations, debates, role playing
- Use contracts, learning packets, independent study.

Evaluation Modifications

- Student is evaluated on progress in reaching learning outcomes, not A-B-C grades.

Remedial Strategies

- Present content through variety of modalities.
- Provide written materials for oral directions and lectures:
  —Notes
  —Advance organizers
  —Cloze outlines
- Shorten listening time.
- Provide group work, peer instruction.
- Designate responsibility to student and carefully define tasks.
- Establish time frames.
- Structure sequence of tasks.
- Provide visuals.
- Connect content to real life.
- Teach memory devices.
- Practice transfer of skills to real-life applications.

Design and Draw a City on a Sheet of Paper that will be Provided. Include in Your City the Things You Believe to Be Important, but the Following Are Requirements

1. State the latitude and longitude of your city.
2. Give a description or drawing of the area's geography and topography.
3. List the advantages and disadvantages of the area that you have chosen.
4. Explain where you will get the necessary resources for life in your city.
5. What forms of transportation are available to and from your city?
6. Will you have an airport? If so, where? What kinds of aircraft will you allow?
7. What kinds of transportation will you encourage and allow in your city?
8. What are the dimensions of your city?
9. What population are you planning for?
10. Draw the boundaries of your city and, in different colors, draw in areas of different zoning and label the zones with an explanation of each zone's limitations.
11. Show government buildings, schools, streets, parks, and open spaces.
12. Draw in police stations and note how many officers are assigned to each.
13. Show the kinds of communications and entertainment you are planning for in your city.
14. Draw in major businesses and employers.
15. Explain the kind of government you will have.
16. Write a brief statement explaining the impact your city will have on the environment in and around it.

Checklist #8. Choice Activities

1. *Scrapbook* must be made from construction paper or other heavy paper. Each clothing item should be labeled and priced. Notebook paper should not be used. Scrapbook should be put together using brads or staples.
2. All information should be typed, computer-generated, or neatly printed using a straightedge. Pencil and notebook paper are not acceptable.
3. The *clothing budget* should be neatly printed or typed using ledger paper and then attached to the scrapbook. Use glue sticks or a small amount of white glue.
4. The *job description* should be a summary of one of the articles in the *Occupational Outlook Handbook*. One paragraph is required using correct paragraph format (topic sentence, supporting detail, closing sentence).

Checklist #10. Choice Activities

1. A *floor plan* should be drafted using plain white paper or graph paper. The purpose of each room and area should be labeled in the floor plan. Project should be mounted on construction paper or poster board. Final product must be in ink or computer-generated. use of white-out is allowed if done neatly.
2. *Descriptions* of equipment and activities should be in paragraph form. Drawings should be provided of equipment used. Neatly clipped pictures of equipment may be used.
3. All written work should be done in ink or computer-generated. Pencil and notebook paper is not acceptable. If ink pen is used, written work must be printed using a straightedge.

Checklist #11. Choice Activities

1. Scrapbook must be made of construction paper fastened together using brads or staples. A minimum of 10 political cartoons from newspaper editorial pages is required.
2. The cartoons must be about a *social issue.*
3. The *written explanation* of each cartoon must be typed or printed in ink on plain white paper. If printing, use a straightedge. Attach the written explanation neatly to the scrapbook with glue stick or a small amount of white glue.
4. **The** *written explanation* should describe the social issue and explain what point the cartoon is making about the social issue.

House 4: Student–Parent Conference

Student Reflection
Review/describe with your parent each piece of work in

Parent Reflection
Has your child communicated clearly during this conference?

What is your best piece?
_____

Is written work logically organized, neat, and pleasing to the eye?

Why? _____

Student Reflection

Is there work in your portfolio which represents your
personal best?

How would you rate the
quality of each piece?

_____

If you could work further on
one piece, what would you
do?

If you could repeat a project,
how would you do it
differently?

What do you still not understand about what you have
studied?

_____
Student Name

Parent Reflection

Does the quality of the completed
work reflect your student's best
effort?

Does work appear to be carefully
edited and revised?

Is your child's evaluation of his
or her work realistic?

Comments*: _____

_____

_____

_____
Parent Signature   Date

Please leave this conference form with the Prime Time teacher.

*Use the back of this form if more space is needed.

Integrated House 4 Quarterly Progress Report

Name _____   Teacher _____

Quarter   1   2   3   4   (Circle One)   * Indicates improvement needed

Needs Improvement ⟶ ⟵ Superior Achievement
• • • • • •

Self-Directed Learner

- Takes responsibility for actions
- Self-assesses progress
- Uses class time productively
- Turns in work on time
- Seeks additional information if needed
- Assignments missing
- Works to potential

Problem Solver

- Demonstrates knowledge of resources
- Considers alternatives/consequences
- Thinks through process before reaching decision
- Applies reasoning in a logical manner
- Works to potential

Community Contributor

- Demonstrates a positive attitude
- Participates in classroom activities
- Displays caring/considerate behavior
- Provides service to school and community
- Follows school rules
- Works to potential

Quality Producer

- Designs quality projects
- Produces neat/legible work
- Meets prescribed requirements
- Works to potential

Teacher's Comments: _____

_____

_____

Parent Signature: _____

Parents' Comments: _____

Collaborative Leader

- Works cooperatively with others
- Shares ideas with class members
- Contributes to group learning
- Works to potential

Creative Thinker

- Envisions original ideas
- Initiates innovative ideas
- Explores new boundaries

Effective Oral Communicator

- Participates in group discussions
- Listens to others during group discussions
- Speaks clearly and audibly when presenting
- Does not interrupt other speakers
- Works to potential

Effective Written Communicator

- Writes clearly and concisely
- Uses correct spelling
- Uses correct punctuation
- Uses correct capitalization
- Organizes written work in a professional manner
- Works to potential

Mathematical Performance

- Completes classwork
- Completes homework
- Transfers mathematical concepts to practical application
- Demonstrates mastery of concepts
- Works to potential

Integrated House 4 Quarterly Progress Report

Name _____ Prime Time Teacher _____

Quarter   1   2   3   4   (Circle One)   Date _____

	Change Needed	Meets Standards	Exceeds Standards

Self-Directed Learner

- Takes responsibility for actions
- Initiates solutions to problems
- Self-assesses progress
- Uses class time productively
- Completes work on time
- Seeks additional information if needed

Problem Solver

- Demonstrates knowledge of resources
- Considers alternatives
- Thinks through process before reaching decision
- Applies reasoning in a logical manner

Community Contributor

- Demonstrates a positive attitude
- Participates in classroom activities
- Displays caring/considerate behavior
- Follows school rules
- Provides service to school and community
- Seeks/secures position in community

Quality Producer

- Designs quality projects
- Produces neat/legible work
- Meets prescribed requirements

Collaborative Leader

- Works cooperatively with others
- Shares ideas with class members
- Contributes to group learning

	Change Needed	Meets Standards	Exceeds Standards

Effective Oral Communicator

- Participates in group discussions   _____ _____ _____
- Listens to others during group discussions   _____ _____ _____
- Self-assesses progress   _____ _____ _____
- Speaks clearly and audibly when presenting   _____ _____ _____
- Does not interrupt other speakers   _____ _____ _____

Effective Written Communicator

- Writes clearly and concisely   _____ _____ _____
- Uses correct spelling   _____ _____ _____
- Uses correct punctuation   _____ _____ _____
- Uses correct capitalization   _____ _____ _____
- Organizes written work in a professional manner   _____ _____ _____

Mathematical Performance

- Completes classwork   _____ _____ _____
- Completes homework   _____ _____ _____
- Transfers mathematical concepts to practical application   _____ _____ _____
- Demonstrates mastery of concepts presented during the quarter   _____ _____ _____

Teacher's Comments: _____

_____

_____

_____

Parent Signature: _____

Parents' Comments: _____

_____

_____

_____

Integrated House 4 Teacher Project Evaluation

Science Projects

Subject Area
Grade levels 7–12, science

School and Contact Person
Martin Luther King, Jr., Middle School
4545 Ammendale Road
Beltsville, MD 20705
(301) 937-6070

Bette Lewis, principal
Michael Martirano

Summary
This unit incorporates the theory of multiple intelligences in the design of monthly developmental science projects. The projects have been formulated around the premise of exploring each individual student's gifted area. Each month a different science project is communicated and explained to the students with the hope that individual creativity will be fostered and each form of intelligence will be explored and challenged.

The assessment conducted by the teacher is based on the student's presentation of the project to the class. The rating of the project is based on creativity, effort, and originality. The presentation is rated on how clearly the project is communicated. Students are asked to prepare a written evaluation, which requires them to reflect on what they have learned, what they thought of the project, and how successful they thought they were.

Unit

Multiple Intelligences Applied to Science

Howard Gardner, in *Frames of Mind* (New York: Basic Books, 1983) identified seven distinct kinds of intelligences that operate independently in the brain:

1. *Linguistic-verbal* is the ability to use words written spoken, or just heard.
2. *Logical-mathematical* has to do with numbers, symbols, and abstract relations.
3. *Musical* is thinking about sounds in their infinite variety.
4. *Spatial* deals with the knack of visualizing shapes or location with movement and dimension.
5. *Bodily-kinesthetic* relates to the muscles and their own movement and meaning.
6. *Interpersonal* is the ability to understand other people's moods and concerns.
7. *Introspective* is the ability to understand oneself and one's own feelings.

The theory states that all of us are born with the potential to develop a multiplicity of intelligences that make us competent people. We all have gifts, and therefore we must explore our most gifted intelligence areas and maximize the focus in that area for what we do best. This will yield greater success. According to Gardner, we should not be asking our students, "How smart are you?" but "How are you smart?"

There are ten projects associated with this unit. Following each unit, the student is required to complete the Project Evaluation Form.

Science Mobile Assignment

The objective of this assignment is for you to design and build a mobile that reflects your interest in any science topic.

1. You must use one coat hanger to build your mobile.
2. You must cover the hollow part of the hanger with paper and decorate it to reflect your topic title.
3. From the bottom part of the hanger, you must hang at least five items in varying lengths that further explain your topic.
4. This is due on September _____ , at which time you will explain your mobile and hang it in the classroom.

Aerospace Collage

The object of this assignment is for you to design and assemble a collage that reflects an aerospace theme.

1. You must place your collage on a 14" x 22" piece of heavy poster board.
2. You must cover the entire front surface of the poster board with pictures, drawings, illustrations, etc., that reflect your selected topic theme.
3. You must exhibit the highest standards of neatness and creativity, and you must put your name in the lower left corner.
4. The due date is October _____ , at which time you will explain it and display it in the classroom.

TV Weather Report

The objective of this assignment is for you to research a weather topic and write a one-page report on the topic. The catch is you must write it as if you are reporting to a TV audience. You are the reporter.

1. You must use a file folder and attach your report to the inside.
2. You must illustrate the outside of the folder to reflect your weather topic.
3. Keep in mind that you must write this as if you are a reporter reading the nightly news.
4. This is due on November _____ , when you will read your report to the class.

Astronomy Shoebox

The objective of this assignment is for you to research an astronomy topic and display, illustrate, depict, and label your topic in 3-D inside a shoebox.

1. You must use a shoebox of normal size to display your topic.
2. You must place your name and topic title on the inside of the lid and outside top of the shoebox. When your shoebox is complete, it should look like a shadow box done in 3-D.
3. This is due on Tuesday, December _____ . On that day you will explain your shoebox display.

Scientific Method Experimentation

The objective of this assignment is for you to select one scientific experiment and complete the experimentation following the steps of the scientific method. (Teacher approval is a must.)

1. You must select one experiment and conduct it using the scientific method to guide your process.
2. You must record your data and draw conclusions from your findings.
3. You must display your experimentation and results on a piece of foam board.
4. This is due on January _____ , at which time you will present your outcomes.

Black Scientist Song/Poem/Report

The objective of this assignment is for you to select one black scientist and complete a one-page report, song, or poem about the person's life and contributions to science.

1. You must write a one-page report or song or poem on the person's life. Your selection must be teacher-approved.
2. You must attach a one-page cover that illustrates the report.
3. Place the report and the illustration in a clear plastic folder.
4. This is due on Thursday, February _____ . You will present your report at this time. See attached sheet for suggested ideas.

Suggested Ideas

Norbert Rillieux	Elijah McCoy
Lewis H. Latimer	Granville Woods
Garrett A. Morgan	Archie Alexander
David Crosthwait	Frederick M. Jones
Louis W. Roberts	Katerine Johnson
Otis Boykin	O. S. (Ozzie) Williams
J. Ernest Wilkins	Rufus Stokes
Virgil Trice	Meridith Gourdine
Annie Easley	James Harris
Caldwell McCoy	Clarence Elder
Cordell Reed	Donald Cotton
Ernest Coleman	Lawnie Taylor
Banjamin Banneker	Charles Drew
George Washington Carver	Mae E. Jemison
Lloyd Augustus Hall	Ron McNair
Percy L. Julian	Joseph Lee
Jan Earnst Matzeliger	

Environmental Poster

The objective of this assignment is for you to design an environmental awareness poster on the topic of your choice.

1. You must use a 14" x 22" piece of heavy posterboard to place your poster on.
2. You must select a topic and convey the topic over the entire poster, using drawings, pictures, illustrations, quotes, etc.
3. Your end result must be self-explanatory to anyone reviewing your work. Neatness and creativity are a must, and you must put your name in the lower left front corner.
4. The due date is Friday, May _____ , at which time you will present your awareness poster.

Element Model

The objective of this assignment is for you to select one element from the periodic chart and construct a model of the element.

1. Your element selection must be approved by _____ .
2. You must build your model either on foam board or in a mobile form.
4. Your model must be titled with the name of your element and an accurate depiction of the protons, electrons, and neutrons.
4. You must complete the attached sheet and secure it to your model.
5. This is due on Wednesday, March _____ .

Element name:	Number of electrons:
Element symbol:	Number of neutrons:
Atomic number:	State at room temperature:
Atomic mass:	Properties:
Number of protons:	

In one paragraph, describe your element. Include its uses, where it is found, and any interesting facts:

Sports and Science

The objective of this assignment is for you to select on athletic activity or phenomenon and explain the impact that science has on the event.

1. You will research the topic and complete a report explaining how science impacts the activity.
2. You will demonstrate the activity to further explain the athletic ability.
3. Refer to the attached sheet for ideas and consult with your teacher for ideas.
4. This is due on Thursday, June _____ , at which time you will present your findings.

Sports and Science Ideas

1. Explain how a pitcher throws a curve ball.
2. Explain how a golfer makes the ball slice or hook.
3. How does a high jumper achieve maximum height?
4. How has science revolutionized a particular sport?
5. How does an ice skater do rapid 360s?
6. Explain the impact of any science principle on a sport.

Project Evaluation Form

Name: _____

Date: _____   M. L. King, Jr., Middle School

Mod _____

1. How did you come up with your idea (conceptualization)?
2. How did your presentation go?
3. What do you think of the quality of your project?
4. What does the project say about your interests, hobbies, style?
5. Did you work with anyone on this project?
6. What grade do you deserve? _____ Why?

_____

Teacher comments: _____

_____

_____

_____

Overall grade: _____

Teacher signature: _____

Date: _____

Science Portfolios

Subject Area
Grades 7–12, science

School and Contact Person
Martin Luther King, Jr., Middle School
4545 Ammendale Road
Beltsville, MD 20705
(301) 937-6070

Bette L. Lewis, principal
Michael Martirano

Summary
The purpose of this unit is to provide a complete and accurate picture of how a student is performing. At the beginning of each year, an individual folder is distributed to each science student. Instructions are given to allow students time in class to personalize the front and back of their folders by decorating them with relevant topics related to science. The purpose of this activity is to allow students to feel ownership of the portfolio. At the end of each science unit, students are given time to select examples of their best science work. The selected work is submitted to the teacher for approval. Once this process is complete, the papers become part of the student's portfolio. The process is ongoing, occurring many times during the year.

At the end of each quarter, students are given the opportunity to reflect upon their learning. During this time, students engage in an activity of analyzing their science work. Students make comparisons of previous work to current work by: (1) looking for evidence of improvement; (2) selecting and ranking their best pieces of work; (3) selecting their best and overall piece of work and sharing it with other members of the class, explaining their reasons for selecting the piece of work; and (4) making connections to previously taught concepts.

The school has studied the use of the portfolio system by comparing grades of students who use the portfolio assessment to those who do not and has found improved grades and improved student attitudes toward science as a result of using portfolios. The benefits of using portfolios have been seen in the active role students play in assessing and selecting their best work. The portfolios allow for the recognition of different learning styles. Portfolios serve as evidence of learning beyond traditional approaches. They provide a record of long-term performance and allow for the incorporation of different written learning activities into courses where it once was thought impossible. For example, in science more focus can be placed on written work in which students are asked to explain how and why things happen, as opposed to focusing on recall. This calls for the utilization of higher order thinking skills and strategies.

Portfolio Selection Rationale

You are given the task of assessing your best piece of science work for your portfolio. Write a letter to your teacher, parents, or principal telling them why you chose the piece for your portfolio.

Questions to Consider

1. Why did you select this piece?
2. How does this piece make you feel?
3. What did you learn from this piece?
4. How does it compare to your work from the beginning of the year?
5. How has your work impacted your attitude toward science?
6. Are you doing well in science? Why or why not?

Science Class

M. L. King, Jr., Middle School
4545 Ammendale Road
Beltsville, Maryland 20705

Date: _____

Dear _____ :

I selected this piece of work because: _____

_____

_____

_____

_____

_____

_____

Sincerely,

Portfolio Rating Form

Name: _____

Date: _____

Mod: _____

M. L. King, Jr., Middle School

Selected Science Work   *Comments*

1. Lab(s):

2. Warm-up(s):

3. Classwork:

4. Test/quiz:

5. Hands-on activity:

6. Miscellaneous:

Water Water Everywhere

Subject Areas
Grades 8–10, all subjects

School and Contact Person
Hastings Middle School
190 East 9th Street
Hastings, MN
(612) 437-6111

Garry Jensen, principal
Cliff Jacobson, eighth-grade environmental science

Summary
The unit teaches about ground and surface water and the variables that affect its quality. Included are half a dozen laboratory experiments plus a highly experimental water-testing unit. Students will gain knowledge about acid rain, groundwater contamination, toxic and biodegradable wastes, and much more. The students will demonstrate competence in testing a local water source (surface or tap) for chemical and biological pollutants. The unit is commercially available from the Hach Company (1-800-227-4224).

Students use the *Student Reading Unit, Water Quality Factors* book, notes, friends, or parents to help answer questions on a parent-graded take-home test and parent-graded speech. The staff at Hastings Middle School feel that these units guarantee success, reinforce learning, and get parents actively involved.

On the take-home test, parents are instructed to score the student's response on a scale from 0 to 4. On the take-home speech, the parents are requested to score the speech on a D, C, B, or A scale. The parent rating counts for 50 percent of the grade. The teacher does the other half. A student may improve a grade on both parts of the take-home with repeated attempts.

Source: This unit is reprinted with permission from the Hatch Company (1994) P.O. 389, Loveland, CO 80539.

Parent-Graded Take-Home Test

Name _____ Hour _____

Directions for Students   Use the *Student Reading Unit, Water Quality Factors* book, notes, friends, or parents to help answer these questions. Be sure they are correct before you give your paper to your teacher. Your teacher will check your paper and give you an answer sheet. Study the answer sheet carefully, then teach any 10 concepts to your parents. CIRCLE the numbers of the 10 concepts you plan to teach.

Your parents should read the information in the box below, then grade each answer using the guidelines below. You may earn a higher grade by redoing any question you get wrong.

Directions for Parents   Your son/daughter will teach 10 concepts to you. Be sure you have the answer sheet so you'll know if the answers are correct. Please grade each answer using the following scale:

A = 4 points, B = 3 points, C = 2 points, D = 1 point, F = 0 points

Place the points earned in the blank and total the score on the last page. Your son/daughter will then return the test to me for recording.

TOTAL SCORE = A = 36–40, B = 32–35, C = 28–31, D = 24–28

Students may improve their grade if they restudy their wrong answers and reteach the concept to you later (I suggest a 24-hour wait). Please initial the blank in front of the question every time the student "redoes" it. Total the score at the bottom and sign the sheet. Thank you for your help.

Direct questions to _____
Teacher's name and phone number

1. _____ points
   a. What causes hard water? _____
   b. Name the two main constituents that make water hard: _____

   _____
   c. What is a buffer? _____
   d. How does a buffer differ from a base? _____
   e. Does our community have hard (or soft) water? _____

2. _____ points
   a. What acid is the second main cause of acid rain? _____
   b. What acid is the second main cause of acid rain? _____
   c. Automobiles are a major cause of acid rain because of gasses they emit? What gas do they contribute? _____
   d. What is the pH of normal rain? _____ Of acid rain? _____
   e. Explain the pH scale. Tell the relationship of one pH unit to another. _____
      _____
      _____

3. _____ points
   a. What is *ecology?* _____
   b. Why is it important to study ecology? _____
      _____

4. _____ points
   What is eutrophication? _____

5. _____ points
   a. Pretend you are the city park director. At the edge of town is a small lake covered with algae. There are selective herbicides to kill weeds but not fish. The town mayor wants you to kill the weeds with these chemicals, but you have another idea. Why should you disagree with the mayor? _____
      _____
   b. What are the two main chemicals in water that cause the growth of algae? _____
      _____
   c. What is the main source of these chemicals? _____
      _____

6. _____ points
   a. What do we mean when we say a substance *bioaccumulates?* _____
      _____
   b. Give examples of some chemicals or metals that bioaccumulate _____
      _____

7. _____ points
   a. What is *synergy?* _____

Parent-Graded Take-Home Test, continued

    b. Give an example of synergy: _____

        _____

    c. How does acid rain affect heavy metals like mercury and lead? _____

        _____

8. _____ points

    a. Explain why "sanitary landfills" really aren't effective. _____

        _____

    b. Biodegradable wastes take many years to decompose in a sanitary landfill. Explain why it takes so long. _____

        _____

9. _____ points

    a. What do we mean when we say we are "mining" our groundwater? _____

        _____

    b. Why shouldn't we mine our groundwater? _____

        _____

    c. Where (in the oceans, rivers, lakes, or underground) is most of the drinking water in our country stored? _____

        _____

10. _____ points

    a. In which of these places is acid rain more serious, in the limestone region of central Indiana or on the granite Canadian shield of Minnesota's Boundary Waters Canoe Area? _____

    b. Explain why acid rain is more harmful in one place than in the other. _____

        _____

11. _____ points

    a. *Scenario:* A city dumps raw waste into a river but is worried about high bacteria levels in the wastge. So they add lots of chlorine to the waste before they dump it. What's wrong with doing this? _____

        _____

    b. You have a septic tank in your yard. You know the micro-organisms in your septic tank eat your home's waste products. One day your septic tank doesn't work and your backyard smells awful. You tell your dad that the chemical toilet bowl cleaner has killed the bacteria in the septic tank. Dad says you're wrong. Are you? _____

Explain. _____

_____

12. _____ points

    a. Name the three stages of wastewater treatment and tell how they differ. _____

_____

_____

    b. What is thermal pollution? _____

_____

    c. How does it affect a river? _____

_____

13. _____ points

    a. Tell how to purify water on a camping trip. _____

_____

    b. Is all bottled water safe to drink? _____

14. _____ points

    Define each of the terms below and use them in a sentence: (Use a separate paper.)

desalinated	iceberg	pack ice	carcinogen
reclamation	impounded	ecologically sensitive	ecology
aquifer	isotope	potable	anaerobic
sludge	pathogen	effluent	turbid

_____ Total score = letter grade _____

Parent signature _____

American Society

Subject Area
Elementary school, grade 5

School and Contact Person
   Bunker Hill Elementary School
   Spring Branch Independent School District
   11950 Taylorcrest
   Houston, Texas 77024
   (713) 465-0036

   Gayle Lambert, principal
   Frances Shoup, instructional consultant
   Nancy Burch, Molly McCreary, Suzanne Rosevelt

Summary
This unit involved students in a reciprocal teaching project. There are three fifth grades in this school, and they divided the time-span of American history into three chronological times. Fifth grade #1 read about the years 1775–1850; they researched and selected important people, events, and discoveries and inventions. Fifth grade #2 accomplished similar tasks for the years 1850–1925. Fifth grade #3 did the same for 1925 to the present day. The entire project took from January to May and included the students reading six historical novels and innumerable books for research.

As the data were collected, the students in cooperative groups developed a mural that covered one wall of their classroom (ceiling to floor) and depicted what they decided were the highlights of their time period. The staff used group evaluation and self-evaluation for assessment as the process unfolded.

When the three murals were finished, the staff asked each student to become an expert on a particular part of the mural. Each student made sure everyone in the class was truly an expert by making a mural test and then teaching each other 100 percent of the answers. When each class was an expert, the classes were mixed up. About one-third of each class was reassigned to another class. The task of the experts now was to instruct everyone in the new group on 100 percent of the answers on the mural test.

As a culminating event, the murals were taken to the school cafeteria where they were secured to one wall for the entire school to share. It was here that "real" teaching took place. Fifth-graders, dressed in the style of their time period, brought in younger students in the school and instructed them about the mural.

The assessment was based on six criteria, each rated on a scale from 1 to 5: teacher observation, national achievement test, research paper, student-made portfolio, student-made mural test, and student self-evaluation.

Fifth-Grade Mural Study Guide

1769–1775

1. When did Patrick Henry give his speech and what did he mean?
2. What did Roger Williams do for our country and what did he believe in?
3. Who invented the Conestoga Wagon? Why was it important?
4. How did Daniel Boone settle Kentucky?
5. Why is the Steam Engine so important?
6. Who was Elizabeth Seton and what did she do?
7. Why was Johnny Appleseed so important?

1776–1780

1. What did the Declaration of Independence mean/ When was it signed?
2. Who is given the credit for making the first American flag?
3. Why did Benedict Arnold become a traitor?
4. How did Israel Putnam help win the Revolutionary War?
5. What did Abigail Adams do to become famous? Why is that so significant?

1780–1800

1. Who started the first political parties and what did each believe?
2. Who asked George Washington to be president and why?
3. When was the Constitution signed and why?
4. Who was the inventor of the cotton gin? How did the cotton gin affect the cotton industry and slavery?
5. What famous duty was Alexander Hamilton given in 1789? Why was it so important?

1800–1823

1. Whom did Jane Long guard Bolivar Point for and why?
2. Why did James Monroe write the Monroe Doctrine in 1823?
3. What did Dolley Madison do to become famous?
4. Who was the fourth president and what was fought during his term?

1823–1850

1. Who explored the Rocky Mountains? What do the mountains stand for and why are those people famous?
2. Why was the Gold Rush so important? Where did it take place?
3. What does the San Jacinto Monument represent? Where is it located?
4. Who used "We hold these truths to be self evident . . ." and what did she mean by them? From what documents did she take them.?
5. What happened in Utah in the late months of 1846?

1834–1862

1. Explain the Underground Railroad. Why was it illegal?
2. What is the Morse Code? What was its purpose?
3. Who was Laura Ingalls Wilder? How did her novels affect the United States?
4. What did Elizabeth Blackwell do and why was it important?
5. What was so important about the novel *Uncle Tom's Cabin?* Who wrote it?

1862–1885

1. What was the major cause of the Civil War?
2. What inspired Alexander Graham Bell to invent the telephone?
3. Why did the United States purchase Alaska? When?
4. How did the invention of the light bulb help change America?
5. What was the Gettysburg Address? Who wrote it? Why was it so important?

1885–1907

1. Where was the first airplane flown and who invented it?
2. How did the world "use" Hawaii?
3. How did the expansion of the railroad across the country affect the United States?
4. What did Nellie Bly do and how did it affect the United States?

1907–1920

1. How was jazz introduced to the United States?
2. Where was Nazism born?
3. Who discovered penicillin and how?
4. When was Charlie Chaplin discovered and how?

1920–1933

1. Why was the flight of Amelia Earhart across the ocean so important?
2. How did Susan B. Anthony get women the right to vote and when?
3. What made Babe Didrikson so great?
4. What was the Great Depression?
5. Why was Eleanor Roosevelt so important and how did she affect our nation?

1917–1934

1. Why were the Americans in World War I?
2. When were Loony Tunes invented? Why was this so important?
3. What caused the Great Depression? How did this affect our nation?
4. Who invented jazz?
5. Where was the Great Flood during the period of 1917–1934? What was the exact date?

1935–1950

1. What country crossed the Rhine River in World War II to invade Germany?
2. What country bombed the *U.S. Arizona?* When and where did it happen? What resulted?
3. Who was the leader who tried to take over Europe in World War II?
4. In what year was the atomic bomb first used? What country dropped the bomb? What country was bombed?
5. The Americans and the Russians united over the Elbe River in World War II. Where is the Elbe River?

1951–1963

1. What disease was cured in 1963? Where was the announcement that the vaccine worked made? What is the status of that disease today?
2. What war was fought in 1951 and who fought in it? Why?
3. What was the purpose of the satellite?
4. Who was Lee Harvey Oswald and how did he die?
5. What record did Wilt Chamberlain set and when?
6. What was the name of Martin Luther King, Jr.'s speech and what was its purpose?

1965–1975

1. Which flight went up in 1969? Why is it famous?
2. Explain the Watergate scandal.
3. What happened to Richard Nixon?
4. What war took place in 1969? Why did the United States enter the war (officially)?
5. What is Chris Everett Lloyd famous for?
6. What did the peace sign stand for before it was a peace sign?

1976–1993

1. Who won Olympic gold medals in 1984 and for what events?
2. How did the *Challenger* blow up and when?
3. What happened to corn and wheat prices in the late 1970s? What is the significance?
4. Where was Desert Storm? Who fought in it? What was the cause?
5. Who was elected president in 1980? How long did he serve?
6. In 1983, who went into space and how was it a first?
7. How do you feel about the fifth-grade integrated unit and what you learned? Did you do your personal best?

Mural Test

Name _____

Date _____ Homeroom _____

Directions

Read all of the following questions. Choose two questions from each time period. You should have a total of six *essay* answers when the test is complete. Be sure to answer in essay form, not in short sentences. Each question should be answered in detail. Each answer is worth 16.5 points. Good luck, historians!!

1769–1850

1. What did Roger Williams do for our country and what did he believe in? Why is this so significant?
2. Why was Johnny Appleseed so important? Be sure to explain in full detail.
4. Who started the first political parties and what did each believe?
5. Who used, "We hold these truths to be self evident . . ." and what was meant by these words? From what document were they taken? Be sure and include why this person would want to talk about the rights of Americans. (Remember what I told you about the treatment of a certain gender?)

1850–1925

1. Explain the underground railroad in full detail. Include why it was illegal and why people were involved in it.
2. Explain the importance of the novel *Uncle Tom's Cabin*. Include who wrote it.
3. How did the expansion of the railroad across the country affect the United States?
4. Who discovered penicillin and how? (Be sure you have your facts straight.)
5. Explain the cause of the Great Depression and the condition of the United States during that time.

1925–1993

1. What happened on December 7, 1941? What were the consequences?
2. What is the purpose of a satellite? Include an example of your explanation other than the one I gave in class.
3. Explain the Watergate scandal. What happened to Richard Nixon?
4. What war took place in the 1960s? What was the official reason for entering the war? Explain.
5. What was Desert Storm? Who fought in it? What was the cause?

Bonus Section (2 points each)

1. Who was Elizabeth Seton and what did she do?
2. How did Israel Putnam help win the Revolutionary War?
3. Why did Benedict Arnold become a traitor?
4. Who explored the Rocky Mountains? You must spell the names correctly.
5. Where was the first airplane flown and who invented it?
6. How long (exactly) did it take Nellie Bly to travel around the world?
7. What was the exact date of the great flood on Galveston Island?
8. Where was the announcement made that the polio vaccine worked?
9. What was the name of Martin Luther King, Jr.'s speech? What was he in favor of, and what year did he make it?
10. What year did Sally Ride fly into space?

Science Thinking Journal

Subject Area
Elementary school, grades 3–6, math and science

School and Contact Person
Susan Lindgren Elementary School
4801 West 41st Street
St. Louis Park, MN 55416
(612) 928-6700

Harry Hoff, principal
Jeff Saslow, staff development specialist

Summary
Students articulate science ideas by keeping a science journal where they write their thoughts after a particular science lesson. The students are prompted by ideas based on seven different creative extensions of the lessons. Each week a student selects his or her best journal entry and indicates why he or she made that selection. This process involves self-evaluation and metacognitive feedback.

Unit

Insist on clear expression. Effective oral and written communication is so important in every facet of life that teachers of every subject and at every level should place a high priority on it for all students.—Project 2061

Science Thinking Journal Ideas

Creative Extension

- Write a one-page story about the magnet that was attractive.
- Create a poem about the solar world.
- Develop two jokes from our metric measurement unit.

A pea seed is like a teacher because . . .

Open-ended

- Knowing what you know about acidity, how would you change your diet and why?
- Where have you seen steam erosion taking place?
- What would happen if you enlarged the cylinder and the amount of water?

- What kind of game can you think of using a flipper for?
- What can you use a pendulum for?

Pictorial

- Draw a picture of the round magnets on a pencil.
- Using the vocabulary words *magnet, repel, attract,* and *force;* label the diagram and in three sentences explain what is happening.
- Using at least five blocks of cartoon paper, create sequential steps (drawing and with words) to tell how we made solar water heaters.

Hands-on

- Explain two ways we separated the materials from the water.
- How did you use the syringe to measure acidity?
- How did you use the filler paper, funnel, scale, and weights to measure the amount of salt dissolved?

Cooperative

- How did you work today?
- Tell how you helped a group member today.
- Tell everything you did for your cooperative job.
- What would have happened if you did not perform your cooperative job today?

Reflective
Explain:

- When yeast is mixed with water and flour, after an hour or so it begins to bubble.
- Some objects have very small capacities (plastic spoons, bottle caps). What would be a good way to measure such small containers?
- What is a variable?
- How could you get your plane to fly halfway down the line when you put a full standard number of winds on the propeller?

Metacognition

- Tell what part of the lesson you understood today.
- What part of the lesson did you have difficulty with (explain where you got stuck).
- What did you know about the task before we started today?
- If you did this lesson over, what would you do differently?
- What surprises did you encounter today?
- What attributes or disposition will help you accomplish this task?

Weather

Subject Area
Elementary grades 4–6

School and Contact Person
Lial Elementary School
5900 Davis Road
Whitehouse, OH 43571
(419) 877-5167

Sr. Margaret Mary Faist, principal
Sr. Mary Cherly Darr, Becky Mills, Christy Anderson

Summary
The goal is for students to realize a connectedness in all subject areas and to realize skills are applicable to everyday life. Students complete three projects.

Windsock   At the end of the unit on weather, students will construct a windsock (art), answer test questions on the sock itself (science and social studies), and describe clouds (language arts).

Postcard   Students design a postcard to show their knowledge of a region or state, including natural resources, wildlife, occupations, and location. This integrates art, social studies, and language arts.

Graphs   After individual surveys, students made picto-bar and line graphs to illustrate weather data and other data. This incorporates science, math, and language arts.

Students are assessed by different methods: direct teacher observation, written tests, oral presentations, the completed project, and conferenciang with the teacher.

Cultural Comparisons

Subject Areas
Grade 5/6 social studies, language arts, music, art, math

School and Contact Person
Broward Elementary School
400 West Osborne Avenue
Tampa, FL 33603
(813) 276-5592

Beverly DeMott, principal
Cheryl Bell, MaryAnn Graham

Summary
Students analyze the culture of Jamaica and that of the United States by comparing and contrasting the historical facts, climate, resources, life-styles, transportation, holidays, cultural heritage, and national heroes. In the process, students will produce book reports, interactive teaching kit activities, portfolios, timelines and charts. Assessment is done by teacher observation, book reports, and peer assessment.

USA: Melting Pot of the World

Subject Areas
Grade 5/6 social studies, language arts, math, music, art

Summary
In this unit, students discover the role immigration played in the United States. Using literature to gain insights and see the world from different perspectives, students understand that their own family histories are part of the U.S. immigration story, and appreciate various cultures. Book reports are written after reading fictional and nonfictional immigration experiences. A debate on such topics as "Should everyone be allowed into the United States?" and "When should people be excluded?" are conclusion of the unit, students will compare what is best about Old and New World Experiences.

Where Do Floridians Come From?

Subject Area
Grades 4/5/6 geography, language arts, math, and science

Summary
Students gain an understanding of the nature of the state of Florida's population by completing this unit. Among the questions are "Why do people need to relocate?" "What parts of the United States do they come from?" and "What are the demographics of the new population?" In addition, students will be able to explain the relationship between the environment and Florida's population growth. The assessment of this unit is demonstrated in the products the students complete. Examples are: constructing a bulletin board displaying the results of the "Where Do We Come From?" survey, displaying the endangered wildlife, writing essays, and writing timelines.

Appendixes

Appendix A
Increasing Parent and
Community Participation
in Schools

*L*isted here are three ways to gain an increase in parent and community participation in school decisions. All three can be used to help a district or school building develop and measure common curriculum standards.

Shared Decision Making

One method to ensure that parents and community members are supportive and contributing to your efforts to improve the school's curriculum is to involve them as stakeholders in some of the decision making. For our purposes, we will confine our discussion to curriculum and assessment issues, but shared decision-making groups can be used for other school-related agenda items as well.

Certainly a school or school district needs to have parents and the community involved in establishing the high school exit standards for its students. These are the visible performance-based standards that students from the community will be able to do upon graduation. A district planning team should be involved in establishing standards. The next step for a school district is to have each school in the district other than the high school(s) establish exit standards for the school. These should be planned backwards and support the high school exit standards. School-based planning teams should be involved in establishing these school-based standards.

The decision about the involvement of our school-based planning team in establishing course standards has been an issue in some districts. This decision should be left to the planning teams themselves. In some cases, the team may feel that the teaching staff should develop these course standards. In other communities, the planning team may want to be involved. If this is the case, then perhaps a small subcommittee can be established for this task.

Composition
These are suggested guidelines. Local districts may want to amend them to meet the local needs.

District Planning Teams

1 building administrative representative
1 building administrative representative
1 school board representative
1 central office administrative representative
2 PTA representatives-at-large
3 parent representatives from each of the school buildings
2 teacher representatives from each of the buildings
1 teachers' union representative-at-large
1 senior citizen
3 business persons from the community—nonparents
2 community representatives-at-large
2 members of the civil service union
2 student representatives

---

21 total membership

Other members may include 1 representative of the religious community, 1 from a taxpayers' watch committee, 1 from the local government, and 1 from higher education.

School Building Planning Teams

Teachers

7 elementary level
8 secondary level
administrators
principal, elementary
principal, secondary
assistant principal, secondary

Parents

4 elementary
6 secondary

Other

1 civil service employee
2 support staff
1 community member—nonparent

Membership

There are two common ways to find members for these communities. The first is to have each constituency group or the head of each group appoint members from that group. The second is to have elections within each constituency group if it is feasible. The chief difficulty with the first procedure is that the parent or community group does not represent a cross-section of the group in the community. As the politics change, so does the committee representation. The second method of selection, elections, tends to minimize the problems with the first method but presents other problems. Among them is the time the parents and community groups need to devote to put together the elections.

The terms of office for the first selection procedure should be two years. After that, one-half of the members, except the principal, need to be replaced on an ongoing basis. Terms of office should be two years.

Training

One of the chief needs of these committees is training in how to work together. The training should be in content as well as in process. The I/D/E/A organization offers an excellent training program in helping a group form a vision and reorganize the school or district to meet this vision. Often, school-based planning teams get involved in peripheral issues such as building beautification, school discipline, or busing patterns, instead of looking at long-term reform. Curriculum is rarely looked at in the initial stages, yet the standards of performance are at the heart of what school is all about. Training in process should be ongoing as well. How to reach consensus, brainstorm, and deal with dissatisfaction among group members should be covered.

Problems

A number of issues have arisen in the operation of school-based planning teams. The chief one is protection of one's turf. This is seen at all levels, and we all are guilty to some degree. teachers may resent parents' involvement in decision making and parents' apparent lack of regard for teacher expertise on many issues, particularly curriculum. Parents may have single-issue agendas or simply represent the needs of their own child and not all students. Administrators are reluctant to let go of their influence and power. This is especially true when the are held accountable. School boards want to review and "study" the school planning teams' recommendations. Boards may even vote down recommendations, leaving committee members resentful and angered. Community members may make decisions based on their own beliefs or politics rather than on what is best for children.

Focus Groups

Advertisers use focus groups to solicit people's opinions. These groups are structured to reflect what a particular community—in this case, your school district. Typically, a group comprises fifteen individuals. Each individual is selected to participate on the basis of membership in some group—Hispanic male, a white female, an African American male, parents of a special education student, parents of a gifted child, a business community member who has no children in the schools, a senior citizen. Together, these types of individuals build a focus group.

Typically, a focus group leader is not from the school community, to prevent bias. The meeting lasts about 90 minutes and is highly structured. A series of questions are asked in a fixed order. Participants are asked to respond to the questions and not get involved in speech making or dialogues with each other. The group leader's task is to focus the meeting on responding to the questions.

The questions themselves are directly related to the information the school district is seeking. For example, if the district planning team is establishing curriculum standards, they would like questions about what standards the community feels should be established. Typical questions are as follows:

- What should high school students be able to do when they graduate?
- How important is it that high school graduates be proficient in a foreign language?
- Should a graduate be able to play a musical instrument?
- How many years of mathematics should high school graduates have?
- What courses should we have now that we do not have? Why?
- Should community service be required as part of graduation?
- Should students complete a number of performance-based exams before they graduate?

A focus group could also respond to questions like these:

- Which issues do you think are the most serious ones facing our schools today?
- Which goals would you like the district to address in the future?

The final task of the focus group leader is to provide a summary of the group's responses to the questions. Many group leaders tape the meetings and also take notes. Sometimes a note taker is used in the meetings. The results are shared with the district planning team, and these responses are used in their discussions.

Questionnaires and Telephone Interviews

These are common ways for district or school planning teams to gather information. In both cases, a representative sample of district residents is used. This usually can be done by district staff, but some districts employ professionals to complete the task. This is an excellent way to use a school–business partnership if your partner works in the area of marketing or public opinion polls. From census data, it is easy to determine the demographics of the district and then to select a representative group of citizens to ask questions. As with most surveys, you will need to plan on sending out or calling four times as many individuals as you need to get a representative sample to respond.

Typical questions are as follows.

Issues

A number of issues are facing our schools today. Please indicate here by a checkmark how serious these issues are for you. You can check the following categories:

Extremely serious
Very serious
Somewhat serious
Not at all serious

A list of issues then is provided for the respondent, either in written form or on the phone.

Expectations

Listed below are a number of suggested expectations for high school graduates that some believe, if realized, could help reach our nation's educational goals under the Goals 2000: Educate America Act passed by Congress. Please rate each one using one of the four criteria listed above.

Specific questions are then developed in areas of reading, math, foreign language, science, technology, and so on. The questions can be as specific as:

How important is it that all high school graduates be able to read and understand:

A VCR manual
An editorial in a newspaper
College textbook

All results should be shared with the district or school planning team and with the community at large.

Appendix B
Blue Ribbon Schools

*T*his is a list of Nationally Recognized 1993 Blue Ribbon Schools that are represented in Section II. The schools are listed by order of appearance in the book and by name of Unit.

School	Unit
The Harrisburg Academy 10 Erford Road Wormleysburg, PA 17011 (717) 763-7811 J. Gregory Morgan, headmaster	Wallops Island field study
Aurora High School West Pioneer Trail Aurora, OH 44202 (216) 562-3501 Linda Robertson, principal	School/business partnership
Holt High School 1784 Aurelius Road Holt, MI 48842 (517) 694-0097 Mr. Thomas D. Davis, principal	Algebra II
Holt High School 1784 Aurelius Road Holt, MI 48842 (517) 694-0097 Mr. Thomas D. Davis, principal	Learning journals in the history classroom
Jefferson High School 1801 South Eighteenth Street Lafayette, IN 47905 (317) 449-3400 Dennis C. Blind, principal	Senior honors British literature portfolio
Jefferson High School 1801 South Eighteenth Street Lafayette, IN 47905 (317) 449-3400 Dennis C. Blind, principal	Senior research portfolio

School	Unit
Bob Jones High School 1304 Hughes Madison, AL 35758 (205) 837-8780 Billy Broadway, principal	Writing as a process
North Allegheny School District 10375 Perrysville Avenue Wexford, PA 15090 (412) 935-5767 Lawrence Butterini, principal	Diet and food facts
Oak Park High School 899 North Kanan Road Agoura, CA 91301 (818) 707-7926 Jeff Chancer, principal	Oak Park 2013
Metro High School 1212 Seventh Street, S.E. Cedar Rapids, IO 52401 (319) 398-2193 Mary Wilcynski, principal	Schoolwide portfolios
Milwaukee Custer High School 5075 North Sherman Boulevard Milwaukee, WI 53209 (414) 461-6600 Robert Peters, principal	Career certificate program (CCP)
Fort Couch Middle School 515 Fort Couch Road Upper St. Clair, PE 15241 (412) 854-3046 Thomas H. Harshman, principal	Expressive arts
Mohave Middle School 5520 North 86th Street Scottsdale, AZ 85250 (602) 423-3700 Carol Erikson, Ed.D., principal	Mini-business community

School	Unit
School	*Unit*
Martin Luther King Jr. Middle School 4545 Ammendale Road Beltsville, MD 20705 (301) 937-6070 Bette L. Lewis, principal	Science projects
Martin Luther King Jr. Middle School 4545 Ammendale Road Beltsville, MD 20705 (301) 937-6070 Bette L. Lewis, principal	Science portfolios
Hastings Middle School 190 East 9th St. Hastings, MN (612) 437-6111 Garry Jensen, principal	Water water everywhere
Bunker Hill Elementary School Spring Branch Independent School District 11950 Taylorcrest Houston, TX 77024 (713) 465-0036 Gayle-Lambert, principal	American society
Susan Lindgren Elementary School 4801 West 41st Street St. Louis Park, MN 55416 (612) 928-6700 Harry Hoff, principal	Science thinking journal
Lial Elementary School 5900 Davis Road Whitehouse, OH 43571 (419) 877-5167 Sr. Margaret Mary Faist, principal	Weather

School	*Unit*

Broward Elementary School
400 West Osborne Avenue
Tampa, FL 33603
(813) 276-5592
Beverly DeMott, principal
	Cultural comparisons
	U.S.A.: Melting Pot of the
	  World
	Where do Floridians come
	  from?

Appendix C
Blue Ribbon Schools Program

Since 1982 the U.S. Department of Education has recognizd outstanding schools throughout the nation. As part of the Blue Ribbon Schools Program, over 2,500 schools from every state have been recognized as outstanding. These schools are diverse; they come from inner cities as well as fural and suburban areas. Private, parochial, and public schools are represented. But these schools share a number of characteristics. The chief one is that they have successfully mobilized their respective resources, staff, and community to meet the educational and social needs of the students entrusted to their care. These schools are special, reflecting all that is outstanding in U.S. education today.

The process of becoming a nationally recognized school begins at the school building level. The staff of the building must decide to look at itself and decide what is working well, what is working O.K., and what needs improvement. An elaborate application form asks a number of questions about he status of education in the school building. Usually, secondary schools and elementary schools are recognized in alternating years. Middle schools have a choice of which category to apply to, but once they apply they must stay with this category. Because of budget difficulties, the Department of Education was not able to recognize elementary schools in 1992, so in 1993 both elementary and secondary schools were recognized. All the schools represented in this book came from the 1993 round of applications. The following criteria were used to judge these schools as outstanding.

Leadership
Teaching environment
Curriculum and instruction
Student environment
Parent and community support
Indicators of success
Organizational vitality
A special area such as history, math, or the arts, which is also usually
selected for evaluation

The process of recognition begins with the chief school officer of each state nominating a certain number of schools recognized. Recommendations are also received from the Council for American Private Education. Once the applications are received in Washington, they are read by a peer review panel, which recommends the most promising schools for site visits. Another single- or two-member peer review team visits the schools, verifies the information submitted by the school, and reports on the school climate and instruction. After a review of the site reports, the original panel makes its recommendations to the U.S. secretary of education, who announces the names of the schools selected. The recognized schools are honored at a national ceremony in Washington, D.C.

Appendix D
Model Sixth-Grade Language Arts Assessments

The reader may be interested in viewing how a core section of a sixth-grade language arts program can be developed using interdisciplinary curriculum and alternative assessments. Listed here are four examples from the sixth grade at the Anne M. Dorner Middle School in Ossining, New York. This school was recognized as a Blue Ribbon school in 1989. The scope of this curriculum is comprehensive in that it incorporates the use of journal writing, interdisciplinary projects, exhibitions, oral reports, and book reports.

Outcome #33
Students will engage once a week in sustained silent reading followed by written analysis, synthesis, evaluation, or stating of opinion in their individual journals.

Assessment Tool
The students will write in their journals once a week a response to a literature-based question. In addition, once a week students will write in their journals a response to a personal question (see the attachament for examples of questions)

The Journal Rubric comprises:

Completed number of entries	25 points
Depth of thought	25 points
Productive use of allotted time	20 points
Demonstrates improvement in indicated areas (i.e. more detail and examples to support ideas)	10 points
Self-motivated writing	10 points
Attention to proper grammar and mechanics	10 points

Literature-Based Journal Questions

---

1. How are you similar to one of the characters in the story?
2. How are you different from one of the characters in the story?
3. How did the story make you feel? Why?
4. What new ideas did the story make you think about?
5. Using the four sentence types (interrogative, exclamatory, imperative, and declarative), analyze which types this author uses most frequently in this chapter. Locate a paragraph that contains at least two of the four sentence types. Copy it verbatim (using quotations and include page numbers) into your journal and label each sentence.
6. Find a paragraph that is particularly descriptive. What is it describing, and what are the words that make it come alive?
7. What is the author saying about human behavior?
8. Predict what will happen next. (Be sure to describe what has just occurred.)
9. Describe something (a character's actions, a problem you can identify with, an incident) in your book that might make you change something in your life.
10. Trace the development of a character ("At first the character was _____ , but then the character became _____ .")
11. This character is like (the name of the character) in _____ (underlined title of work) because . . .
12. Imagine that a character in your book met a character from another book you have read. Describe this meeting.
13. The character I most admire is _____ because . . .
14. Describe the mood of this chapter. use adjectives to describe the feeling you get as you read this chapter.
15. Pretend you are the author of the book. Prepare a speech to be given before a group of students. Explain why you wrote the book and what you hope the reader gained.

Outcome #34
Students will apply and demonstrate mastery of English skills through written interdisciplinary projects such as whale reports, Egyptian dictionaries, and research reports on prehistoric civilizations.

Journal Questions (Personal)

- Do you think boys or girls have it easier?
- If you could have a round-trip ride in a time machine and travel any distance into the past or future, where would you want to go?
- Would you like to have an identical twin? What about it would be best? Worst?
- Are you in a hurry to grow up? What does it mean to be "grown up," and when do you think it will happen to you?
- If you could permanently trade lives with one of your classmates, brothers, or sisters, would you? If so, whom would you pick and why?
- What are you most proud of having done? What would make you even prouder?
- Would you rather be a rich and famous movie star or a great doctor who saves a lot of people but is not wealthy or well known?

Outcome #34
Students will apply and demonstrate mastery of English skills through written interdisciplinary projects such as whale reports, Egyptian dictionaries, and research reports on prehistoric civilizations.

Assessment Tool
Each student will complete a report on the *origins of humans*.

Origins of Humans: Research Report

Name: _____   Date: _____

Social Studies/English   Period: _____

You will be required to complete the following six stages:

1. **Bibliography:**
   Three sources, properly documented and alphabetized

   30 points total
   (10 points each)

2. **Notes:**
   Twelve main ideas from three sources   45 points total
                                                   (15 points each)

3. **Outline:**
   First word in each line must be capitalized.   25 points total
   Use only a short phrase or word for each   (5 points each)
      topic.

4. **Report:**
   Use the main topics from your outline (Roman numerals) as a
   structure for each of your paragraphs. Your report should have
   a total of five paragraphs—an introduction, three body paragraphs, and a conclusion. Use transitional words (see sheet in
   packet) and clear topic sentences.

5. **Student Assessment**   **Teacher Assessment**

_____	Topic sentences	20 points total _____
_____	Use of transitional words	10 points total _____
_____	Introduction	10 points total _____
_____	Body paragraph #1	10 points total _____
_____	Body paragraph #2	10 points total _____
_____	Body paragraph #3	10 points total _____
_____	Conclusion	10 points total _____
_____	Mechanics	20 points total _____
_____	Bibliography	30 points total _____
_____	Notes	45 points total _____
_____	Outline	25 points total _____
_____	**Total**	**200 points total** _____

6. Include this page as the last page of your final report.

Social Studies/English Origins of Humans: Research Report

Bibliography Format

Name: _____

Interview of Class
Last name, First name, Middle initial. Title of teacher or source of notes, Month, year.

Example
Maurer, Richard E. Social Studies Teacher Class Notes and Instruction, October 1995.

_____, _____, _____. _____
_____ , _____ _____. _____
_____ .

Reference Book
Last name, First Name, Middle INitial. *Underlined Title of Book.* City Published: Name of Publishing Company, Copyright date.

Example
Maurer, Richard E. *The Joy of Teaching English.* Ossining: Anne M. Dorner Publishing Company, 1995.

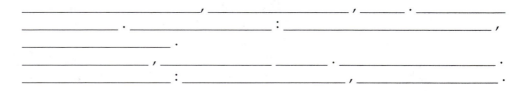

Film
Underlined Title of the Film. Type of film (Filmstrip, cassette, video). Publisher of film, year published. Length of film.

Example
How to Earn an A on Your Report. Filmstrip. Warner Brothers, 1993. 57 min.

_____ . _____ . _____ ,
_____ .
_____ . _____ . _____ .
_____ .

Magazine
Last name, First Name Middle Initial. "Title of Article in Quotation Marks." *Underlined Title of Magazine*, Volume number of magazine (Year published): Page number(s).

Example
Smith, Thomas A. "The History of Homo Sapiens." *Time*, 54 (1993): 23–27.

Encyclopedia
   A. When the author's name is given:

      Author's last name, first name. "Title of Article." *Underlined Title of Encyclopedia.* City Published, Year.

Example
Spinrod, Hyron. "Man." *World Book Encyclopedia.* Ossining: Macmillan Press, 1993.

   B. When the author's name is *not* given:
      "Title of Article." *Underlined Title of Encyclopedia.*
      City Published: Publisher, Year.

Example
"Man." *World Book Encyclopedia.* Ossining: Macmillan Press, 1993.

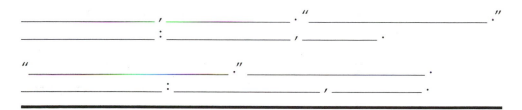

Origins of Humans: Research Report: Note-Taking Sheet

Name: _____   Date: _____
Social Studies/English   Period: _____

First Source: _____

1. _____
2. _____
3. _____
4. _____
5. _____
6. _____
7. _____
8. _____
9. _____
10. _____
11. _____
12. _____

Second Source: _____

1. _____
2. _____
3. _____
4. _____
5. _____
6. _____
7. _____
8. _____
9. _____
10. _____
11. _____
12. _____

Outcome #35

Students will present at least three oral reports incorporating the following skills: evaluating, predicting, and analyzing based on research conducted or books read.

Assessment Tool

Each student will present an oral book report.

Book Report and Craft Demonstration Rubric

Name: _____   Date: _____

Period: _____

I. Book information Title (underlined), Author, Publishing Company, Copyright Date.	20 points _____	
II. Report questions answered Craft chosen? Why? History of craft? Popularity today? Interesting facts you learned?	20 points _____	
III. Visual display A. Neatness	20 points _____	
B. Note cards with steps clearly written	20 points _____	
C. Picture and/or explanation of each stage of project	20 points _____	
D. Example of finished product	20 points _____	
IV. Oral presentation A. All materials needed for demonstration	20 points _____	
B. Delivery of speech 1. Volume of voice	10 points _____	
2. Eye contact with audience	10 points _____	
3. Enthusiasm and interest shown	10 points _____	
4. Information presented in an organized manner	10 points _____	
5. Each stage explained and demonstrated	10 points _____	
6. Appropriate length (10 minutes)	10 points _____	
Total	**200 points** _____	

Outcome #36
Each student will complete monthly book reports focusing on different genres and will demonstrate mastery of higher level vocabulary, spelling, and grammatical usage.

Assessment Tool
Each month a book report will be completed.

Rubric for Autobiography/Biography Book Report

Name: _____ Date: _____
Period: _____

Categories	Points Earned
1. Neat cover and report	(15) _____
2. Title (must be underlined), Author, Publisher, copyright date, number of pages.	(10) _____
3. Description of person about whom the book is written (physical and personality)	(15) _____
4. Explanation of why the book was written about this person	(15) _____
5. Description of two other important people in this person's life	(15) _____
6. Description of setting or settings of book	(15) _____
7. Recommendation	(15) _____
8. Spelling	(15) _____
9. Capitalization/punctuation	(20) _____
10. Paragraphs	(15) _____
Total possible points	(150) _____

Your grade

Comments:

Parent's signature _____

Rubric for Writing Piece

Name: _____   Date: _____
                                            Period: _____

Categories   *Points Earned*

_____ Brainstorming   (10)   _____

_____ Rough Draft   (25)   _____

_____ Revisions   (15)   _____
        Response to suggestions

_____ Final Draft
        Spelling   (15)   _____

        Capitalization   (15)   _____

        Punctuation   (15)   _____

        Clarity   (15)   _____

        Description   (15)   _____
          (adjectives)

        Paragraphs   (15)   _____
          (including topic sentences)

        Neat   (10)   _____
          (use pen and write with script or type)

Total possible points: 150   Your grade _____

Comments:

Parent's signature _____

Index

Algebra, curriculum on, 130
Alleman, J., 34
Alternative assessments:
  community members and, 82
  costs of, 78
  course standards and, 71–72
  design of, 76–79
  identifying needs for, 79–83
  parents and, 82
  performances as, 62, 65, 67–70,
    73–74, 78, 80, 107
  portfolios as, 62, 67–70, 78, 80, 107
  products, 62, 63–64, 70, 78, 80, 107
  purposes of, 60–62, 80
  qualities of, 71–77
  standardization of, 77
  states and, 78
  technical issues and, 77–78
American Association for the
    Advancement of Science
    (AAAS), 8
  *Benchmarks for Science Literacy:
    Project 2061*, 8
  Project 2061, 16
American history, standards for, 40
American Teacher, The, 8
Anastasi, A., 116
Apprenticeship, 20
Arizona, 7, 70
Arnold, J., 33
Art, curriculum on, 15, 181–182
Assessment, 23, 44–45, 85, 132–133.
    See also Alternative
    assessment; Authentic
    assessment
  definition of, 58–60
  relevancy of, 72
Assessment tasks, 57, 79-85, 119
  measurement of, 89–118
  scoring for, 120
Association for Supervision and
    Curriculum Development, 91
Atwell, Nancy (*In the Middle:
    Writing, Reading, and Learning
    with Adolescents*), 92–93
Authentic assessment, 20. *See also*
    Alternative assessment
  competency tests and, 3–4
  definition of, 3–4
  history of, 4–9, 19
  interdisciplinary curriculum and,
    24, 53
  measurement of, 89
  multiple intelligences and, 15
  teachers and, 9
Authenticity (generalizability), 116

Baker, E. L., 76, 117
Baron, M., 42
Beane, J. A., 17, 33

Behaviorism, 12
Benchmarks, 107, 112
  four-corner measurement, 108
Beyer, B. K., 48, 51
Biology, curriculum on, 122, 127
Block, J. H., 44
Bloom, B. S., 27, 90
Blue Ribbon schools, 230–235
Boschee, F., 42
Boyer, E., 33
Brain research, 11–13
British Standard Assessment Tasks
    (SAT), 61
Brooks, J. G., 18
Brooks, M., 18
Brophy, J., 34
Brown, C. S., 67
Burns, R. B., 44
Bush, President George, 7
Business:
  curriculum on, 120, 128, 183
  needs of, 53, 73

Caine, G., 17
Caine, R. N., 17
California, 7, 70
Career Certificate Program, 174–180
Career Pathways Certificate, 11
Carnegie Council on Adolescent
    Development, 10
Carr, J., 34
Carrol, J. B., 44
Carter, M. A., 67
Certificate of Employability, 119,
    174–175
Chao, C., 34
Chittenden, E., 60
Clinton, President, 7
Coalition for Essential Schools, 8, 78,
    170
Cognition, 47
Cognitive psychology, 4, 11–13, 16,
    20
Commission on Excellence, 4
Community participation, 5, 6, 24,
    41–42, 91, 93–94, 121, 215–219
Community service, 73
  and multidisciplinary unit, 66
Competency tests:
  and authentic assessment, 3–4
Computer studies, 63
Conation, 47
Constructive paradigm, 17–19, 73
Content validity, 115–116
Cooperative learning, 51–53, 73, 120,
    130, 146
Costa, A., 47
Council for American Private
    Education, 234
Council for Basic Education, 38

Council of Chief State School
    Officers, 38
Course Outcome Development
    model, 36–38
Course standards, 81, 27–31, 32,
    36–37, 39, 40–41, 71–72, 79, 90
Critical thinking skills, 47–51, 73
Cronbach, L. J., 58
Cuomo, Mario, 10
Curriculum standards, 8–9

Darling-Hammond, L., 5, 9
Davis, A., 78
DeBono, E., 47
Desai, L. E., 67
Developmental psychology, 4, 11–13,
    20
Dimensions of Learning model, 91
Duff, S. C., 52
Dunbar, S. B., 76

Education Commission of the States
    (1983), 4
Education reform. *See also* Standards
  administrators role in, 5
  community groups and, 5, 6, 24,
    41–42
  educators' role in, 5, 42–43
  federal government and, 7–8, 10
  opposition to, 41–43
  parents' role in, 5, 6, 24
  state governments and, 11
  teachers' role in, 5–6, 8, 31, 43
Education Week, 38
Educators, opposition to reform,
    42–43
Effective Schools, 8
Efthim, H. E., 44
Elementary schools, 33, 36–37, 40,
    121
  curriculum on American society,
    210
  interdisciplinary curriculum, 219,
    220, 221, 222
  journal writing curriculum, 217,
    236
  language arts curriculum, 236
  life science curriculum, 41
  mathematics curriculum, 217
  research reports in, 239–245
  science curriculum, 217
English, curriculum on, 8, 35, 65, 71,
    81, 121. *See also* Elementary
    schools; High Schools; Middle
    Schools
Environmental theme, 63, 199–200
Epistemology, 47
Evaluation, 58–59, 85
  parent–community, 91, 93–94, 121
  peer, 91, 93–94, 117–118, 121

student self-evaluation, 91–93, 121

teacher, 94–95

Exit standards, 3, 25–26, 32, 36, 37, 39–40, 79, 90, 165

Experiment Evaluation Checklist, 94–95

Face validity, 116

Federal government, 7–8, 10, 38

Felknor, C., 79

Feur, M. J., 63

Fogarty, R., 34

Foxfire Outreach, 8

Frames of Mind: The Theory of Multiple Intelligences (Gardner), 13

Fuhrman, S. H., 6, 9

Fulton, K., 63

Gardner, H., 13, 15, 33, 67

Generalizability (authenticity), 116

Geography, curriculum on, 66

Geology, curriculum on, 66

Glazer, S. M., 67

Goals 2000: Educate America Act, 7, 38, 229

Goodman, K. S., 18, 67

Goodman, Y. M., 18, 67

Guskey, T. R., 78

Hafner, A. L., 73

Haney, W., 59

Harp, B., 67

Hawaii, 41

Hawley, W., 6

High schools, 36–37, 121, 122, 128

curriculum on English, 122, 128, 148, 153, 174

history curriculum, 141

interdisciplinary curriculum, 156, 159, 165, 170, 174, 205

language arts curriculum, 39

mathematics curriculum, 64, 130, 174

ROPE (Rite-of-Passage) in, 66, 106

science curriculum, 158, 195, 202

social studies curriculum, 174

technical education curriculum, 174

writing curriculum, 123, 156, 170–171

Hill, B. C., 58

Hirsch, E. D., 477

History:

curriculum on, 8, 19, 141

standards for, 40

Hood, W. J., 18, 67

Instructional programs:

cooperative learning, 51–53, 73, 120, 130, 146

critical thinking skills, 47–51, 73

proficiency learning, 44–47

Integrated curriculum, 121

Interdisciplinary curriculum, 15–17, 119. *See also* Elementary

Schools; High schools; Middle schools

standards for, 23–53

themes, choosing, 33-37, 79

International Thinking Assessment Network, 5

Jacobs, H. H., 17, 34

Johnson, D. W., 51

Johnson, R. T., 51

Journal writing, 141–147, 217, 236

Judson, G, 42

Kahneman, D., 12

Kellaghan, T., 78

Kelly, T., 42

Kentucky, 7, 40, 68, 70

Kirst, M. W., 4

Kohlberg, W. H., 10

Language arts, curriculum on, 33, 63, 64, 71, 79, 81. *See also* Elementary schools; High schools; Middle schools

Learning theory, 11–13

Life science, standards for, 41

Lindsay, P. H., 100

Linn, R., 76, 117

Linn, R. L., 76

Madaus, G. F., 78

Madden, N. A., 93

Mansilla-Boix, V., 33

Mapping procedures, 34–36

Maryland, 7, 70

Maryland Center for Thinking Studies, 49

Maryland Geographic Alliance, 92

Marzano, R. J., 91

Mathematics, 3, 27–28, 32, 35, 63, 65, 68, 71, 90, 117, 119. *See also* Elementary schools; High schools; Middle schools

Maurer, R. E., 17, 34

McCabe, M. E., 67

McDonald, J. P., 62, 77

McKernan, J., 42–43

McTighe, J., 91, 111

Measurements, 23, 108–110, 118

benchmarks and, 107–108, 110

literature review of, 103

types of, 101–107

Megacognition, 47

Metropolitan Life Insurance Company, 8

Michalko, M., 47

Michigan, 7

Middle schools, 36–37, 49

art curriculum, 181

business curriculum, 183

creative expression curriculum, 181

environment curriculum, 63

geography curriculum, 66

geology curriculum, 66

home economics curriculum, 181

industrial technologies curriculum, 181

interdisciplinary curriculum, 65, 205

language curriculum, 38

music curriculum, 181

science curriculum, 195, 202

video curriculum, 38

Minimum mastery levels, 74

Mitchell, R., 6

Multiple choice tests, 6, 53, 74

Multiple intelligences, 13–15, 120, 195

Nation at Risk, A: The Imperative of Educational Reform, 4, 10

National Assessment of Educational Progress, 5, 78

National Center on Education and the Economy, 10

National Commission on Excellence in Education, 4

National Council for Science Standards, 41

National Council of Teachers of English (NCTE), 5

National Council of Teachers of Mathematics (NCTM), 5, 8, 16, 71, 130

National examination system, 70

National History Standards Project, 40

National Research Council, 5

National Standards in American Education: A Citizen's Guide (Ravitch), 38

Neuropsychology, 13

New American Schools Development Corporation, 16

New Standards Project, 8, 70, 78

New York State, 70

Education that Works: Creating Career Pathways for New York State Youths, 11

language arts curriculum, 39

Newmann, F. M., 18

Nolan, K., 5

Norman, D. A., 100

O'Day, J., 9

O'Neil, H. F., 117

Olson, L., 42

Outcome-based education movement (OBE), 25, 42–43. *See also* Partners for Quality Learning

Parents, 82, 91, 93–94, 118, 121

education reform and, 5, 6, 24

school participation and, 215–229

standards and, 24, 25, 30–31, 79

Partners for Quality Learning, 43

Performance Assessment Matrix, 52

Performance assessments, 111–117

Performance skills, 91, 120

Perkins, D., 17, 34

Peters, T. J., 73

Physics, assessment for, 102–103

Piaget, J., 12–13

Pickering, D., 91

Popham, W. J., 78
Portfolios, 62, 67–70
    designing assessments, 69–70
    interdisciplinary, 170, 183
    research, 153–155
    science, 202–204
    writing, 61, 68, 70, 72, 105,
        123–126, 148
Portfolio Assessment
        Clearinghouse, 68
Portfolio News, 68
Predictive validity, 116
Presseisen, B. F., 47
Professional Standards for
        Teaching Mathemat-
        ics, 119
Proficiency learning, 44–47
    assessment component in,
        44–45

Program standards, 25, 26–27, 32,
        36, 37, 40

Raters. *See* Evaluation
Ravitch, D., 38
Reflection, 23
Reich, R. B., 73
Reigeluth, C., 34
Reliability, 111–115
    by raters, 112–113
    test, 113–114
Report cards, 59
Reporting, 59–60, 85
Research projects, 153–155
Resnick, L., 5
Resnick, L. B., 70
Restak, R. M., 12
Rhoades, J., 67
ROPE (Rite of Passage Experience),
        66, 106
Rubrics (scoring), 95–100
    analytic, 96, 120
    holistic, 95–96, 120
    narrative, 120
point allocation, 120
    scales and, 101
Ruptic, C., 58

Sanders, J. R., 60
Scales, 118
    confusion, 101
    development of, 100–101
    direct, 101
Scholastic Aptitude Test (SAT), 6
School-to-Work Opportunity Act, 10

Science, curriculum on, 8, 35, 65, 81,
        120. *See also* Elementary
        schools; High schools; Middle
        schools
Science Plus: Technology and Society,
        97, 121
Scientists, African-American,
        198–199
Scoring. *See* Rubrics
Simpson, E. J., 91
Sizer, T., 33, 43
Skinner, B. F., 12
Slavin, R. E., 51, 93
Smith, F. C., 10
Smith, M. S., 9
Social studies, curriculum on, 33, 35,
        64
Socratic seminars, 107
Spady, W., 42
Special education, 105
Sports, 200–201
Standardized testing, 9
Standards:
    for assessment tasks, 119
    community groups and, 24–25, 30,
        79
    controversies about, 41–43
    for courses, 81, 27–31, 32, 36–37,
        39, 40–41, 71–72, 79, 90
    demand for, 4–9, 19, 24–25
    development of, 25–28
    establishment of, 23
    exit, 3, 25–26, 32, 36, 37, 39–40, 79,
        90, 165
    federal government and, 38
    for interdisciplinary curricula,
        23–53
    and other countries, 5, 19
    parents and, 24, 25, 30–31, 79
    program, 25, 26–27, 32, 36, 37, 40
    state governments and, 38
    unit, 25, 32, 37–38
State Education Leader, The, 8
State governments, education and, 4,
        8, 11, 38, 78
Stevens, R. J., 93
Stevenson, C., 34
Students:
    accountability of, 24
    anxiety and, 82
    feedback from, 83
    performance assessment and, 117
    preparation for, 81–82
    test scores of, 6

Teachers, 120
    constructive paradigm and, 18
    educational reform and, 5–6, 8, 31,
        43
    opposition to reform, 43
    performance assessment and, 117
    standardized testing and, 6
Teachers' union, 43
*Teaching Thinking Skills: A Handbook
        for Elementary School Teachers*
        (Beyer), 48
*Teaching Thinking Skills: A Handbook
        for Secondary School Teachers*
        (Beyer), 48
Test reliability, 113–114
Tests. *See* Measurements
Thinking skills. *See also* Critical
        thinking skills
    high-order, 91
Tierney, R. J., 67
Tucker, M., 70
Tversky, A., 12

United States, 9–10, 19. *See also*
        Federal government
United States Department of
        Education, 10, 19, 234–235
United States Department of Labor,
        10, 19
    Commission on Achieving Neces-
        sary Skills (SCANS), 10
Unit standards, 25, 32, 37–38

Validity (generalization), 114–117
    content, 115–116
    face, 116
    predictive, 116
Van Patten, J., 34
Vars, G. F., 15, 34
Vermont writing portfolio, 61, 68, 70,
        72, 105
Viadero, D., 43

Wehlage, G., 18
Whole language movement, 18
    assessment and 18–19
Wiggins, G. P., 81, 100, 115, 117
Work Force 2000, 4, 9–11, 20
Worthen, B., 9
Worthen, B. R., 60
Writing programs, 61, 68, 70, 72, 105,
        123, 126, 148, 156, 170–171.
        See also Journal writing